Cubeo Grammar
Studies in the Languages of Colombia 5

Summer Institute of Linguistics and
The University of Texas at Arlington
Publications in Linguistics

Publication 130

Publications in Linguistics is a series published jointly by the Summer Institute of Linguistics and the University of Texas at Arlington. The series is a venue for works covering a broad range of topics in linguistics, especially the analytical treatment of minority languages from all parts of the world. While most volumes are authored by members of the Institute, suitable works by others will also form part of the series.

Series Editor

Donald A. Burquest
Summer Institute of Linguistics
University of Texas at Arlington

Volume Editor

Rhonda L. Hartell

Production Staff

Bonnie Brown, Managing Editor
Margaret González, Compositor
Hazel Shorey, Graphic Artist

Cubeo Grammar
Studies in the Languages of Colombia 5

Nancy L. Morse
and
Michael B. Maxwell

A Publication of
The Summer Institute of Linguistics
and
The University of Texas at Arlington

©1999 by the Summer Institute of Linguistics, Inc.
Library of Congress Catalog No: 98-89597
ISBN: 1-55671-044-5
ISSN: 1040-0850
Printed in the United States of America
All Rights Reserved

09 08 07 06 05 04 03 02 01 00   10 9 8 7 6 5 4 3 2 1

No part of this publication may be reproduced, stored in a retrieval system, or transmitted in any form or by any means—electronic, mechanical, photocopy, recording, or otherwise—without the express permission of the Summer Institute of Linguistics, with the exception of brief excerpts in journal articles or reviews.

Copies of this and other publications of the Summer Institute of Linguistics may be obtained from

International Academic Bookstore
Summer Institute of Linguistics
7500 W. Camp Wisdom Rd.
Dallas, TX 75236-5699

Voice: 972-708-7404
Fax: 972-708-7433
Email: academic_books@sil.org
Internet: http://www.sil.org

Contents

Abbreviations ix

1 Introduction 1
   1.1 Phonemes 2
   1.2 Allophones 3
   1.3 Syllable, tone, and stress 6
   1.4 Morphophonemics 7
      1.4.1 Nasal spreading 7
      1.4.2 Morphophonemic variation between /r/ and /d/ 9
      1.4.3 Stress shift 11
      1.4.4 Vowel coalesence 13
      1.4.5 Epenthesis of /j/ 13

2 Verbs 15
   2.1 Verb classes 15
      2.1.1 Dynamic verbs 15
      2.1.2 Stative verbs 16
      2.1.3 The copular verb clitic 16
   2.2 Verb morphology 17
      2.2.1 Class-changing suffixes 17
      2.2.2 Inflectional suffixes 19
      2.2.3 Derivational suffixes 54
   2.3 Auxiliary verb constructions 60
      2.3.1 Progressive aspect 60

2.3.2 Continued action aspect 63
　　　2.3.3 Independent purpose clause 65
　　　2.3.4 Compound causative 67
　2.4 Gerundive complements 69
　2.5 Clausal complements 69
　2.6 Object incorporation 70

3 Nouns 73
　3.1 Noun classes 73
　　　3.1.1 Inanimate nouns 73
　　　3.1.2 Animate nouns 77
　　　3.1.3 Pronouns 80
　　　3.1.4 Deverbal nouns 85
　3.2 Noun phrases 90
　　　3.2.1 Possessives 91
　　　3.2.2 Adjective and quantifier modification 91
　　　3.2.3 Noun phrases in apposition 94
　3.3 Noun affixes and clitics 96
　　　3.3.1 Demonstrative prefixes 96
　　　3.3.2 -xɨ diminutive 96
　　　3.3.3 -xã associative 99
　　　3.3.4 -REka certainty 99
　　　3.3.5 -pe similarity 100
　　　3.3.6 -wa separation 103
　　　3.3.7 -bĩã and -bã identity 104
　　　3.3.8 -ka partitive 109
　　　3.3.9 Case marking suffixes 110

4 Other Word Classes 123
　4.1 Adjectives 123
　　　4.1.1 Adjectives versus nouns and stative verbs 123
　　　4.1.2 Nonderived adjectives 124
　　　4.1.3 Derived adjectives 124
　　　4.1.4 Indefinite adjectives 124
　　　4.1.5 Possessive adjectives 125
　　　4.1.6 Adjective inflection 126

Contents   vii

    4.1.7 Comparison of adjectives 128
  4.2 Quantifiers 129
  4.3 Adverbs 131
    4.3.1 Nonderived adverbs 131
    4.3.2 Derived adverbs 132
    4.3.3 Adverb inflection 134
    4.3.4 Comparison of adverbs 134
  4.4 Postpositions 134
    4.4.1 Uninflected postpositions 135
    4.4.2 Inflected postpositions 136
  4.5 Conjunctions 137
  4.6 Interjections 139

5 Clause Structure 141
  5.1 Word order in the clause 141
  5.2 Question words 144
  5.3 Quotations 144

6 Subordination 147
  6.1 Argument structure of subordinate clauses 147
  6.2 Tense marking in subordinate clauses 148
  6.3 Relative clauses 151
    6.3.1 Relativization of the subject 152
    6.3.2 Relativization of objects 156
    6.3.3 Relative clauses based on *'bA-* 158
  6.4 Adverbial clauses 160
    6.4.1 Temporal adverbial clauses 160
    6.4.2 Locative adverbial clauses 174
    6.4.3 Logical adverbial clauses 174
    6.4.4 Event clauses 182

Appendix 1: Affixes and Glosses 185

Appendix 2: Practical Orthography 195

References 197

Abbreviations

ACST	accustomed	F, f	feminine
ADVZ	adverbalizer	FOC	focus
AFTER	after	FRUS	frustrative
AG	agentive	FUT	future
AN	animate	GER	gerund
ASC	associative	GOAL	goal, limit
ASM	assumption/assumed	HPAST	historical past
AUTH	authoritative	IDENT	identical
BEFORE	before	IF	conditional
BEN	benefactive	IMP	imperative
BT	backbone tag	IN	inanimate
CAUS	causative	inc	inclusive
CERT	certainty	INDEF	indefinite
CLS	classifier	INST	instrument, accompaniment
CNCS	concession		
COND	conditional	INTNS	intensifier
DES	desiderative	INTNT	narrator intent
DIM	diminutive	INTR	interrogative
DS	different subject	IRR	irrealis
DUB	dubative	ITER	iterative
DYN	dynamicizer	LOC	locative, temporal
EMPH	emphatic	M, m	masculine
exc	exclusive	N/H	nonrecent past/ present habitual
EXCLM	exclamation		

NARR^FOC	narrator focus	REP	reportative
NEG	negative	RP	recent past
NFUT	nonfuture	S	singular
NMLZ	nominalizer	SELF	self, alone
NON3	1st-, 2nd-person inanimate subject	SEP	separation
		SG	singular inanimate noun
NRFUT	near future	SIM	similarity
NRP	nonrecent past	SINCE	since
OBJ	object	SS	same subject
OPT	optative	STV	stativizer
P	plural	UNIQUE	unique, one of a kind
PART	partitive	VB	verb
PERS	any person	WHEN	when
PL	plural inanimate noun	WHICH	which
POS	possessive	WHILE	while
PROB	probable	1	first person
PST	past	2	second person
PSV	passive	3	third person
PUR	purpose		
R/D	recent past/ present durative		

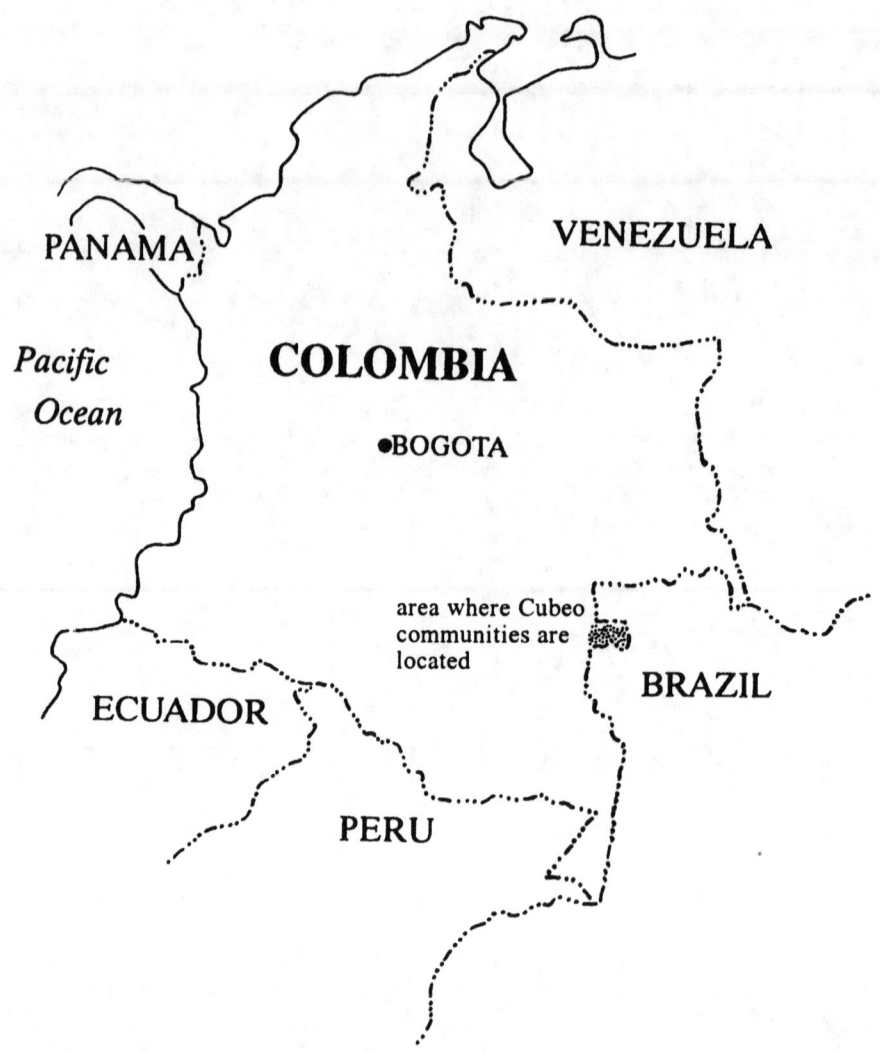

1
Introduction

The Cubeo people live principally along the Vaupés, Cuduyarí, and Querarí Rivers in the northwestern Amazon River Basin. The majority (an estimated 6,000) live in southeast Colombia in the Vaupés territory. Approximately 300 to 500 more live across the border in Brazil.[1]

The area in which the Cubeos live is jungle interrupted by little other than a network of rivers. Although explorers have entered the area since the early sixteenth century, and the Cubeos have had contact with rubber hunters and many others, the Cubeo language and culture have remained largely intact.

The largest Cubeo village, Tapurucuara, on the Querarí River, has a population of about 300. Most Cubeo villages, however, consist of about 15 to 35 people in two or three houses on the bank of a river or stream. The distance between these small settlements poses a problem for the schooling of the children, since only the larger villages have schools. Children from villages without a school must go away to boarding schools if they want to study, which is not very satisfactory to many Cubeo parents.

The food staples of the Cubeo people are fish (over 100 different species) and cassava. The women work in fields that have been cleared and burned by the men. Using tumplines, the women carry baskets of manioc tubers, sometimes weighing 30 kilograms or more, from the field to their houses, often walking an hour or more with their load. Then, the time-consuming process of converting poison manioc roots to cassava cakes begins. This involves the use of grating boards, a basket and tripod

---

[1]The data for this study was gathered by J. K. and Neva Salser (1964–1976), Nancy L. Morse (1980 to present), and Judith Ferguson (1984–1986) under the auspices of the Instituto Lingüístico de Verano, which is under contract with the government of Colombia. All are grateful to the Cubeo people who so kindly taught their language.

for straining, a woven manioc squeezer, a basket for sifting, and a huge clay skillet. The carrying baskets and clay skillets are made by the women, but the men make all the other baskets. The men also hunt and fish, build the houses, make the dugout canoes and paddles, and the nets and traps for fishing.

According to a comparative study of Tucanoan languages (Waltz and Wheeler 1972:128–29), the Cubeo language has phonological and lexical similarities with both Eastern and Western Tucanoan languages and, thus, should be classified in a third category, Middle Tucanoan. According to Ardila (1988:12), Cubeo is one of two languages, the other being Tanimuca, for which "su ubicación en la familia lingüistica Tucano queda aún por definir."

The percentage of the Cubeo population that is fluent in Spanish is estimated at 10 to 20% of children ages five to twelve, 70 to 80% of young adults, and 15 to 20% of older people.

A Cubeo belongs to one of three phratries and may marry a Cubeo who does not belong to his/her phratry or someone from one of the other language groups in the area. Because of the intermarriage among language groups in this area, it is not unusual to find Cubeos who speak three or more indigenous languages in addition to their own.

1.1 Phonemes

Cubeo has six oral vowels /a e i o u ɨ/ and six corresponding nasalized vowels /ã ẽ ĩ õ ũ ɨ̃/ shown in (1). (The /ɨ/ is a high central unrounded vowel.) The phoneme written here as /e/ and its nasalized counterpart /ẽ/ are phonetically open: [ɛ] and [ɛ̃].

(1) Vowel phonemes

		Front	Central	Back
High	oral	i	ɨ	u
	nasalized	ĩ	ɨ̃	ũ
Nonhigh	oral	e	a	o
	nasalized	ẽ	ã	õ

The consonant phonemes of Cubeo are shown in (2). The /w/ and the /j/ have allophones at other points of articulation (see §1.2). Cubeo is unusual in having a velar fricative /x/ but no strident fricatives. Among the older Cubeos, Spanish borrowings containing the *s* sound are pronounced instead with the alveopalatal affricate /tʃ/ before vowels; the *s* disappears word final in such borrowings: [xeˈtʃu] from Spanish *Jesús*.

Introduction

(2) Consonant phonemes

	Bilabial	Alveolar	Alveopalatal	Velar
Stop voiceless	p	t		k
voiced	b	d		
Affricate			tʃ	
Fricative				x
Flap		r		
Semivowel	w		j	

1.2 Allophones

While there are no vowel allophones in Cubeo, many of the Cubeo consonants have allophones conditioned by the nasality of the environment. The voiceless consonant /x/ has the variant [ŋ̊] before a nasalized vowel as in (3).

(3)　/xɨ̃ˈxõrɨ/ [ŋ̊ɨ̃ˈŋ̊õɾɨ]　　　　squirrel
　　　/ˈxuxiko/ [ˈxuxiko]　　　　species of fish

Similarly, /r/ has the allophone [ɾ̃] before a nasal vowel and [ɾ] before an oral vowel.

(4)　/koˈrexakɨ/ [koˈɾexakɨ]　　wait!
　　　/kõˈrẽko/ [kõˈɾ̃ẽko]　　　　woodpecker

The voiced stops /b/ and /d/ occur as the nasal variants [m] and [n], respectively, either word initial or following a nasalized vowel, provided the following vowel is nasalized; and as [m͡b] and [n͡d] either word initial or following a nasalized vowel, provided the following vowel is oral as in (5)–(7)

(5)　/bãˈkaRõ/ [mãˈkaɾ̃õ]　　　jungle
　　　/dãˈxõko/ [nãˈxõko]　　　crab
　　　/xõˈbẽbIko/ [xõˈmẽmĩko]　she stirred
　　　/dẽˈdẽbIko/ [nẽˈnẽmĩko]　she sucked

(6)　/ˈkɨ̃ba/ [ˈkɨ̃m͡ba]　　　　　comb
　　　/bãˈxibewɨ/ [mãxim͡bewɨ]　I don't know

(7) /'xīRɨ/ ['xĩndɨ]   egg
     /'dudukɨ/ ['ndudukɨ]   chigger

In other environments (i.e., following an oral vowel), /b/ and /d/ are realized as voiced stops.

The voiceless stops /p/ and /t/ have prenasalized allophones when they appear word initial or following a nasalized vowel, if the following vowel is nasal.

(8) /kō'pĩjo/ [kō'mpĩjo]   tooth

(9) /tãi'tēdɨ/ [tãi'ntēdɨ] fly (noun)

The phoneme /j/ has eight allophones: [j j̃ ð ð̃ dʒ ɲ ndʒ ɲ̃]. The semivowel [j] occurs after the high front vowels /i ĩ/, before an oral vowel.

(10) /bĩ'bĩjo/ [mĩ'mĩjo]   hummingbird

The nasalized semivowel [j̃] occurs after the high front vowels /i ĩ/ before a nasalized vowel.

(11) /ĩ'jōrɨ̃/ [ĩ'j̃ōrɨ̃]   did you take (it)?

The voiced interdental fricative [ð] occurs between the nonhigh vowels /a ã e ẽ o õ/, provided the second vowel is oral.

(12) /do'je/ [do'ðe]   species of fish *(dormilón)*
     /ã'rãjo/ [ã'r̃ãðo]   leg
     /ka'jaxĩẽ/ [ka'ðaxĩẽ]   nearby

The preceding nonhigh vowel may be in the preceding word if the /j/ begins a word closely associated (possibly cliticized) to that preceding word.

(13) /dō'jobo/ [nō'ð̃obo]   after that, lit., that after
     /dẽ je'bai/ [nẽ ð̃e'bai]   their place

The nasal interdental fricative allophone [ð̃] occurs between nonhigh nasalized vowels.

(14) /ã'jã/ [ã'ðã] snake
    /kõ'jēĩbē/ [kõ'ðēĩmē] necklace

The voiced alveopalatal affricate [dʒ] occurs elsewhere before an oral vowel, that is, after a high back or central vowel [u], [ū], [ɨ], or [ɨ̄], and before an oral vowel. The nasal alveopalatal allophone [ɲ] occurs elsewhere before a nasalized vowel; that is, after a high back or central vowel [u], [ū], [ɨ], or [ɨ̄] and before a nasalized vowel, or utterance initial before a nasalized vowel as in (15).

(15) /a'bukuja/ [a'bukudʒa] cassava serving basket
    /jã'bĩ/ [ɲã'mĩ] night

The allophones with nasal onset [n͡dʒ] and [n͡j] occur utterance initial before an oral vowel in free variation with each other.

(16) /jɨí/ [n͡jɨí] ~ [n͡dʒɨí] kapok

Salser (1971) posited a separate phoneme /ð/, whereas we have claimed that [ð] is an allophone of /j/. Our analysis faces a single counterexample in the common verb root /ja-/ 'do, make', which unexpectedly retains the [ð] utterance initial, e.g., [ðabexakɨ] 'don't do it!', and sometimes word initial even though the preceding word does not end in a nonhigh vowel, e.g., *pōbɨ ða-Rī* (burrow make-GER) 'burrow making'. As discussed above, [j] would be expected in this environment (cf. *xewɨ-ja-Rī* (edge-make-GER) 'sharpening'). Aside from this one verb, then, [ð] can be treated as an allophone of /j/.

The phoneme /w/ has as allophones the voiced labiodental fricative [v], the semivowel [w], the voiced bilabial fricative [β], and the nasal semivowel [w̃].

The allophone [v] occurs before the oral front vowels /i e/, as well as between two /a/s.

(17) /we'a/ [ve'a] corn
    /ka'wa/ [ka'va] buzzard

The allophone [w] occurs before nonfront vowels and word initially before /a/.

(18) /kɨ'wɨ/ [kɨ'wɨ] I am
    /wa'o/ [wa'o] black howler monkey

The allophone [β] occurs in free variation with [w] before /a/.

(19) /waˈxa/ [waˈxa] ~ [βaˈxa] capuchin monkey

The allophone [w̃] occurs before nasalized vowels.

(20) /ˈwãrĩ/ [ˈw̃ãrĩ]   pig
      /wĩˈɨ̵bE/ [w̃ĩˈɲɨ̵mẽ]   he is sniffing/smelling

1.3 Syllable, tone, and stress

A syllable in Cubeo consists of (C)V. Two levels of pitch, low (unmarked in phonemic examples) and high (marked with an acute accent over the vowel in the examples of this section), contrast in Cubeo: /kábűká/ 'ear' and /kábãve/ 'torch'; /xájɨbU/ 'I'm looking at' and /ãjɨbU/ 'I'm eating'. Low pitch has two variants, mid (unmarked in the following examples) and low ([ˋ] in the following phonetic examples). Low pitch occurs word final and on syllables preceding a vowel (except on dipthongs, where mid pitch is found); mid pitch occurs elsewhere: /xoékɨ/ [xòˈékɨ́] 'axe', /ãíje/ [ãˈíjè] 'food', /vekó/ [veˈkó] 'parrot', and /ãdúi/ [ãˈnúí] 'there' (Salser 1971).

The stressed syllable (marked with a [ˈ] before the stressed syllable in the phonetic examples of this section) is the first syllable with high pitch in a phonological word. In the majority of Cubeo words, this is the second syllable of the word, and the primary stress always falls on one of the first four syllables. Stress (equivalently, the position of the first syllable with high pitch) is contrastive as shown in (21).

(21) /kuˈjawɨ/   I bathed (recently)
      /ˈkujawɨ/   I ran (recently)

In addition to the difference in pitch, stressed vowels are slightly longer than unstressed vowels in normal speech and significantly lengthened in emphatic speech.

In the remainder of this book, pitch is not marked; stress is marked only when it does not fall on the second syllable, or in other words, when it falls on the first or third syllable.

1.4 Morphophonemics

1.4.1 Nasal spreading

Most morphemes are of one of three types:

1. Inherently nasal (many roots, as well as suffixes such as -xã 'associative', -xĩ 'diminutive', -Rã 'animate plural', -kũ and -jãbĩ 'classifiers', -Rĩ 'gerund');
2. Inherently oral (many roots, as well as suffixes such as -pe 'similarity', -ke 'accompaniment, instrument', -du 'frustrative', and the classifiers -bo, -Rɨ, -we, -bɨ, and -jo); and
3. Unmarked for nasality (suffixes only, e.g., -RE 'direct/indirect object', -wɨ 'nonthird person', and -bA 'interrogative').[2]

Most roots belong to classes one or two; there are no roots belonging to class three (i.e., there are no roots which are unmarked for nasality). However, a few roots are partly oral and partly nasal, e.g., /bã'kaxa-/ [mã'kaxa-] 'defecate', /kõ'bãxi-/ [kõ'mãxi-] 'be accustomed to', /bã'xi-/ [mã'xi-] 'know, be able to', and /xo'roxĩ-/ [xo'roxĩ-] 'get angry'. There is no evidence that these roots are bimorphemic in present day Cubeo.[3]

Suffixes beginning with consonants that lack nasal allophones can only be inherently nasal or inherently oral, while suffixes beginning with consonants that have nasal variants (viz., /b d j w x r/) can belong to any of these three classes. The impossibility of predicting which class a suffix beginning in a nasalizable consonant will belong to is illustrated by the suffixes -wa 'accustomed aspect' and -wA 'causative' in (22) and (23).

(22) dɨ̃-wA-Iy-Abẽ → /dɨ̃-'wã-ĩj-ãbẽ/ → [dɨ̃'w̃ãĩjãmẽ]
go-CAUS-STV-N/H^3ms
He takes (someone/something) (lit., he causes (someone/something) to go).

(23) 'dɨ̃-wa-bI → /'dɨ̃-wa-bi/ → ['dɨ̃wabi]
go-ACST-3ms
He customarily goes.

A few suffixes are partly oral and partly nasal, that is they contain both inherently oral and inherently nasal vowels. An example is -kebã

---
[2]In this book, vowels unmarked for nasality are represented by upper case letters.
[3]The interlinear glosses of verbs throughout this book will not overtly mark the infinitive form with 'to' though this should be understood.

'assumed' (discussed in §2.2.2.4). There is no evidence in present day Cubeo for further breaking -kebã down into separate oral and nasal suffixes. Furthermore, the suffix -ta (which indicates focus at the discourse level) is itself oral, but conditions nasal spreading.

Nasalization spreads from a nasal vowel to the right across morpheme boundaries onto vowels which are unmarked for nasality, providing only vowels unmarked for nasality and nasalizable consonants (/b d j w x r/) intervene. Some examples are given in (24) and (25).

(24) a. bue-bIko → /bu'e-biko/ → [bu'ebiko]
She studied recently.

b. dɨ̃-bIko → /dɨ̃-'bĩko/ → [nɨ̃'mĩko]
She went recently.

(25) a. bue-jɨ-bE → /bu'e-jɨ-be/ → [buédʒɨbe]
He is studying.

b. dɨ̃-jɨ-bE → /dɨ̃-'jɨ̃-bẽ/ → [nɨ̃'ɲɨ̃mẽ]
He is going.

Nasal spreading is blocked by an inherently oral suffix (or an inherently oral vowel in a suffix of mixed nasality) as in (26).

(26) a. jɨ̃ã-bo-RE → /jɨ̃'ã-bo-re/ → [ɲɨ̃'ãm͡bore]
knee (accusative case)

b. õpõ-bɨ → /õ'põ-bɨ/ → [õ'm͡põm͡bɨ]
shotgun cartridge

c. dɨ̃-Rĩ-du-bi → /dɨ̃-'rĩ-du-bi/ → [dɨ̃'rĩn͡dubi]
He tried to go (but couldn't).

Note that the oral stops which occur between the nasal vowel on the left and the inherently oral vowel on the right appear phonetically as their prenasalized allophones.

In some cases, as with the frustrative morpheme du, one might propose that a morpheme beginning in a nasalizable consonant, but which blocks nasal spreading is in fact a separate word. (Nasal spreading is blocked by word boundaries.) However, this is not a general solution, since many of the morphemes which unexpectedly block the spread of nasalization are clearly suffixes, for example the classifiers -*bo,* -*Rɨ,* -*we,* -*bɨ,* and -*jo,* and the accustomed aspect suffix -*wa* discussed above.

In addition to suffixes which unexpectedly block nasal spreading, the verb '*bA-* 'be' has the status of an independent word in that it (and the suffixes following it) act as a word for purposes of the assignment of stress. Nonetheless, when preceded by a word ending in a nasalized vowel, '*bA-* is itself subject to nasal spreading, and thus appears to be encliticized to that word.

(27) a. *ixi-bõ*   '*bA-I-bIko* (['mãĩmĩ͡ko])
         be^sick-PSV^FS^NMLZ be-STV-3fs
         She was sick.

   b. '*xi-jo-ko*   '*bA-I-bIko* (['baibiko])
      POS-younger^sibling-FS be-STV-3fs
      She is my younger sister.

Finally, the morpheme *di-* 'this/that previously identified' unexpectedly has a nasalized allomorph *dĩ-* before the diminutive suffix -*xĩ.* This is an isolated situation, rather than an instance of a more general rule of leftward spreading of nasalization, since there are numerous instances of non-nasal vowels before the diminutive suffix, and of the oral allomorph of *di-* before suffixes containing nasal vowels.

1.4.2 Morphophonemic variation between /r/ and /d/

Suffixes of which the initial consonant is the flap /r/ (or under an alternative analysis, the alveolar stop /d/) exhibit morphophonemic variation conditioned by the preceding vowel. After the front vowels /i ĩ e ẽ/, such suffixes begin with /d/, but after other vowels, they begin with /r/. An example is the inherently nasal suffix -*Rĩ* (gerund).[4]

(28) a. *a-Rĩ* → /a-'rĩ/ → [ɑ'r̃ĩ]
         say-GER
         saying

   b. *ĩ-Rĩ* → /ĩ-'dĩ/ → [ĩ'nĩ]
      get-GER
      getting

---

[4] The capital *R* is used here to indicate an archiphoneme ambiguous between /r/ and /d/.

Another example of the archiphoneme R is the inherently oral classifier suffix, -Ri 'small, three-dimensional object' in (29).

(29) a. ūjū-Ri → /ū'jū-ri/ → [ū'ɲũɾɨ]
    avocado-CLS:3D
    avocado

b. ɨjei-Ri → /'ɨjei-di/ → ['ɨdʒeidɨ]
    tree^grape-CLS:3D
    tree grape

Finally, some suffixes have this morphophonemic variation and, in addition, are unmarked for nasality. This results in four morphophonemic variants of a single suffix. An example is -RE (object marker).

(30) a. ibã-Rõ-RE → /i'bã-rõ-rẽ/ → [i'mãrõ̃rẽ]
    town-CLS:place-OBJ
    town

b. jãbĩ-RE → /jã'bĩ-dẽ/ → [ɲã'mĩnẽ]
    night-OBJ
    night

c. oko-RE → /o'ko-re/ → [o'koɾe]
    water-OBJ
    water

d. kɨi-RE → /kɨ'i-de/ → [kɨ'ide]
    manioc-OBJ
    manioc

The verbs da- 'come' and dɨ̃- 'go' also become Ra- and Rɨ̃-, respectively, when cliticized to a verb ending in -kɨ or -ko as in (31).

(31) toiwa-ko-Ra-xA-ko   toiwa-I-we-Rã
    write-FS-come-IMP-FS   write-STV-CLS:flat-LOC
    Come write on the blackboard.

Apart from this clitic construction, these verb roots are da- and dɨ̃-, respectively.

Introduction

The /r/ very nearly approaches being an allophone of /d/, but there are a few examples of contrast, e.g., /ˈdudukɨ/ 'chigger' and /ˈturubo/ 'species of plant'. Apart from these few examples, /d/ always occurs following the front vowels (/i ī e ẽ/) and word initial. The /r/ usually occurs following nonfront vowels. The only instances of /r/ following a front vowel are onomatopoetic words or words borrowed from Spanish, e.g., /ˈperu ˈperu/ [ˈperu ˈperu] 'twinkle twinkle/flash flash', /ˈtferu/ [ˈtʃeru] 'sound of panpipes', and /tferutfu/ [tʃerutʃu] 'wood saw' (Spanish *serrucho*); and the only instances of word initial /r/ are in words borrowed from Spanish, particularly proper nouns such as *Roberto*.

1.4.3 Stress shift

Nonhigh vowels attract the primary stress of a word from an immediately preceding stressed vowel, which may be high or nonhigh. One example of this are the two-syllable noun roots that are pluralized by the addition of the suffix -A shown in (32).

(32) /kōˈpījo/   tooth   /kōpī-ˈA/   teeth
     /pɨˈrɨ/   hand   /pɨrɨ-ˈA/   hands
     /kōˈrījo/   blade of grass   /kōrī-ˈA/   grass

(The *-jo* suffix is a classifier which means 'slender, pointed, cylindrical'; it does not appear in the plural forms above for reasons which will be discussed in §3.1.1.) Another example of stress shift is one- and two-syllable verb roots conjugated in the regular past tense, as seen by comparison with other tenses and with nominalized forms in (33).

(33) /xi-ˈA-bẽ/   he gave
     /ˈxi-bI/   he gave recently
     /ˈxi-jɨ-bE/   he gives
     /ˈxi-I-Rō/   a gift

Note that the stress shifts only one syllable to the right; the already shifted stress is not further attracted from the /ˈA/ onto the /ẽ/.

(34) /kojɨ-ˈA-bẽ/   he told
     /koˈjɨ-bI/   he told recently
     /koˈjɨ-jɨ-bE/   he tells
     /koˈjɨ-I-Rō/   a tale/story

(35) /bue-ˈA-bẽ/ he studied/taught
/buˈe-bI/ he studied/taught recently
/buˈe-jɨ-bE/ he studies/teaches
/buˈe-I-Rō/ a class/lesson/course of study

Still another example of stress shift are two-syllable verb roots taking the causative suffix -O as in (36)–(38).

(36) /xaˈjɨ-wɬ/ I tossed/spilled recently.
/xajɨ-ˈO-wɬ kaju-ˈxĩ-Rã-RE/ I fed chickens recently.

(37) /xaˈtu-wɬ xia-jo-kũ-RE/ I boarded a canoe recently.
/xatɨ-ˈO-wɬ ˈdã-RE/ I transported them recently.

(38) /koˈre-wA-wɬ/ I counted recently.
/kore-ˈO-wA-wɬ/ I realized recently.

A final example of stress shift is the abstract general nominalized form of two-syllable stative verb roots, as seen by comparison with the abstract specific nominalized form and the conjugated verb forms. (The singular inanimate nominalizer, glossed (IN^SG^NMLZ), is used to form abstract specific nominalizations, and the plural inanimate nominalizer, glossed (IN^PL^NMLZ), is used to form abstract general nominalizations, as explained in §3.1.4.)

(39) /xidɨ-ˈE/ fearfulness (general nominalization)
/xiˈdɨ-Rō/ a fear (specific nominalization)
/xiˈdɨ-wɬ jɨ/ I'm afraid.

(40) /xɨxɨ-ˈE/ coldness (general nominalization)
/xɨˈxɨ-Rō/ something cold (specific nominalization)
/xɨˈxɨ-wɬ jɨ-RE/ I'm cold (lit., it is cold to me).

(41) /xũã-ˈE/ redness (general nominalization)
/xũˈã-Rō/ something red (specific nominalization)
/xũˈã-wɬ/ It's red.

1.4.4 Vowel coalesence

When two identical vowels are juxtaposed across morpheme boundaries, the two vowels coalesce. For example, when the suffix -*I* 'stativizer' is added to the verb root *kopai-* 'to return', the two /i/s collapse into a single /i/: *kopaidõ* [kopɑinõ] 'a returning' (with the further addition of the suffix -*Rõ* (NFUT^SG^NMLZ), which forms a specific abstract nominalization) and *kopaije* [kopɑije] 'returnings' (with the addition of the suffix -*E* (NFUT^PL^NMLZ), which forms an abstract general nominalization).

(42) and (43) are examples of this morphophonemic change with the vowels /a/ and /e/.

(42) *da-RExa-Abẽ* → /dɑrexɑbẽ/
come-HPAST-N/H^3ms
he came long ago

(43) *ape-E-RE* → /ɑpede/
other-IN^PL^NMLZ-OBJ
other (things)

1.4.5 Epenthesis of /j/

When the vowel /i/ precedes a distinct vowel across morpheme boundaries, a /j/ is epenthesized. This is very common with the stativizing suffix -*I*, which has the allomorph -*Ij* before vowels (see §2.2.1), but also occurs with other morphemes, e.g., *kai-* 'all' becomes *kaij-E* 'all of them' when the -*E* (PL^NMLZ) is added.

2
Verbs

2.1 Verb classes

Cubeo has two sizable verb classes, referred to in this book as DYNAMIC and STATIVE. The terms stative and dynamic do not, unfortunately, have exactly the same meaning for the grammar of Cubeo that they do for other languages; while typical stative verbs in Cubeo, such as *ki̵-* 'be, exist, live', are what would be considered stative universally, some verbs which fall into the stative class are less obviously stative, e.g., *doba-* 'sit'. Likewise, while there are prototypical dynamic verbs in Cubeo, such as *da-* 'come' and *wai-* 'happen', others are less obviously dynamic, e.g., *o-* 'cry'. Nonetheless, the distinction between the stative and dynamic verb classes is crucial to understanding the verb morphology of Cubeo. As one example, the same set of suffixes used on a dynamic verb stem implies the recent past tense, but on a stative verb stem implies the present durative.

While the dynamic/stative verb system described here has similarities to what has been called active/agentive case marking systems (see Mithun 1991 for a review), the system of Cubeo differs in that a system of affixes freely switches both transitive and intransitive verbs between these two classes, without affecting the active/passive status of the verbs.

A third verb class consists of one member, the clitic verb meaning 'be', which is very restricted in form.

2.1.1 Dynamic verbs

Most Cubeo verbs are dynamic. These are largely verbs of action, including intransitive verbs, such as *di̵-* 'go' and *da-* 'come', transitive verbs, such as *xoa-* 'wash', and ditransitive verbs, such as *'xi-* 'give'.

The past tenses are formed by adding the past tense suffixes directly to a dynamic verb. A dynamic verb may be converted into a stative verb stem by the addition of certain suffixes; when the past tense affixes are added after such a stativizing suffix, the result is instead a verb in the durative or habitual tense/aspect.

2.1.2 Stative verbs

Verbs in this class generally express a mental or physical state of some sort. Some typical stative verb roots include ʹbA- 'be', kɨ- 'be, exist, live', doba- 'sit', ixi- 'hurt', bēā- 'be well', and ɨrōxi- 'smell bad'.

The defining characteristic of a verb of the stative class is the different use of certain suffixes from the way they are used with dynamic verbs. For instance, in order to form the past tenses, a suffix must be added which converts the stative root into a dynamic stem. In the absence of such a dynamicizing suffix, the suffixes which indicate a past tense on a dynamic verb instead mark the durative and habitual tense/aspects.

2.1.3 The copular verb clitic

The third class of verbs in Cubeo consists of just one verb, the copular clitic -bU 'be', which attaches to nouns (including nominalized verbs). It has only four different forms: -bE (declarative third-person animate singular), -bEbu for the probable evidential (this form occurs only in the second and third persons), -bA for the interrogative mood, and -bU, which is used in all other cases. The copular clitic does not occur with the assumed evidential.

Both the verb ʹbA- 'be' in (44a) and the clitic -bU in (44b) may function in an equative construction.

(44) a. bia   ʹbA-wɨ   di-E
           hot^pepper be-NON3 this-IN^PL^NMLZ
           This is hot pepper.

     b. bia-bU   di-E
           hot^pepper-be this-IN^PL^NMLZ
           This is hot pepper.

Like the stative verb kɨ- in (45a), the copular clitic may also be used to mean 'be in a place, live, exist', as in (45b).

(45) a. 'ārī kɨ-RI   Juan
       where exist-INTR Juan
       Where is Juan?

   b. 'ārī-bA   Juan
      where-be^INTR Juan
      Where is Juan?

The construction used in (45a) is typical of the Eastern Tucanoan languages. The construction used in (45b) might be a borrowing from Curripaco, an Arawakan language; the Cubeos have frequent contact with the Curripacos.

The copular clitic verb is also used to form several of the verb tenses and in the passive, as described later in this chapter.

2.2 Verb morphology

The morphology of independent verbs of Cubeo, discussed in this section, is quite complex. This is not only because there is a large number of suffixes which encode a variety of grammatical information—all verbal affixes in Cubeo are suffixes, except the directional *xa-* 'away from the speaker' and *da-* 'toward the speaker'—but also because the individual suffixes often overlap in function. For instance, the person of the subject is encoded both by what are here called person markers, and by tense/aspect markers. For that reason, and because of occasional morphophonemic processes, decisions about morpheme breaks are often arbitrary.[5]

2.2.1 Class-changing suffixes

A number of inflectional suffixes alter the stativeness of verb stems. When added to a dynamic verb stem, the stativizer suffix *-I* (before consonants) or *-Ij* (before vowels; see §1.4.5 regarding this allomorphy) causes the resulting stem to be stative. In addition to this affix, the following suffixes also cause the resulting stem to be stative: *-bE* 'negative' (see page 30), *-ijɨ* 'desiderative' (see page 27), *-xE* 'conditional' (see page 51), and *-xɨ* 'present tense irrealis' (see page 26).

When added to a stative verb stem, the dynamicizer suffix *-te* (cognate with the dynamic verb root *te-* 'do') causes the resulting stem to be

---

[5]The reader is encouraged to refer to the appendices which list alphabetically all of the prefixes, suffixes, and classifiers, giving their meaning, abbreviated form, and where to find further discussion.

dynamic. The following suffixes also cause the resulting stem to be dynamic: *-RExa* 'historical past' (see page 45), *-Rɨ-du* 'frustrative' (see page 28), *-wA* 'causative' (see page 57), *-ka* 'benefactive' (see page 58), and *-Ikõxẽ* 'authoritative' (see page 59).

The stativizer suffix *-I* and the dynamicizer suffix *-te* precede suffixes marking tense and aspect.

Some examples of the use of class-changing suffixes follow.

Example (46) illustrates how the same tense/aspect affixes on a dynamic stem imply recent past, while on a stative stem they imply present durative.

(46) a. *ẽbẽ-karã*
    descend-N/H^1pexc
    We descended. (*ẽbẽ-* is a dynamic verb root)

  b. *ẽbẽ-I-karã*
    descend-STV-N/H^1pexc
    We are descending.

  c. *di-jābɨ-RE*   *'kɨ-te-bI*
    this-CLS:building-OBJ live-DYN-3ms
    He lived in this house. (*kɨ-* is a stative verb root)

  d. *kɨ-bI*
    live-3ms
    He exists, he lives.

In example (47) the dynamic verb *ja-* 'do, make' is first stativized by the negative suffix *-bE*, then dynamicized by the dynamicizer suffix *-te*.

(47) *jɨ ja-bE-te-wɨ*
    I   do-NEG-DYN-NON3
    I didn't do (anything).

Examples (48)–(50) illustrate the stativizing or dynamicizing effects of some of the desiderative, frustrative, and causative suffixes.

(48) a. *da-ijɨ-bI*
    come-DES-3ms
    He wants to come.

b. *da-ijɨ-te-bI*
   come-DES-DYN-3ms
   He wanted to come.

(49) a. *bue-Rɨ-du-bI*
   study-GER-FRUS-3ms
   He tried to study.

   b. *bue-Rɨ-du-I-bI*
   study-GER-FRUS-STV-3ms
   He tries to study.

(50) a. *dɨ-wA-bI*
   go-CAUS-3ms
   He carried (lit., he caused to go).

   b. *dɨ-wA-I-bI*
   go-CAUS-STV-3ms
   He carries (lit., he causes to go).

2.2.2 Inflectional suffixes

Verbal affixes used in independent clauses are discussed in this section. The morphology of verbs in subordinate clauses is discussed in chapter 6.

2.2.2.1 Mood. Cubeo distinguishes three moods: indicative, interrogative, and imperative. Cubeo also has irrealis, desiderative, and frustrative suffixes, but since these are not, for the most part, mutually exclusive with the indicative, interrogative, and imperative suffixes, we consider them separately (see §2.2.2.2). (There is also a suffix used with conditionals which can occur with the indicative and interrogative, and, therefore, we treat it as an aspect marker; see "conditional aspect" on page 51.)

Indicative. The indicative mood is used to make statements.

(51) *dɨ-Abẽ*
   go-N/H^3ms
   He went.

The indicative mood is unmarked, i.e., it is indicated by the absence of the interrogative and imperative suffixes. However, some of the person/gender/number suffixes (e.g., those of the recent past and present durative, shown in the table in (130) on page 40) occur only in the indicative, and may, thus, be considered markers of the indicative mood.

Interrogative. The interrogative mood is used in both content questions and yes/no questions.

The choice of interrogative suffixes is dependent on the person of the subject, the tense, and the aspect. There seems to be some variability, perhaps between generations, in the choice of these suffixes; in the following, we describe the most common patterns.

The first-person interrogative of the near future tense is formed by simply attaching the suffix *-xi* to the stem; this suffix is here glossed 'FUT^1^INTR'. It is unclear from our data whether there is a first-person interrogative of the indefinite future tense distinct from the first-person interrogative of the near future. This is perhaps not surprising, as first-person interrogatives are often quite unnatural, and this is particularly true in the future tense. The near future tense, unlike the indefinite future, is often used to indicate intent (see page 1947), so it makes sense that the near future would be more common on second-person interrogatives.

The first-person interrogative, the third-person animate interrogative of the present tense, and the third-person animate interrogative of the indefinite future tense are formed by replacing the normal person/number suffixes with the suffix *-bA*, glossed 'INTR'. (This is the interrogative form of the copular verb; note that the present tense and the indefinite future tense are formed on nominalized stems.)

The second-person interrogative of the indefinite future tense, the present tense, the nonrecent past tense/habitual aspect and the recent past tense/durative aspect are all formed with the suffix *-Rĩ*, replacing the normal person/number suffixes. (However, we have also observed what appear to be second-person assumed recent past questions with the suffix *-bA*; see example (63a).) Thus, in the indefinite future tense, *-Rĩ* replaces the declarative person/number suffixes (see page 47 and table (130) on page 40). In the present tense *-Rĩ* replaces the declarative copular verb (see §2.1.3).

In the nonrecent past/habitual, *-A-Rĩ* replaces the person/gender/number suffixes (table (140) on page 42). (*-A* can be analyzed as a suffix marking the nonrecent past and habitual tenses. In most cases, we do not gloss it separately. However, separating *-A* simplifies the presentation of the interrogative suffixes, so for the interrogative mood we distinguish it as a separate affix. It is therefore not shown in the table of

Verbs

interrogative suffixes below.) In addition to these forms, which are unmarked for evidential status, we have also observed (example (63b)) second-person nonrecent past/habitual interrogatives with the 'assumed' evidential -*kebā* followed by the interrogative suffix -*RI*; the latter suffix is not otherwise used in the second-person nonrecent past interrogative.

Finally, in the recent past/durative, -*Rĩ* replaces the person/number suffix (table (130) on page 40). In the recent past/durative questions we have recorded, the interrogative suffix always follows one of the 'assumed' evidentials given in (129) on page 39. The distinction between witnessed and assumed evidential status thus seems effectively to be neutralized in second-person interrogatives for the recent past/durative, although it is unclear why the recent and nonrecent past tenses should differ in this way.

For all other persons and tenses, the interrogative is formed by replacing the normal person/number suffixes with the suffix -*RI*, preceded by the suffix -*A* in the nonrecent past and present habitual. (Note that on a stem ending in *a*, the nonrecent past and recent past interrogatives will often be identical, since the -*A* suffix marking the nonrecent past will coalesce with the final *a* of the stem.) The -*RI* suffix may also be used with the other combinations of person/tense, except for the first person of the future tenses.

The affixes marking the interrogative are summarized in the table in (52); the suffix -*RI* is used in the entire shaded area.

(52) Interrogative suffixes

Person	Near Future	Indefinite Future	Present Tense	RP/Durative, NRP/Habitual	All other tenses and aspects
1	-*xi*	??			
3 animate			-*bA*		
inanimate				-*RI*	
2			-*Rĩ*		

The examples in (53)–(63) illustrate the interrogative mood.

(53) a. *da-kɨ-Rɨ̃*   *bɨ̃*
    come-R/D^MS^ASM-INTR 2s
    Did you come? (typical greeting for a host/hostess to a male visitor; recent past, since *da-* is a dynamic verb)

   b. *doba-kɨ-Rɨ̃*   *bɨ̃*
    sit-R/D^MS^ASM-INTR 2s
    Are you sitting? (typical greeting of a visitor to his/her host, durative aspect, since *doba-* is a stative verb)

(54) *kɨ-wA-te-Rã-Rɨ̃*   *bɨ̃xã tãũ-tɨra-RE*
    exist-CAUS-DYN-R/D^PL^ASM-INTR 2p   metal-CLS:circular-OBJ
    Did you have money? (recent past)

(55) a. *tɨ-RI*   *ɨ̃*
    fall-INTR 3ms
    Did he fall? (recent past, since *tɨ-* is a dynamic verb)

   b. *tɨ-A-RI*   *ɨ̃*
    fall-N/H-INTR 3ms
    Did he fall? (nonrecent past)

(56) a. *doba-te-RI*   *õ*
    sit-DYN-INTR 3fs
    Did she sit down? (recent past)

   b. *doba-te-A-RI*   *õ*
    sit-DYN-N/H-INTR 3fs
    Did she sit down? (nonrecent past)

   c. *bue-I-RI*   *õ*
    study-STV-INTR 3fs
    Is she studying? (durative)

   d. *bue-Ij-A-RI*   *õ*
    study-STV-N/H-INTR 3fs
    Does she habitually study? (habitual)

(57) *oka-ki-RI*
rain-FUT-INTR
Is it going to rain? (indefinite future)

(58) a. *ixi-RI   bĩ-RE*
hurt-INTR 2s-OBJ
Do you hurt? (lit., Does it hurt you?)

b. *ixi-te-RI   'ĩ-RE*
hurt-DYN-INTR 3ms-OBJ
Did he hurt? Was he in pain? (lit., Did it hurt him? recent past)

c. *ixi-te-A-RI   ĩ-RE*
hurt-DYN-N/H-INTR 3ms-OBJ
Did he hurt? Was he in pain? (lit., Did it hurt him? nonrecent past)

(59) *aipije-RE   piri-bio-Rāxi-RI-ka   bĩxã*
how^many-OBJ hand-tie-NRFUT^PL-INTR-DUB 2p
When in the world are you going to get married? (lit., When are you going to get hand-tied? At one time, as part of the marriage ceremony one of the groom's hands was tied to one of his bride's hands; near future.)

(60) *'ārī   bēbē-Rāxārā-bA   dã*
where work-INDEF^FUT^PL-INTR 3p
Where will they work? (indefinite future)

(61) *xabo-ki-Rĩ   bĩ*
rule-NFUT^MS^NMLZ-INTR 2s
Are you the chief/headman? (present tense)

(62) *eda-RI   dã*
arrive-INTR 3p
Did they recently arrive? (recent past, since *eda-* is a dynamic verb; nonrecent past would be homophonous, but *eda-A-RI* morphemically)

(63) a. *ārɨ̃-bE-te-RE-bA*   *bɨ̃xã*
remember-NEG-DYN-R/D^ASM-INTR 2p
Did you evidently forget? (recent past)

b. *bue-kebã-RI*   *ɨ̃*
study-ASM-INTR 3ms
Did he evidently study? (nonrecent past)

Finally, the interrogative form of the conditional tense is formed with both the interrogative form *-bA* of the copular verb and the interrogative suffix *-RI*, followed by the discourse suffix *-ka* as in (64).

(64) *jai-'xe-bA-RI-ka*   *ɨ̃*   *kaja-te-kɨjɨ*   *põẽ-wA-RE*
die-COND-be^INTR-INTR-DUB 3ms help^do-FUT^MS^NMLZ person-PL-OBJ
When in the world would he die, in order to help people?

Imperative. The imperative mood is used in the second person to give commands, in the third person as a sort of optative, and in the first-person plural as a hortative ('let's...').

The imperative in all persons is marked by the suffix *-xA* 'imperative'. This suffix follows the negative suffix (if present).

In the second person, the imperative suffix is followed by a gender/number suffix: *-kɨ* 'masculine singular', *-ko* 'feminine singular', *-Rõ* 'inanimate singular', *-Rã* 'animate plural', or *-je* 'inanimate plural'; or in the unusual situation in which an inanimate object is being addressed, by a classifier (optionally pluralized).

Examples of second-person imperatives are shown in (65)–(67).

(65) *doba-xA-kɨ*
sit-IMP-MS
Sit down! (said to a male)

(66) *o-bE-xA-ko*
cry-NEG-IMP-FS
Don't cry! (said to a female)

(67) *ã-Rã-Ra-xA-Rã*
eat-PL^NMLZ-come-IMP^AN^PL
Come (in order) to eat! (said to more than one person)

Verbs

The two elicited examples in (68) and (69) illustrate the use of classifiers in second-person imperatives with personified agents.

(68) ti̵-xA-Rõ   ji̵xã-RE
     fall-IMP-IMP^IN^SG^NMLZ 1pexc-OBJ
     Fall on us! (said to a mountain)

(69) pākā-bE-xA-bi̵
     make^waves-NEG-IMP-CLS:oblong
     Don't make waves! (said to a lake)

In the third person, the imperative suffix -xA is followed by the gender/number suffixes described above for the second-person imperatives, followed in turn by the suffix -Rĩ (homophonous with the gerundive suffix). Some examples are given in (70)–(72).

(70) bẽã-xA-ko-Rĩ   bĩ-bã-RE-pa-ko
     be^well-IMP-FS-GER 2s^POS-child-OBJ-parent-FS
     May your wife be well! (typical leave-taking of a man whose wife is not present)

(71) ke   'bA-xA-ko-Rĩ
     thus be-IMP-FS-GER
     May she be thus! (response by the husband to the previous phrase)

(72) ji̵-RE kari wai-'bE-xA-je-Rĩ
     1s-OBJ today happen-NEG-IMP-IMP^IN^PL-GER
     May what will happen to me today not happen!

There are two forms of the first-person plural imperative. In the short form, which implies more urgency, the verb stem is followed by the suffixes -RE-wi̵ (OBJ-PL). The longer form consists of the suffixes -Rã-xA-RE-wi̵ (-IMP^AN^PL-IMP-OBJ-PL).

(73) di̵-RE-wi̵
     go-OBJ-PL
     Let's go right now.

(74) Vícto-I   kɨrãbɨ̃ dɨ̃-Rã-xA-RE-wɨ
    Víctor-POS house go-IMP^AN^PL-IMP-OBJ-PL
    Let's go to Víctor's house.

The suffix -wɨ may be omitted from both the long and short forms of the first-person plural imperative in speech. For instance, (75) is commonly heard in church services.

(75) kojɨ-RE
    talk-OBJ
    Let's pray.

2.2.2.2 Affixes of propositional attitude. The affixes of propositional attitude include irrealis, desiderative, and frustrative, all of which can occur together. Another such affix is -xIda 'optative frustrative', (see page 30); it is quite rare, and its coocurrence restrictions are unclear.

Irrealis mood. The irrealis mood indicates that the action of the verb is uncertain; it perhaps took place, is taking place, or will take place. Its meaning is related to that of the probable evidential, but it differs in that it implies even less certainty. The irrealis mood obligatorily occurs together with the witnessed evidential.

The irrealis mood in the past tenses is formed by attaching the non-present irrealis suffix *-itʃɨ* to a dynamic verb stem; this suffix is followed by the usual past tense suffixes (see pages 38–44). (The irrealis suffix appears between the *-RExa* (historical past) suffix and the nonrecent past tense suffix.) An example is given in (76).

(76) ke   bA-RU õ pare ɨ-RE-te-jO   ʹbA-te-itʃɨ-Ako
    thus be-IF 3fs a^lot want-OBJ-do-NFUT^FS^NMLZ be-DYN-IRR-N/H^3fs
    Therefore, maybe she was a really fussy/moody one.

Similarly, the irrealis mood in the habitual and durative aspects is formed by attaching the irrealis suffix *-xɨ* to a stative verb stem, followed by the usual person/number suffixes. Example (77) is from a text, while (78) and (79) were elicited.

(77) jɨ du-A-Rɨ̃   ja-bE-kɨ   ʹbA-xɨ-wɨ jɨ bɨ̃-RE
    1s remove-CAUS-GER do-NEG-NFUT^MS^NMLZ be-IRR-NON3 1s 2s-OBJ

> 'xãki bãxã ji a-I-kaki   'jo-pe
> INTNT 1pinc 1s say-STV-N/H^1ms this-SIM
>
> "Maybe I am not the one who causes to remove from you (what is causing your illness)," we, that is I, say like this.

(78) a. *bue-I-xi-bI   Mitú-RE*
   study-STV-IRR-3ms Mitú-OBJ
   Maybe he studies in Mitú.

   b. *bue-I-xi-Abẽ   Mitú-RE*
   study-STV-IRR-N/H^3ms Mitú-OBJ
   Maybe he habitually studies in Mitú.

(79) *toro-xi-bã   õ-I   biki-wA   õ-I   piri-bio-Ij-E*
   be^happy-IRR-3p 3fs-POS adult-PL 3fs-POS hand-tie-STV-IN^PL^NMLZ

   boxe
   payment
   Maybe her parents are happy because she's getting married.

The irrealis mood in the near future tense is formed by inserting the nonpresent irrealis suffix *-itfi* between the near future suffix and the person/gender suffix (see page 47).

(80) *jĩxẽ   'orexa-RU   jĩxã-RE   ĩ-ki-Ra-kixi-itfi-bI*
   1pexc^POS call-IF 1pexc-OBJ get-NFUT^MS^NMLZ-come-NRFUT^MS-IRR-3ms

   Biri
   Gregorio
   If we call out, maybe Gregorio will come to get us.

The irrealis mood does not occur with the indefinite future tense.

Desiderative. The desiderative expresses the desire of the subject to do the action. It is formed by attaching the suffix *-iji* to a verb after any derivational suffixes and after the accustomed aspect affix (see page 52). The form of the suffix is *-ji* after a verb ending in the vowel *i* and *-iji* elsewhere. The desiderative suffix is followed by the usual tense and person suffixes, or by a nominalizer (see §3.1.4 concerning nominalized verbs). The affixed stem is stative.

The desiderative suffix is probably related to the stative verb root *i-* 'want, desire, love'. Two examples of the desiderative are given in (81) and (82).

(81) i-Rā   pōe-wA   'xapia-ijɨ-bE-te-kebā-wɨ   Carlo-I
      this-PL person-PL   listen-DES-NEG-DYN-ASM-PERS Carlos-POS

      kojɨ-Ij-E-RE
      tell-STV-IN^PL^NMLZ-OBJ
      The people evidently didn't want to listen to what Carlos said.

(82) 'dɨ̄-wa-ijɨ-RIwɨ-bU   Mitú-I
      go-ACST-DES-NFUT^PL^NMLZ-be Mitú-LOC
      They customarily want to go to Mitú.

In (83), the desiderative occurs together with the irrealis. For other examples, see (87) and (197).

(83) bue-ijɨ-itʃɨ-Ako
      study-DES-IRR-N/H^3fs
      Maybe she wanted to study.

Frustrative. The frustrative (or counterexpectation) suffix expresses the idea that the intent to perform the action was frustrated, that the action had an unexpected and probably undesired result, or that the action is an unexpected one.

The frustrative is formed by attaching the suffix *-Rī* 'gerund' (discussed in §6.4.1) plus the suffix *-du* 'frustrative' to a verb. The frustrative suffixes follow derivational suffixes, the accustomed aspect suffix (see page 52), and the negative suffix whenever any of these appear (see §2.2.2.3).

The frustrative suffix is inherently oral, i.e., it blocks nasal spreading (cf. §1.4.1), and the resulting stem is dynamic. (The *-du* suffix does not undergo the *d/r* alternation that most other suffixes beginning in /d/ undergo, because it always follows the vowel /i/.) A frustrative verb may be nominalized (see §3.1.4).

The frustrative has not been found to occur with the negative in the present or future tenses, probably for semantic reasons.

Some examples of the frustrative are given in (84)–(89). In (84) and (85), the actions of the verb are not accomplished.

(84) kū-Rī-du-Abẽ   jɨ-RE
     bite-GER-FRUS-N/H^3ms 1s-OBJ
     He (an animal) tried to bite me (but didn't).

(85) ɨxɨ-'A koapa dī-xī-kɨ   bue-wa-Rī-du-I-bI
     year-PL every this-DIM-MS study-ACST-GER-FRUS-STV-3ms
     Every year this boy tries to study (but fails).

Example (86) is from a text about a fisherman who put bird meat on his hook as bait, but the fish cut the whole line and got away. In this case, the action of the verb was carried out, but the desired results weren't achieved.

(86) 'bī-xī-kɨ   juja-Rī-du-kakɨ
     bird-DIM-MS hang-GER-FRUS-N/H^1ms
     I hung bird (meat) on (the hook), but (the fish got away).

Example (87) is from a text about a hunter who went some distance expecting to be able to get meat for his family, but the tapir he tried to shoot got away. He has both reasons for using the frustrative suffix: he did not get the results he expected, and his performance of the action was frustrated.

(87) dō-I   'ɨ-RE   ōpō-boa-ijɨ-Rī-du-RExa-kakɨ
     that-LOC 3ms-OBJ explosion-kill-DES-GER-FRUS-HPAST-N/H^1ms
     Over there, I wanted to shoot him (the tapir) (but didn't).

Note that the object ōpō 'explosion' is incorporated into the verb boa 'kill'; note also the cooccurrence of the desiderative and frustrative.

The next example is from a text about two men from the jungle who were visiting in the plains and tried to make baskets from reeds that weren't quite the same as the ones in the jungle.

(88) pɨe-bɨ-A   ja-ijɨ-RIwɨ   'bA-Rī-du-karã
     basket-CLS:oblong-PL make-DES-NFUT^PL^NMLZ be-GER-FRUS-N/H^1pexc
     We were ones who tried to make reed baskets (lit., who were frustratedly wanting to make reed baskets).

Finally, note the cooccurrence of the frustrative and irrealis in (89).

(89) bue-RI-du-itfɨ-Ako
   study-GER-FRUS-IRR-N/H^3fs
   Maybe she tried to study (but couldn't).

Also see examples (194) and (198).

Optative frustrative. The suffix *-xIda* expresses at the same time the desire to do something and the belief that the desired action will not occur. Compare the examples in (90).

(90) a. āibā-Rā-RE   boa-'xIda   dā
       animal-PL-OBJ kill-OPT^FRUS 3p
       They would like to hunt some animals (but probably can't).

   b. āwɨ-'E   ixi-wɨ   jɨ-RE. ke   ba-RU   ā-xIda
      be^hungry-IN^PL^NMLZ hurt-NON3 1s-OBJ thus be-IF eat-OPT^FRUS

      jɨ a-I-wɨ   jɨ
      1s say-STV-NON3 1s
      I'm hungry. Therefore I'm saying, "I'd like to eat (but won't be able to)."

2.2.2.3 Negative. To form a negative, the suffix *-bE* is attached to the verb following any derivational suffixes and the desiderative suffix, but preceding all other suffixes. The negative suffix turns a dynamic verb into a stative verb stem (see §2.2.1). Examples of the negative suffix in various tenses, aspects, and moods are given in (91)–(103). See also example (178).

(91) 'ɨ-RE   bāxi-bE-wɨ   jɨ
     3ms-OBJ know-NEG-NON3 1s
     I don't know him.

(92) kojɨ-bE-te-RI   ɨ̃
     tell-NEG-DYN-INTR 3ms
     Didn't he explain (what happened)?

(93) ĩ-bE-xA-ko
     touch-NEG-IMP-FS
     Don't touch! (said to a little girl)

(94) a. bɨoxa-bE-te-wɨ   kãrẽxã xi   tarea-RE
       finish-NEG-DYN-NON3 yet   1s^POS homework-OBJ
       I didn't finish my homework yet.

   b. kopai-da-bE-te-ko-be   kãrẽxã
      return-come-NEG-DYN-R/D^FS^ASM-R/D^3s^ASM yet
      She evidently didn't come home yet.

(95) toroxɨ-bE-kɨ-bEbu
     be^happy-NEG-NFUT^MS^NMLZ-be^PROB
     He probably isn't happy.

(96) boa-ˈbE-te-bI-jA
     kill-NEG-DYN-3ms-REP
     They say he didn't kill (any fish).

(97) ˈje-RE   boxe-ja-bE-te-Abẽ   jɨ̃xã-RE
     what-OBJ payment-make-NEG-DYN-N/H^3ms 1pexc-OBJ
     He didn't pay us anything.

(98) bue-bE-kɨjɨ-bẽ   ape-ɨxɨ   bA-kiˈrõ
     study-NEG-FUT^MS^NMLZ-FUT^3s other-CLS:year be-FUT^IN^SG^NMLZ
     He won't study next year.

(99) monsenor ˈɨ-RE   dɨ-Ikõxẽ-bE-RU dɨ-bE-xE-bU
     the^bishop 3ms-OBJ go-AUTH-NEG-IF go-NEG-COND-be
     If the bishop hadn't commanded him to go, he would not have gone.

(100) ke   te-Iwɨ   ˈbA-kawɨ   i-Rã   ˈwãrɨ-wA
      thus do-NFUT^PL^NMLZ   be-NFUT^PL^NMLZ this-PL pig-PL

      pɨkõ-bũ-A   kɨ-bE-ibã-jA
      tail-CLS:vine-PL exist-NEG-N/H^3p-REP
      Those who had done thus are said to be those pigs who don't have tails.

(101) *oka-bE-wɨ   kari*
rain-NEG-NON3 now
It's not raining now.

(102) *Víctor dɨ̃-bE-kixi-bI   Mitú-I   i-sumana*
Víctor go-NEG-NRFUT^MS-3ms Mitú-LOC this-week
Víctor isn't going to go to Mitú this week.

(103) *ĩ   kɨ-bE-xɨ-bI*
3ms live-NEG-IRR-3ms
Maybe he isn't (here).

2.2.2.4 Evidentials. There are four evidential categories in Cubeo: witnessed, assumed, probable, and reportative. All four evidentials are used in the indicative mood, but only the unmarked witnessed and the assumed evidential occur in the interrogative mood. Evidential status is not marked in the imperative mood.

The same suffixes which indicate the evidential status (except for the reportative evidential) also indicate the tense/aspect of the verb. For this reason, and because the tense/aspect system of Cubeo is so complex, in this section we discuss mostly the function, not the form, of the witnessed, assumed, and probable evidentials. (See §2.2.2.5, for a discussion of the form of the suffixes which indicate both evidential and tense/aspect.) Following the discussion of the function of the individual evidentials, the use of the evidentials in a text is illustrated.

Witnessed. The witnessed evidential indicates that the speaker's knowledge of the action comes from his sense perception(s), e.g., sight, hearing, etc. Witnessed information is, by implication, the most reliable. In (104), the speaker reports what he smelled and saw.

(104) *pare ɨrõxɨ-te-Awĩ   di-jãbĩ   dẽ   ãĩbã*
very smell^bad-DYN-N/H^IN^3 this-CLS:building 3p^POS animal

   boa-I-jãbĩ.   'kɨ-te-Ibã   kawa-wA   dõ-RE.
kill-STV-CLS:building exist-DYN-N/H^3p buzzard-PL that-OBJ

  tuba-te-Ibã *xokɨ-kɨ* *pɨedõ-I*
  perch-DYN-N/H^3p wood-CLS:tree on^top^of-LOC
  This slaughter house of theirs smelled terrible. Buzzards were there. They were perched on top of a tree.

 Assumed. The assumed evidential indicates that the speaker assumes the action expressed by the verb took place, based on evidence. Being based on evidence, rather than having directly witnessed the action, information conveyed by the assumed evidential is considered less reliable than if it were expressed by the witnessed evidential.

 The assumed evidential is marked by the suffix *-kebã* in the past tenses. While this suffix is not found in the present or future tenses, a similar distinction is made in the present tense by the use of the auxiliary verb *'bA-* 'be' (see §2.3.1).

 Some examples of the use of the assumed evidential are given in (105)–(111). The first four are in the nonrecent past while the last three are in the recent past.

(105) *u* *da-kebã-wɨ*
   sloth come-ASM-PERS
   The sloth evidently came. (The sloth refers to a yearly cold spell which is explained by a myth about a sloth.)

(106) *xawe-I-ta* *põẽ-te-RExa-kebã-wɨ* *'ke-RA*
   already-LOC-GOAL person-become-HPAST-ASM-PERS thus-UNIQUE
   A long time ago (our ancestors) evidently were born thus.

(107) *di-jābī-RE* *kɨ-RExa-kebã-wɨ* Pachi *'bA-kɨ*
   this-CLS:building-OBJ live-HPAST-ASM-PERS Pachi be-NFUT^MS^NMLZ
   In this house, the late Pachi evidently lived a long time ago.

 In (108), a tape recorder had been given to the linguists to get fixed, but they had not yet gotten it fixed. The owner assumed they had forgotten.

(108) *ãrɨ̃-bE-te-kebã-wɨ*
   remember-NEG-DYN-ASM-PERS
   They evidently forgot.

(109) *'kewe* *ãĩbã-xī-kɨ-RE* *ea-kɨ-be*   *'a-Abẽ*
   Kevin animal-DIM-MS-OBJ find-R/D^MS^ASM-R/D^3s^ASM say-N/H^3ms

jɨ-RE
1s-OBJ

"Kevin evidently found a little animal," he said to me.

(110) xokɨ   kaij-E   xātā-RE-bu
wood all-IN^PL^NMLZ fall-R/D^ASM-NON3^ASM
All the trees evidently fell.

(111) dɨ̃-bE-te-kɨ-be
go-NEG-DYN-R/D^MS^ASM-R/D^3s^ASM
He evidently didn't go.

Probable. The probable evidential indicates that the speaker considers the action probable, based on his feelings. It is more subjective and less certain than either the witnessed or assumed evidentials.

In the probable evidential, there is no distinction between the recent and nonrecent past tenses, although the historical past tense suffix can appear. Some examples of past tense probable evidentials are given in (112) and (113). (The bracketed structure in (112) is a relative clause.)

(112) ape-kɨ   jawi   'bA-te-jɨ-bẽ   [põẽ-wA-RE
other-MS jaguar be-DYN-R/D^MS^PROB-R/D^3s^PROB person-PL-OBJ

ã-I-põẽ-kɨ]   ã-RExa-Ibã   jɨ-RE
eat-STV-AG^NMLZ-MS eat-HPAST-N/H^3p 1s-OBJ

"He probably was another jaguar, a people-eating one," they said to me a long time ago.

(113) je   põẽ-kɨ   bA-RE'xa-jɨ-bẽ   dẽ
what person-MS be-HPAST-R/D^MS^PROB-R/D^3s^PROB 3p^POS

kɨ-Rõ-RE
exist-IN^SG^NMLZ-OBJ

What kind of person probably was in their place a long time ago!

In (114), the sentence quoted by the speaker was itself spoken by a man who awoke in jail after having been very drunk, thinking he had probably killed someone in a fight.

(114) *boa-'jɨ-bū jɨ 'a-Abē-jA*
kill-R/D^MS^PROB-NON3^PROB 1s say-N/H^3ms-REP
"I probably killed (someone)," he reportedly said.

Probable present tense verbs seem to appear only with second- and third-person subjects. This may be because, while one might have occasion to say 'I/we probably did…' (in the past tense), one is unlikely to say 'I am/we are probably doing…'. Some examples of present tense probable evidentials are given in (115)–(118).

(115) *tɨ̃õ-Ij-Abē ɨ̃ xebẽbo jābɨ̃ ku-jɨ*
snore-STV-N/H^3ms 3ms paca night walk-NFUT^MS^NMLZ

'bA-kɨ. kari ke te-jɨ-bEbu
be-NFUT^MS^NMLZ now thus do-NFUT^MS^NMLZ-be^PROB
The paca habitually snores; he is nocturnal (lit., who was walking about at night). Now he is probably doing that.

(116) *'kū-wA-bEbu bɨ̃-RE 'a-Abē jɨ-RE*
worm-PL-be^PROB 2s-OBJ say-N/H^3ms 1s-OBJ
"You probably have worms," he said to me (lit., worms are probably to you).

(117) *'ke-wɨ-RA-bEbu dā abuxu-wA*
thus-PL-UNIQUE-be^PROB 3p demon-PL
That's probably all of the demons.

(118) a. *Timoteo-bEbu 'dā-RE põē-wA-RE dɨ̃-Rāxiwɨ-RE*
Timoteo-be^PROB 3p-OBJ person-PL-OBJ go-FUT^PL^NMLZ-OBJ

bāxi-kɨ
know-NFUT^MS^NMLZ
Timoteo is probably the one who knows which people are going to go.

b. *'ke-bEbu*
thus-be^PROB
It's probably like that

The probable evidential seldom appears in the future tense. One example is given in (119).

(119) eda-kɨjɨ-bE   curso xipo-xĩ-ka-i
   arrive-FUT^MS^NMLZ-FUT^3s^DUB course head-DIM-DUB-LOC
   He will probably get here just before the course (starts).

Reportative. The reportative evidential indicates that the speaker was told the information. This does not necessarily indicate that the speaker doubts the information, merely that the speaker does not vouch for its accuracy.

Unlike the other evidentials, which are indicated by a suffix that combines tense and evidential status, the reportative evidential is indicated by a separate suffix, *-jA* (reportative). This suffix is attached to a verb in the witnessed evidential status, after all other suffixes. The reportative evidential appears with all other tenses and aspects except the conditional aspect (see page 51) and the near future tense (see §2.2.2.5). Examples of the reportative evidential are given in (120)–(123).

(120) põ-Awĩ-jA   ĩ-RE
   explode-N/H^IN^3-REP 3ms-OBJ
   It (a gun) exploded at him, so they say.

(121) japi-bɨ   ixi-wɨ-jA   ĩ-RE
   stomach-CLS:oblong hurt-NON3-REP 3ms-OBJ
   His stomach hurts, so they say (lit., stomach hurts to him).

(122) a. *da-jO-bU-jA*
    come-NFUT^FS^NMLZ-be-REP
    She says she's coming.

   b. *bɨoxa-kojo-bẽ-jA*   ij-ɨxɨ
    finish-FUT^FS^NMLZ-FUT^3s-REP this-CLS:year
    Reportedly she will finish this year.

(123) *dĩ-itʃɨ-Ibã-jA*
   go-IRR-N/H^3p-REP
   It's said that maybe they went.

Verbs

Illustrations of the use of evidentials in text. The examples in this section are excerpted from a text recounting the history of the Cubeo village Tapurucuara. The writer begins with the assumed evidential, because the information is general knowledge (even though someone must have told the author).

(124) *di-Rɨbɨ̃   'kari ape-ko   bue-I-põẽ-ko*
 this-CLS:time BT   other-FS teach-STV-AG^NMLZ-FS

  eda-RExa-kebã-wɨ
  arrive-HPAST-ASM-PERS

  At that particular time, another woman teacher evidently arrived.

The author then switches to the witnessed evidential, implying that he had arrived in the village by then.

(125) *ke   te-Rĩ   'kari ape-wɨ   bue-I-põẽ-wA   bãkapõẽ-wA*
 thus do-GER BT   other-PL teach-STV-AG^NMLZ-PL Curripaco-PL

  eda-RExa-Ibã
  arrive-HPAST-N/H^3p

  Thus doing, other teachers who were Curripacos arrived a long time ago.

At this point, the scene changes to another location where the author had not been, and so the verbs in (126) are now in the reportative form. Finally, the remainder of the story takes place in Tapurucuara and is again in the witnessed form.

(126) *kɨrã-tãkũ-we-I   jai-'RExa-Ibã-jA   pɨka-Rã*
 rock-CLS:rapids-CLS:flat-LOC die-HPAST-N/H^3p-REP two-PL

  'bA-kawɨ
  be-NFUT^PL^NMLZ

  At the rapids two late ones reportedly died a long time ago.

The title of another text is "What our late ancestors told us." It is almost exclusively in the reportative as in (127).

(127) xobo-RE aru bokobĩ-bo-A-RE   ā-Rĩ   'dẽ-bā-Rã
dirt-OBJ and termite-CLS:round-PL-OBJ eat-GER 3p^POS-child-PL

jai-'RExa-Ibã-jA   obe-RIwɨ   xɨejo-wA
die-HPAST-N/H^3p-REP be^many-NFUT^PL^NMLZ child-PL

Eating dirt and termite nests, a whole lot of their children reportedly died a long time ago.

2.2.2.5 Tense and aspect. Cubeo independent finite verbs may be marked morphologically as any of eleven tense/aspects: historical past, nonrecent past, recent past, present, near future, indefinite future, conditional, durative, habitual, iterative, and accustomed. These tense/aspects are discussed in the following subsections. Several additional aspects are indicated by compound verb constructions (see §2.3).

As discussed earlier, some suffixes which mark tense/aspect also indicate the evidential status. Only the form of evidential marking is discussed here, however, not its function (see §2.2.2.4 for a discussion of the function of evidential marking).

Recent past tense and present durative. The recent past and the present durative are formed with the same set of suffixes, and so are discussed together here. They are distinguished by the fact that the recent past is formed on a dynamic stem, while the present durative is formed on a stative stem.

The recent past is used when the speaker considers the action to have taken place recently, particularly for events which took place within the past week. Nevertheless, the use of this tense is variable. Likewise, the nonrecent past (discussed in the next section) can be used for events which took place as recently as two or three days prior.

The present durative indicates that the action of the verb is in process, progressing, or continuing. It is in this sense a present tense; it differs from the true present tense (see page 45) in that the emphasis of the present durative is on the action, whereas the emphasis in the present tense is on the actor.

The indicative mood of the recent past tense is formed by attaching to a dynamic stem a suffix which indicates the evidental status and gender/number of the subject, followed by a suffix which indicates the evidential status and person/number of the subject. The present durative is formed by adding the same set of suffixes to a stative stem.

In the interrogative mood of the recent past and present durative, the suffix -RI or -Rɨ̃ is attached to the dynamic or stative stem in place of the person/number suffixes used in the indicative (see page 20).

Rarely, a stative root will take the stativizing suffix before the third-person durative suffixes or nominalizers, as in (128). The result may imply an emphasis on the on-goingness of the action or state.

(128) a. *kɨ-I-bI*
live-STV-3ms
He lives.

b. *kɨ-Ij-E*
live-STV-IN^PL^NMLZ
life

The stativizing suffix *-I* is never found on verbs bearing some other stativizing suffix, such as the negative suffix.

The recent past and present durative suffixes which mark the evidential status and gender/number of the subject are given in the table in (129), and the suffixes which mark the evidential status and person/number of the subject in the indicative are given in the table in (130). These suffixes are used with all persons, except that for verbs marked with the assumed evidential, the indicative of first- and second-person subjects always takes the suffix *-RE* (glossed in the table as 'assumed, inanimate subject').

Since the same person/gender suffixes used in the witnessed forms of the recent past and present durative are also used in the near future tense (see page 47), these suffixes are glossed in the examples with only the person/gender features, e.g., 'NON3'. The forms used with the assumed and probable evidentials are only used in the recent past and present durative, and are glossed as 'R/D...ASM' or 'R/D...PROB'. (The suffix *-RE* is simply glossed 'R/D^ASM'.)

(129) Recent past and present durative suffixes for
evidential status and gender/number

Gender/Number	Witnessed	Assumed	Probable
Masculine singular	∅	-kɨ	-jɨ
Feminine singular		-ko	-jO
Plural		-Rã	-jArã
Inanimate		-RE	-jE

-RE also occurs in first- and second-person animate.

(130) Recent past and present durative suffixes for evidential status and person/number

Person/Number	Witnessed	Assumed	Probable
1, 2, 3 inanimate	-wɨ	-bu	-bũ
3 masculine singular	-bI	-be	-bẽ
3 feminine singular	-bIko		
3 plural		-bã	

(131) and (132) are examples of the recent past. Note that the unmarked witnessed suffix is not indicated. Other examples of evidentials in the recent past are given in (109)–(112) and (114).

(131) dɨ̃-bI
go-3ms
He went recently.

(132) 'kɨ-te-bI
exist-DYN-3ms
He was recently here.

Examples (133)–(138) are in the present durative.

(133) kɨ-bI
exist-3ms
He exists/lives.

(134) ĩ   do-Rĩ   ko-Rĩ   bõã-kɨ-RE   xẽ-I-bI
3ms penetrate-GER sink-GER fish^PL-MS-OBJ grab-STV-3ms
Diving, entering (the river), he (a bird) is grabbing a fish.

(135) wɨ-I-kũ   ẽbẽ-Rĩ   da-I-wɨ
fly-STV-CLS:hump descend-GER come-STV-NON3
The plane is landing.

(136) oko   da-I-wɨ
    water come-STV-NON3
    It's raining.

(137) jawɨbĩ bĩ   ã-I-Rõ-RE   ã-I-bĩ
    dog   2s^POS   eat-STV-IN^SG^NMLZ-OBJ   eat-STV-3ms
    The dog is eating your food!

(138) tataro-wA   'ko-wɨ-A-RE   'bãrẽ dũ-I-bã
    butterfly-PL   flower-CLS:tube-PL-OBJ   also   suck-STV-3p
    The butterflies are also sucking the flowers.

Nonrecent past tense and present habitual. The nonrecent past and the present habitual are formed with the same set of suffixes, and so are discussed together here. They are distinguished by the fact that the nonrecent past is formed on a dynamic stem, while the present habitual is formed on a stative stem.

The nonrecent past is used for actions which took place in what the speaker judges not to be the recent past (see page 38), i.e., usually at least a few days or a week ago. The nonrecent past may also be used for events which took place in the last few days, but where the speaker is concerned more with the action than with the time of the action. If the event took place in the more distant past, usually more than twenty years ago (but sometimes as little as ten years ago), the historical past (see page 45) will more often be used.

The present habitual is used to express action that is viewed as usual, expected, habitual, or invariable; it is also used to express general truths.

As is the case with the durative tense/aspect, a stative root will occasionally take the stativizing suffix before the habitual tense/aspect suffixes, resulting in an emphasis on the ongoingness of the action or state, as in (139).

(139) kɨ-Ij-Abẽ
    live-STV-N/H^3ms
    He habitually lives...

The formation of the nonrecent past in the indicative depends on the choice of evidential. The witnessed evidential form of the nonrecent past is marked by one of the suffixes from the list in (140). For the probable evidential, there is no distinction between the nonrecent past and the recent past, nor between the habitual aspect and the present durative aspect (see page 39 for these forms). The assumed evidential form of the nonrecent past is formed by adding to a dynamic stem the suffixes *-kebã-wɨ*, for all persons in the indicative, and *-kebã-RI* for all persons in the interrogative. (The suffix *-wɨ* in the indicative form is used elsewhere as a nonthird-person subject marker; the suffix *-RI* is the most common form of the interrogative marker.)

(140) Witnessed nonrecent past and present habitual suffixes for person, gender, and number (indicative mood)

1 masculine singular	*-kakɨ*
1 feminine singular	*-kako*
1 plural exclusive	*-karã*
1 plural inclusive, 2, 3 inanimate	*-Awɨ̃*
3 masculine singular	*-Abẽ*
3 feminine singular	*-Ako*
3 plural	*-Ibã*

The present habitual in the indicative is formed by adding these same suffixes to a stative stem. We gloss the suffixes as 'N/H' (nonrecent past/present habitual) + person, e.g., 'N/H^3p'. The suffix *-Awɨ̃* is glossed variously as 'N/H^1pinc', 'N/H^2', or 'N/H^3^IN', depending on its use in the particular example.

The interrogative of the nonrecent past or present habitual is formed by attaching the suffix *-A-RI* to a dynamic or stative stem, for all persons and numbers. In the second-person nonrecent past, with the unmarked witnessed evidential, the suffix *-A-Rɨ̃* is also possible.

In addition to the morphophonemic alternation between *-Ij* (before vowels) and *-I* (elsewhere), when the stativizer suffix occurs before the witnessed form of the third-person plural suffix (which begins with *-I*), the stativizer suffix becomes *-jA*.

(141) ã-jA-Ibã
 eat-STV-N/H^3p
 They habitually eat.

Before the interrogative suffix *-RI*, the nonrecent past and present habitual tenses are marked by *-A* for all persons. This suggests that the suffixes given in (140) could be further broken down, at least for certain persons.

Examples (142) and (143) are of the nonrecent past. (142) is an excerpt from a text telling about a Cubeo family's arrival at an airport. It is in the first-person exclusive, since the person to whom the man was speaking was not part of his family traveling party.

(142) ẽbẽ-karã   'kari. xõjã-karã   'kari. wɨ-I-kũ-I
 descend-N/H^1pexc BT   get^out-N/H^1pexc BT   fly-STV-CLS:hump-LOC

 ẽbẽ-I-Rõ   'dũ-te-karã   obe-bE
 descend-STV-IN^SG^NMLZ stand-DYN-N/H^1pexc be^many-NEG

 bãũbẽ-xɨ-E.   ke te-Rɨ̃-ta   xatu-karã
 rapidly-DIM-IN^PL^NMLZ thus do-GER-FOC board-N/H^1pexc

 xãtũrũ-I-kũ-I.   ape-kɨ   bãũbẽ jɨ̃xã-RE pɨ
 roll-STV-CLS:hump-LOC other-MS rapidly 1pexc-OBJ as^far^as

 'ãrĩ   jɨ̃xẽ   kɨ-Rãxɨ-I-Rõ-I-ta
 where 1pexc^POS live-NRFUT^PL-STV-IN^SG^NMLZ-LOC-GOAL

 ea-karã
 arrive-N/H^1pexc

We landed. We got out. We stood around at the airport only a little while. Then, we got in a car. Someone else quickly (taking) us as far as where we would be living, we arrived.

The excerpt in (143) from a text telling about the Cubeo tobacco ritual is in the first-person inclusive, because the person to whom the man was speaking was also a participant in the ritual.

(143) bãxẽ   dɨ-E   kɨ-wA-bE-RU   'ke-RA   bẽ
 1pinc^POS this-IN^PL^NMLZ exist-CAUS-NEG-IF thus-UNIQUE well

 bãxɨ-bE-te-itfɨ-Awɨ̃   bãxã
 know-NEG-DYN-IRR-N/H^1pinc 1pinc

If we didn't have this, we really might not know.

Examples (144)–(148) are present habitual.

(144) *kɨ-Abẽ*
exist-N/H^3ms
He exists, he lives.

(145) *aru   ã-Ij-Abẽ   'kū-wA-RE*
and eat-STV-N/H^3ms worm-PL-OBJ
And he (a fish) habitually eats worms.

(146) *xia   'xiwɨ-I   kɨ-Abẽ   ĩ*
river inside-LOC live-N/H^3ms 3ms
He (a fish) habitually lives in the river.

(147) *ɨ-bE-Rĩ-ta   bɨxi-bE-Ibã   dĩ-Iwɨ   'kari*
want-NEG-GER-FOC make^noise-NEG-N/H^3p go-NFUT^PL^NMLZ BT
But when they (wild pigs) go (move about), they don't make noise.

(148) *di-E   xẽ-Ij-E   kɨ-bE-Rĩbĩ-A-RE*
this-IN^PL^NMLZ hang-STV-IN^PL^NMLZ exist-NEG-CLS:time-PL-OBJ

   kai-Rõ   wo-RE   ku-Ij-Abẽ   xoe-we   aru
   all-CLS:place seek-OBJ walk-STV-N/H^3ms toucan-CLS:flat and

   'ewa-xĩ-E-RE
   kind^of^nut-DIM-IN^PL^NMLZ-OBJ

   'duri-xã-jo-A-bERExa-Ij-E-RE
   kind^of^fruit-DIM-CLS:cone-PL-CLS:genus-STV-IN^PL^NMLZ-OBJ

   wo-Rĩ   ã-RE   ku-Ij-Abẽ   aru ūbã-xĩ-ko-RE
   seek-GER eat-OBJ walk-STV-N/H^3ms and tree^frog-DIM-FS-OBJ

   ea-Rĩ   ã-Ij-Abẽ   ĩ   'bĩ   bābã-xĩ-Rã-RE   'bãrẽ
   find-GER eat-STV-N/H^3ms 3ms bird child-DIM-PL-OBJ also

   ã-Ij-Abẽ   aru 'bĩ-xĩ-kɨ-I   'xĩ-Rɨ-A-RE   'bãrẽ
   eat-STV-N/H^3ms and bird-DIM-MS-POS egg-CLS:3D-PL-OBJ also

   wo-Ij-Abẽ   aru waro-bo-RE   'bãrẽ
   seek-STV-N/H^3ms and kind^of^plant-CLS:round-OBJ also

    wo-Ij-Abẽ   *xoe-we*
    seek-STV-N/H^3ms toucan-CLS:flat

When these fruits (previously referred to) are not (in season), the toucan continues looking everywhere. And looking for a kind of nut, a kind of fruit, he continues eating. And finding a little tree frog, he eats (her). He also eats baby birds. And he looks for birds' eggs also. And the toucan also looks for a certain kind of plant.

Historical past tense. The historical past is typically used to indicate that an action took place long ago, usually at least twenty years ago, but sometimes as recently as ten years earlier. The historical past tense is particularly likely to be used if the speaker wishes to focus on the antiquity of the event.

The historical past is generally formed by adding to the (possibly negated) verb stem first the historical past suffix *-RExa*, then the suffixes of the nonrecent past (see page 41). However, the interrogative of the historical past is formed by adding the interrogative suffix *-RI* immediately after the *-RExa* suffix. The suffix *-RExa* converts a stative verb into a dynamic verb, since the meaning of the tense suffixes after *-RExa* is always that of past tense, not present habitual (as would be the case if those tense suffixes were added to a stative stem).

(149) is an example of the historical past tense.

(149) *eda-Rĩ*   *'xā-jOwA-RExa-kakɨ* *jɨ* *'dā-RE* *põẽ-wA-RE*
     arrive-GER see-CAUS-HPAST-N/H^1ms 1s 3p-OBJ person-PL-OBJ

    'jɨ-ka-wɨ-RE *jawi*   *kaxe-RE*
    1s-PART-PL-OBJ jaguar skin-OBJ

Arriving, a long time ago I showed them, the people, my people, the jaguar skin.

Present tense. The present tense is used to indicate a present action, but with emphasis on the actor, whereas the present durative (see page 38), which also indicates an ongoing action, puts emphasis on the action itself.

The present tense in the indicative mood is formed by nominalizing a (possibly negated) verb stem with a nonfuture nominalizer, and then attaching a form of the enclitic copular verb 'be' (see §2.1.3). The present tense in the interrogative mood is formed with the same nominalizers, but with the interrogative suffix of the copular verb (see page 20).

The nonfuture nominalizing suffixes differ for stative and dynamic verb stems; their active forms are given in the table in (150). (For the passive forms of the nonfuture nominalizing suffixes, see table (179) in §2.3.1.)

(150) Nonfuture nominalizers

	Dynamic verbs	Stative verbs
Animate masculine singular	-jI	-kɨ
Animate feminine singular	-jO	-ko
Animate plural	-Iwɨ	-RIwɨ
Inanimate singular	-I-Rõ	-Rõ
Inanimate plural	-Ij-E	-E

The dynamic nonfuture nominalizers are probably derivable, at least historically, from a combination of the stativizing suffix *-Ij* (cf. §2.2.1) plus the stative nominalizers, but with several morphophonemic changes evident in the animate forms. The animate plural form for stative verb roots, *-RIwɨ*, contains a suffix *-RI*, perhaps the same *-RI* suffix which stative verbs take before a classifier (see §3.1.4). The remainder of this suffix, *-wɨ*, appears as a plural suffix on partitives (§3.3.8) and on certain quantifiers (§4.2), where it probably performs a nominalizing function as well. The fact that the *-RI* is separable from the *-wɨ* is shown by the fact that the latter part can be replaced by a classifier in certain constructions, e.g., *ãbẽ-te-ijɨ-RI-kũ-wakari* (be^bad-do-DES-NMLZ-CLS:hump-CNCS^SS) 'although (the plane) was wanting to go bad'.

The present tense is similar to the progressive aspect (see §2.3.1) in both its form and function. The progressive aspect differs from the present tense discussed in this section in that the form of the verb used in the progressive is not enclitic, and in that the progressive aspect is compatible with a wide variety of tenses.

Some examples of the present tense in the witnessed evidential form are given in (151)–(153).

(151) *xoro   xoa-jO-bU   jɨ*
      dishes wash-NFUT^FS^NMLZ-be 1s
      I'm washing dishes.

(152) a. *xabɨ-'OwA-Rĩ juju-jO-bE   õ*
         wait-CAUS-GER hang-NFUT^FS^NMLZ-be^3s 3fs
         Resting (lit., causing to wait), she's hanging (in her hammock).

Verbs

    b. *ã-Iwɨ-bU*   *jɨ̃xã*
       eat-NFUT^PL^NMLZ-be 1pexc
       We're eating.

(153) *pɨe-kuru-bɨ-I-ta*   *ībã-E-bU*
     basket-CLS:bag-CLS:oblong-LOC-GOAL be^inside-IN^PL^NMLZ-be
     (The batteries) are in the pocket (of an apron).

The clitic form of the verb 'be' is sometimes left off in informal speech, as in (154).

(154) *xia-jo-we*   *tõẽ'tõ-jɨ̵*
     river-CLS:cone-CLS:flat carve-NFUT^MS^NMLZ
     He is (or I (masculine) am or you (masculine singular) are) carving a canoe paddle.

(155) *bī-pa-ko*   *kɨ-RI*   *kɨ-ko*
     2s^POS-parent-FS live-INTR live-NFUT^FS^NMLZ
     Is your mother living? Yes, she's living.

For examples of the present tense in the probable evidential form, see §2.2.2, (115)–(118).

Near future tense. The near future tense may be used with events that are expected to occur in the near future, usually in the next week or two. It occurs only with animate subjects, and often indicates intent. No distinctions of evidential status are made in the near future tense.

    The indicative of the near future tense is formed by adding one of the near future suffixes shown in the table in (156) to a verb stem, followed by an animate person/number marker taken from the same set of person/number suffixes used in the recent past for the (unmarked) witnessed evidential (see the table in (130)). The interrogative of the near future is formed with the same near future suffixes shown below, but with an interrogative suffix instead of a person/number suffix (see page 20). However, the first-person interrogative is formed by simply attaching the suffix *-xi* to the stem.

(156) Near future suffixes

    Masculine singular   -kixi
    Feminine singular   -koxi
    Plural   -Rãxi

Examples of the near future tense are given in (157) and (158).

(157) kari-xɨ̃-E   da-kixi-wɨ
now-DIM-IN^PL^NMLZ come-NRFUT^MS-NON3
I'll come (back) right away.

(158) kopai-Rã-xA-RE   kɨ̃rãbɨ̃-I   xi-pa-ko-xã   'bãrẽ bãũbẽ
return-IMP^AN^PL-IMP-OBJ house-LOC 1s^POS-parent-FS-ASC also rapidly

    kopai-Rãxi-bã
    return-NRFUT^PL-3p

Let's go home right away. My mother and the ones with her are going to go home soon also.

Indefinite future tense. The indefinite future tense is used for actions at an indefinite time in the future. This contrasts with the near future tense (discussed in the preceding section), in which the emphasis is on the nearness of the event or on the intention of the agent.

The indefinite future tense in the indicative mood is formed by adding a future nominalizer, followed by a person/number suffix; these suffixes are shown in the tables in (159) and (160).

The indefinite future tense in the interrogative mood, with an animate subject, is formed with the same animate nominalizers, but with the interrogative suffixes of §2.2.2 in place of the person/number suffixes shown in (160). For the interrogative mood with an inanimate subject, a short form of the future nominalizers, -ki, is used before the interrogative suffix. (Note that with inanimate subjects, singular and plural are not distinguished on the verb.) We are uncertain whether there is a first-person interrogative of the indefinite future tense distinct from that of the near future tense.

In the animate plural forms of the indefinite future tense, a distinction is made between greater and lesser probabilities of the event (similar to the use of evidentials in nonfuture tenses). In the indefinite future tense construction, the use of the nominalizer -Rãxiwɨ (glossed 'FUT^PL^NMLZ') plus the accompanying person/number suffix indicates the speaker has some doubt as to whether the event in question will occur. To form the

Verbs

indefinite future tense in the animate plural without implying doubt, the suffix -Rãxārã (glossed simply 'INDEF^FUT^PL', as it is not a nominalizer) is used instead of the nominalizer plus person/number suffixes. (In other constructions formed with the future nominalizers, the suffix -Rãxɨwɨ is always used, and does not imply doubt.)

Similarly, the person/number suffixes -bE 'third-person singular, doubtful' and -bU 'other persons, doubtful' (both forms of the clitic verb 'be') are used to express doubt, whereas the other person suffixes listed in the table (identical to the person/number suffixes used in the recent past probable in the table in (130) on page 40) are used for more probable events. (All these person/number suffixes are here glossed as future tense suffixes, despite these other uses, to avoid confusion with their other usages.)

(159) Indefinite future nominalizers

Masculine singular	-kɨjɨ
Feminine singular	-kojo
Animate plural of doubt	-Rãxɨwɨ
Inanimate singular	-kirõ
Inanimate plural	-kije

(160) Indefinite future person/number suffixes

1, 2, and inanimate	-bũ
3 singular animate	-bẽ
3 plural animate	-bã
Non3 singular of doubt	-bU
3 singular of doubt	-bE

Several of these nominalizers may clearly be subdivided (although we gloss them as one suffix for simplicity). The masculine singular -kɨjɨ may be divided into -kɨ, which is either the nonfuture masculine singular nominalizer (in the form which appears after stative verbs) or the masculine singular (noun) suffix, and -jɨ is the nonfuture masculine singular nominalizer (in the form which appears after dynamic verbs). Likewise, the feminine singular nominalizer -kojo may be divided into -ko, which is either the nonfuture feminine singular nominalizer (in the form which appears after stative verbs) or the feminine singular (noun) suffix, and -jo, the nonfuture feminine singular nominalizer (in the form which appears after dynamic verbs). The animate plural nominalizer -Rãxɨwɨ might be divisible into -*Rãxi* 'near future plural' and -*Iwɨ* 'nonfuture animate plural nominalizer'.

The breakdown of the inanimate nominalizers -*kirõ* 'singular' and -*kije* 'plural' is less clear. While they end in the singular and plural nonfuture inanimate nominalizers -*Rõ* and -*E*, respectively, -*ki* is not used elsewhere as an inanimate suffix, except as the short form of the inanimate indefinite future in the interrogative mood. (The *j* in the plural future nominalizer is epenthetic; see §1.4.5).

Examples of the indefinite future tense are in (161) and (162).

(161) *aru   dõ   'jobo-RE   xiwa-I   Vaupés dɨ-Rãxãrã-bũ*
      and that after-OBJ up^river-LOC Vaupés go-INDEF^FUT^PL-FUT^NON3
      And after that we'll go up river on the Vaupes...

(162) *ã-kɨjɨ-bẽ   jɨ-RE   a-Rĩ   'dapia-RExa-kakɨ   xi*
      eat-FUT^MS^NMLZ-FUT^3s 1s-OBJ say-GER think-HPAST-N/H^1ms 1s^POS

   ũbẽ-I
   soul-LOC
   "He will eat me," I thought in my soul. (said by a man who was lost in the jungle and came upon a jaguar)

Example (163) shows the future tense in the apodosis of a conditional, to express a future condition.

(163) *ãdõ-RE   jɨ   ĩ-jɨ   bA-RU   jawi*
      that-OBJ 1s get-NFUT^MS^NMLZ be-IF   jaguar

   eta-kɨjɨ-bũ   jɨ
   leave-FUT^MS^NMLZ-FUT^NON3 1s
   If I get that (shiny thing), I will turn into a jaguar.

The probable future, shown in (164), is relatively rare.

(164) *eda-kɨjɨ-bE   curso   xipo-xĩ-ka-I*
      arrive-FUT^MS^NMLZ-FUT^3s^DUB course head-DIM-DUB-LOC
      He will probably get here just before the course (starts).

Conditional aspect. The conditional aspect is used in the apodosis (independent clause) of a conditional sentence to express a hypothetical or contrary-to-fact condition (see §6.4.3 concerning conditional clauses).

The conditional in the indicative mood is formed by attaching the conditional suffix *-xE* to a verb, followed by the default form of the clitic verb *-bU* 'be' (i.e., the form used in the indicative mood for other than the third singular). The stem resulting from the attachment of the *-xE* suffix is stative.

(165) *bɨ-RE dū-RU āb̄ē-I ixɨ-xE-bU bɨ-RE*
2s-OBJ suck-IF badly-INTNS hurt-COND-be 2s-OBJ
If he (a horsefly) were to bite you, it would hurt very badly.

(166) *dārē-bE-RU ape-kaxe boxe-ja-I-Rō*
sew-NEG-IF other-CLS:cover payment-make-STV-IN^SG^NMLZ

xaɨ-xE-bU
be^necessary-COND-be
If I didn't mend (this pair of pants)...it would be necessary (for you) to buy another (pair).

(167) *bāūbē-RA dārē-xE-bU*
rapidly-UNIQUE sew-COND-be
She would sew them very quickly.

Note that the protasis in (167) is implicit.

(168) *ˈkɨ-xɨ́-kɨ ˈtaro-RE kɨ-kɨ ˈō-RE xē-xE-bU*
small-DIM-MS swing-OBJ exist-NFUT^MS^NMLZ 3fs-OBJ grab-COND-be
If the little boy were in the swing, he would grab her (a butterfly).

The interrogative form of the conditional aspect is formed with the suffix *-xE* (conditional) followed by the interrogative form of the copular verb 'be', *ˈbA-*, followed by the interrogative suffix *-RI* and then the discourse suffix *-ka* (see page 24), as shown in (169).

(169) *pare ɨ-be-kɨ bA-RU j̃ɨxā-RE jai-ˈxE-bA-RI-ka*
a^lot love-NEG-NFUT^MS^NMLZ be-IF 1pexc-OBJ die-COND-be^INTR-INTR-DUB

jɨ̃xã-RE boxe
1pexc-OBJ payment

If he hadn't loved us a lot, would he have died on our behalf?

Nominalized verbs in the conditional aspect are formed by first attaching the conditional suffix -xE, then nominalizing the verb (see §3.1.4).

Iterative aspect. The iterative aspect is used for repeated actions. It differs from the present durative which focuses on the action, from the progressive aspect which focuses on the agent, and from the continued action construction which focuses on the continuation of a single action. The iterative aspect indicates repetitions of an action and is compatible with all tenses. It is formed by reduplicating the last syllable of the root, as shown in (170) and (171).

(170) ape-kɨ   ɨ̃bɨ̃   tota-ta-RExa-Abẽ   õpõ-jɨ̃-ke   'ɨ̃-RE
 other-MS man hit-ITER-HPAST-N/H^3ms explosion-CLS:funnel-INST 3ms-OBJ
 Another man hit him repeatedly with a gun.

(171) oko   tɨ-tɨ-Awɨ̃
 water fall-ITER-N/H^IN^3
 It was continuously raining.

Accustomed aspect. The meaning of the accustomed aspect is very similar to that of the present habitual (see page 44): both encode action that is viewed as usual, expected, habitual, or invariable. One difference is that the present habitual has only a present tense meaning, while the accustomed aspect can occur with virtually any tense, including the present durative. The accustomed aspect cannot, however, occur with the present habitual, presumably because the near synonymy of these aspects would make their combination redundant. The accustomed aspect suffix also does not occur with the homophonous causative suffix (see page 57), although the accustomed aspect can appear in the compound verb causative construction (see §2.3.4).

The accustomed aspect is formed by attaching the suffix -wa to the verb stem preceding all other suffixes, except the negative. The accustomed aspect suffix blocks nasal spreading (cf. §1.4.1), and is unstressed; when it is attached to a normally unstressed monosyllabic root, the verb root is stressed, as in (172).

(172) ˈdɨ-wa-bI
    go-ACST-3ms
    He customarily goes.

The accustomed suffix is more commonly found on certain verb roots. For instance, the accustomed aspect suffix is not usually attached to the verb *ja-* meaning 'do, make', although the suffix can be attached to an auxiliary verb in a compound verb construction in which the main verb is *ja-*, as in (173).

(173) a. *ja-Rĩ   kõbãxɨ-Iwɨ-bU*
        do-GER be^accustomed^to-NFUT^PL^NMLZ-be
        They are accustomed to doing...

    b. *ˈ*ja-wa-Iwɨ-bU*
        do-ACST-NFUT^PL^NMLZ-be
        They are accustomed to doing...

Further examples of the accustomed aspect are given in (174)–(178).

(174) ˈārĩ-I-ta   bɨ̃xẽ-bɨkɨ-wA   ea-wa-RI   ij-E
    where-LOC-GOAL 2p^POS^PL-adult-PL find-ACST-INTR this-IN^PL^NMLZ

    ẽtã-RE   ke   te-Rĩ   dã bei   bãbã-xĩ-Rã   a-Ibã-jA
    tapioca-OBJ thus do-GER 3p mouse child-DIM-PL say-N/H^3p-REP

    jɨ̃xẽ-bɨkɨ-wA   ˈĩ-wa-bã   ãdĩ-kɨ-I   xokɨ-kɨ-I
    1pexc^POS-adult-PL get-ACST-3p that-CLS:tree-LOC wood-CLS:tree-LOC

    eta-wa-wɨ̃   ɨra-Rõ   ẽtã
    leave-ACST-NON3 big-IN^SG^NMLZ tapioca
    "Where did your parents customarily find this tapioca?" Then the mice children reportedly said, "Our parents customarily got it from that bush; a lot of tapioca generally comes out."

(175) *awiˈa bo   da-Ij-E   baxu-RE   dɨ-kɨjɨ-bẽ*
    sun   heat come-STV-IN^PL^NMLZ exact-OBJ go-FUT^MS^NMLZ-FUT^3s

ˈa-wa-I-bI   ˈbajɨ
say-ACST-STV-3ms father

"Right when the sun comes up, he will go," Dad has customarily said.

(176) ˈwo-wa-jA-bã   dẽ   xabo-kɨ-RE
      seek-ACST-STV-3p 3pˆPOS chief-MS-OBJ
      They have customarily elected their chief.

(177) a las siete ˈkari bãxẽ   dõbɨ-wA   xio-RE   ˈdɨ-wa-jA-bã dã
      at the seven BT 1pincˆPOS woman-PL garden-OBJ go-ACST-STV-3p 3p
      At seven o'clock, our women are customarily going to the garden.

(178) a. kari-RE ˈxapura-bE-wa-bã ˈkari
         now-OBJ sound-NEG-ACST-3p BT
         Nowadays they don't sound (aren't heard) anymore.

      b. dɨ-bE-wa-Abẽ
         go-NEG-ACST-N/Hˆ3ms
         He wasn't accustomed to going./He didn't usually go.

      c. ˈdɨ-wa-kixi-bI
         go-ACST-NRFUTˆMS-3MS
         Customarily, he will go.

2.2.3 Derivational suffixes

2.2.3.1 Denominal verbs. Denominal verbs are quite rare in Cubeo. One of the few examples of a suffix which derives a (stative) verb from a noun is -xɨ 'have a bad odor or taste of X', where X is the noun. For example, biko-xɨ- 'have an odor of smoke' (biko 'smoke'), bixo-xɨ- 'have an odor of vomit' (bixo 'vomit'), and kojo-xɨ- 'have an odor of diarrhea' (kojo 'diarrhea'). While most verbs derived using this suffix can be related to a noun, the process is not productive, nor do all such verbs derive from a noun: awa-xɨ- means 'have an odor of hot pepper', but the apparent root awa- is not found elsewhere; upiˈa-xɨ- 'have a sour odor' appears to derive from upiˈa-, which is a verb (not a noun) meaning 'be sour or acid'. For some such verbs, there is a noun root from which the verb appears to derive, but the meaning has changed: ēbū-xɨ- means 'have a fishy odor or taste', but the root ēbū- means 'red howler monkey'.

Verbs

2.2.3.2 Valency-changing suffixes. *Passive.* The active voice in Cubeo is unmarked; only the passive voice is marked by suffixes. It is formed by attaching a passive nominalizer agreeing in gender and number with the derived subject to a stative verb stem. The passive nominalized verb may appear in a compound verb construction in which it is followed by a tensed (conjugated) form of the phonologically independent verb meaning 'be' (see §2.3.1). Alternatively, the passive nominalized verb may be followed by the clitic verb meaning 'be', marked with tense and person/gender suffixes. However, inanimate passives are always formed with the independent verb 'be', never occurring with the clitic form of the verb.

The passive nominalizers are shown in (179). Note that the passive inanimate nominalizer is homophonous with the active inanimate nominalizer, and the passive is not used with plural inanimate derived subjects. Examples of passives are given in (180)–(186). Other examples can be seen in (210) and (216).

(179) Passive nominalizers

Masculine singular	-bĩ
Feminine singular	-bõ
Plural	-bārā
Inanimate singular	-Rõ

(180) põē-wA-RE   boa-Iwɨ   'bA-kawɨ
       person-PL-OBJ kill-NFUT^PL^NMLZ be-NFUT^PL^NMLZ

   xako-I-bārā   bA-RE'xa-Ibā-jA   dā
   put^in^jail-STV-PSV^PL^NMLZ be-HPAST-N/H^3p-REP 3p
   Ones who killed people were reportedly put in jail.

The agent of a passive sentence may optionally be indicated by an NP in the instrumental case, as in (181).

(181) xebēbo 'bārē ā-I-bĩ-bE   ĩ.   jābĩ-I
      paca   also   eat-STV-PSV^MS^NMLZ-be^3s 3ms night-LOC

   boa-I-bĩ-bE   ĩ.   xārāwɨ-RE
   kill-STV-PSV^MS^NMLZ-be^3s 3ms day-OBJ

boa-I-bɨ̃-bE ɨ̃ jawibɨ̃-ke
kill-STV-PSV^MS^NMLZ-be^3s 3ms dog-INST

The paca also is one that is eaten. By night he is killed. During the day he is killed by a dog.

(182) ɨra-jabe-ke dẽ õpõ-jabe-ke
big-CLS:seed-INST 3p^POS explosion-CLS:seed-INST

boa-I-bɨ̃-bE ɨ̃
kill-STV-PSV^MS^NMLZ-be^3s 3ms

He is killed with big shot, their shotgun shot.

Inanimate passives (i.e., passives in which the derived subject is inanimate) are used exclusively in procedural texts, in the sense of 'it is done this way'. As discussed above, inanimate passives are always formed with the independent verb 'be', rather than with the clitic verb 'be'. The agent is never made explicit in inanimate passives, as shown in (183).

(183) aru di-bɨ kobo-bɨ korika-I
and this-CLS:oblong kind^of^fish^trap-CLS:oblong middle-LOC

tedẽ-xã-we ja-I-Rõ ʹbA-Awɨ̃
passage-DIM-CLS:flat make-STV-IN^SG^NMLZ be-N/H^IN^3

And in the middle of this fish trap, a little passageway is made.

(184) aipe te-I-Rõ ʹbA-RI-ka dõ
how do-STV-IN^SG^NMLZ be-INTR-DUB that

How in the world can that be done?

(185) ʹdõ-pe a-Rɨ̃ xɨo-I-Rõ ʹbA-Awɨ̃
that-SIM say-GER cure-STV-IN^SG^NMLZ be-N/H^IN^3

a-jO-bE ʹa-Abẽ jɨ-RE Jaime
say-NFUT^FS^NMLZ-be^3s say-N/H^3ms 1s-OBJ Jaime

"Like this saying, 'It's cured,' she is saying," Jaime told me.

(186) aru ke te-Rɨ̃ bãxẽ bõã-RE ʹkari xaxo-wA-Rɨ̃ bɨoxa-Rɨ̃
and thus do-GER 1pinc^POS fish^PL-OBJ BT fish-CAUS-GER finish-GER

Verbs

    bã-wA-Rĩ   ʹ*dã-RE kãrẽxã*
    ascend^from^the^port-CAUS-GER 3p-OBJ   yet

    xɨjo-wA-Rãxɨ-bãrã   *bãbã-Rɨ̃bɨ̃*   *kajawa*
    smoke-CAUS-NRFUT^PL-PSV^PL^NMLZ first-CLS:time rack

    ja-I-Rõ   ʹ*bA-Awɨ̃*
    make-STV-IN^SG^NMLZ be-N/H^IN^3

And doing thus, after catching our fish, taking them up from the port, they are ones that will be smoked, first having made a rack.

Causative. The morphological causative in Cubeo is highly lexicalized. First, it is restricted to certain verbs in Cubeo. Second, Cubeo has four causative suffixes: *-wA, -A, -O,* or *-OwA,* and it is not possible in general to predict from the properties of a root which (if any) of these causative suffixes it will take. There are some generalizations, however, which can be made both about which causative a root will take and about morphophonemic changes that take place:

1. The suffix *-wA* is the most common.

2. If the root is monosyllabic and ends in a back round oral vowel (*u* or *o*), the suffix *-A* is used. Examples: *ku-A-* (hunt-CAUS) 'cause (dogs) to hunt', *xu-A-* (nest-CAUS) 'set a trap', *ju-A-* (drip-CAUS) 'pour', *do-A-* (put^on-CAUS) 'dress'.

3. Most monosyllabic nasalized verbs take the suffix *-O*. Examples: *kã-O-* (sleep-CAUS) 'put to sleep', *ẽ-O-* (burn-CAUS) 'set fire (to something)', *xẽ-O-* (hang-CAUS) 'hang up'. Exceptions to this generalization include *dɨ̃-wA-* (go-CAUS) 'take' and *pã-wA-* (remain-CAUS) 'split off'.

4. If the *-wA* suffix is added to a verb root ending in *u*, the *u* changes to *o*. For example: *xatu-* 'go aboard', *xato-wA-* (board-CAUS) 'transport'.

5. If the *-wA* suffix is added to a verb root ending in *ã*, the *ã* changes to *õ*. For example: *dãkã-* 'be standing', *dãkõ-wA-* (stand-CAUS) 'rise, stand up'.

6. If one of the causative suffixes *-O, -OwA,* or *-A* is added to a verb root stressed on the second or third syllable, the first syllable of the

suffix is stressed; sometimes the root stress is thereby lost. Examples: *bɨ'kɨ-* 'be big', *bɨkɨ-'OwA-* 'raise'; *ko're-* 'wait, expect, hope', *kore-'OwA-* 'know, realize, recognize'; *xa'ju-* 'spill', *xaju-'A-* 'throw water (on someone in a curing ceremony)'.

Finally, the morphological causitive is lexicalized in that the meaning is sometimes noncompositional: *kɨ-* is a verb meaning 'be'; but its causitivized form *kɨ-wA-* means 'have'. Similarly, the verb *kore-* means 'guard, take care of'. There are two morphological causitives of this verb; *kore-wA-* means 'count, measure', while *kore-'OwA-* means 'know, understand, realize'.

The morphological suffixes cause the resulting stem to be dynamic. Some examples of morphological causatives taken from texts are given in (187)–(190).

(187) xia-jo   da-wA-xA-kɨ   xia-jo   da-wA-xA-kɨ
      river-CLS:cone come-CAUS-IMP-MS river-CLS:cone come-CAUS-IMP-MS

      a-jO   bA-te-'Ako-jA
      say-NFUT^FS^NMLZ be-DYN-N/H^3fs-REP
      "Bring a paddle, bring a paddle," she reportedly was saying.

(188) oka-Rĩ   jabo-Rĩ   bexa-wA-RExa-Abẽ-jA   ĩ
      rain-GER flood-GER go^downstream-CAUS-HPAST-N/H^3ms-REP 3ms
      Raining, flooding, he reportedly caused (it) to go downstream.

(189) di-xarabo-ke   xẽ-I-Rɨ-A-RE   tɨ-wA-bI   jĩxã-RE
      this-CLS:forked-INST hang-STV-CLS:3D-PL-OBJ   fall-CAUS-3ms 1pexc-OBJ
      With a long forked stick, he caused the fruit to fall (from a tree) for us.

(190) jawibĩ-wA-RE   ã-O-jɨ-bE
      dog-PL-OBJ   eat-CAUS-NFUT^MS^NMLZ-be^3s
      He is feeding the dogs (lit., causing the dogs to eat).

Benefactive. The benefactive is used to indicate that the subject performs the action on behalf of another individual, often the speaker. The beneficiary may often be overtly expressed in the sentence with a noun phrase case-marked with the *-RE* 'object' suffix. The benefactive form of a verb is produced by adding the suffix *-ka* to the verb, following the morphological causative suffix and accustomed aspect suffix (if present),

Verbs

and preceding all other suffixes. The resulting stem is dynamic. Some examples of the benefactive are given in (191)–(194).

(191) ′kaju-ko-RE   kuxu-ka-ko-Rɨ-xA-ko
      chicken-FS-OBJ chase-BEN-FS-go-IMP-FS
      Go (in order to) chase the hen (for me)!

(192) oko-RE   da-wA-ka-xA-ko   jɨ-RE
      water-OBJ come-CAUS-BEN-IMP-FS 1s-OBJ
      Bring me some water!

(193) xārāwɨ-A koapa bēbē-Rā-Rɨ-wa-ka-Iwɨ-bU
      day-PL   every work-PL^NMLZ-go-ACST-BEN-NFUT^PL^NMLZ-be

      xio-RE
      garden-OBJ
      Every day they go (in order) to work in the garden (for us).

(194) ′dā-RE dɨ-wA-ka-Rɨ-du-wɨ   ij-E   xɨtɨra-RE
      3p-OBJ go-CAUS-BEN-GER-FRUS-NON3 this-IN^PL^NMLZ toasted^manioc-OBJ
      We tried to take this toasted manioc to them (for you) (but couldn't).

Authoritative. The authoritative form of a verb is analogous in meaning to a causative; it means to order, command, or permit someone to do the action of the verb. The object of the command, understood as the agent of the action, optionally appears in the sentence as a noun phrase with the *-RE* 'object' case marker. The authoritative suffix has the additional effect of changing a stative verb into a dynamic verb.

(195) ′dā-RE doba-Ikõxẽ-Abẽ
      3p-OBJ sit-AUTH-N/H^3ms
      He commanded them to sit.

The authoritative is formed by adding the suffix *-Ikõxẽ* to a verb, following other derivational suffixes and the accustomed aspect, if these appear. The regular tense and person markers are added after the authoritative suffix. The form of the suffix is *-kõxẽ* after a verb ending in the vowel *i*, and *-Ikõxẽ* elsewhere.

The authoritative suffix is cognate with, and presumably derived from, the lexical verb root *kõxẽ-* 'order, command'. However, the verb root is phonologically bound to the authoritative marker, and so it is here considered a morphological construction rather than a compound verb construction. Some examples of the authoritative suffix are given in (196)–(198).

(196) *bue-wa-Ikõxẽ-I-bɨ*   *xɨejo-wA-RE*
     study-ACST-AUTH-STV-3ms child-PL-OBJ
     He customarily commands the children to study.

(197) *'dẽ-bɨkɨ-wA*   *bue-Ikõxẽ-ijɨ-bE-te-Ibã*   *Mitú-I*
     3p^POS-adult-PL study-AUTH-DES-NEG-DYN-N/H^3p Mitú-LOC
     Their parents didn't want to permit (them) to study in Mitú.

(198) *xɨ* *a-Ikõxẽ-bE-Rɨ-du-jA-bã*   *jɨxã-RE*
     yes say-AUTH-NEG-GER-FRUS-STV-3p 1pexc-OBJ
     They are trying to not permit us to believe. or They are trying to command us not to believe.

2.3 Auxiliary verb constructions

As is common with languages of the OV type, auxiliary verbs in Cubeo normally appear at the end of the verb phrase. One auxillary verb construction has already been discussed, the passive formed with the phonologically independent verb 'be' (see §2.2.3). Other auxiliary verb constructions are discussed in the following subsections.

In addition to the syntactic (and therefore productive) structures discussed in this section, the verb *kopai-* 'return' may be procliticized to the verbs *da-* 'come' and *dɨ̃-* 'go'; the meaning is compositional (someone comes/goes returning'), although *kopai-* is the only verb that participates in this construction.

2.3.1 Progressive aspect

In general, the progressive aspect is used to indicate continuing action. Its specific meaning depends on the particular form of the main (or lexical) and auxiliary verbs, as discussed below.

The progressive aspect is formed by nominalizing a lexical verb and following it (or sometimes preceding it) with an inflected form of the independent verb *'bA-* 'be'. The nominalizer agrees in gender and number with the subject of the verb. All inflectional suffixes are attached to the verb (which is stative), but derivational suffixes and the negative suffix *-bE* are attached to the lexical verb preceding the nominalizer suffix.

The progressive aspect may be formed with either the future nominalizers or the active nonfuture nominalizers. (The active nonfuture nominalizers are given in the table in (150) on page 46, and the future nominalizers in the table in (159) on page 49.) The meaning of the progressive aspect construction depends on the particular nominalizer chosen and on the tense of the auxiliary verb. If the auxiliary verb is in a past tense, and the main verb is nominalized with a nonfuture nominalizer, the progressive aspect indicates a continuing action in the past.

(199) *Alberto kṹĩ-wA-RE tito-jɨ*
 Alberto turtle-PL-OBJ shoot^with^an^arrow-NFUT^MS^NMLZ

  bA-te-'Abẽ
  be-DYN-N/H^3ms
  Alberto was shooting turtles with an arrow.

(200) *ĩ bA-te-'Abẽ 'xã-jOwA-jɨ 'kari kaij-E*
 3ms be-DYN-N/H^3ms see-CAUS-NFUT^MS^NMLZ BT all-IN^PL^NMLZ

  kɨ-E-RE dõ-RE
  exist-IN^PL^NMLZ-OBJ that-OBJ
  He was showing (us) all the things that were there.

(201) *'jo-pe dẽ te-Rãxɨ-Ij-E-RE daro-Iwɨ*
 this-SIM 3p^POS do-NFUT^PL-STV-IN^PL^NMLZ-OBJ send-NFUT^PL^NMLZ

  bA-te-'kebã-wɨ di-E-RE butfi-RE
  be-DYN-N/H^ASM-PERS this-IN^PL^NMLZ-OBJ tobacco-OBJ
  When they were going to do like this, they were evidently sending that tobacco.

When an auxiliary verb in the past tense is used with a main verb bearing a future nominalizer, this indicates a continuing action in the future relative to a point in the past. That is, while *bue-jɨ bA-te-'Abẽ* (study-NFUT^MS^NMLZ be-DYN-N/H^3ms) means 'he was studying', *bue-kijɨ bA-te-'Abẽ* (study-FUT^MS^NMLZ be-DYN-N/H^3ms) means 'he was going to study (after doing something else)'. Two examples from a text are given in (202) and (203).

(202) *boxe-jA-bE-kɨjɨ*   *bA-te-'Abẽ*   *'ɨ-RE*   *pɨ*
payment-make-NEG-FUT^MS^NMLZ be-DYN-N/H^3ms 3ms-OBJ until

    ɨ-I   *xebe-Ij-E-ta*
    3ms-POS finish-STV-IN^PL^NMLZ-GOAL

He was not going to pay him until he finished (the work).

(203) *'xākɨ dō-I*   *xɨtɨra-RE*   *ō-I*   *ēdū-wA-Rĩ*
INTNT that-LOC toasted^manioc-OBJ 3fs-POS get^wet-CAUS-GER

    epe-Ij-E   *'bA-ke-RE*   *'xā-jOwA-kojo*
    put-STV-IN^PL^NMLZ be-NFUT^IN^PL^NMLZ-OBJ see-CAUS-FUT^FS^NMLZ

    bA-te-'kebā-wɨ   *'bākidā*
    be-DYN-N/H^ASM-PERS machine

Having wetted some toasted manioc, when (the nurse) had placed it (on a glass slide), she was going to show (it) with a machine (microscope).

If the auxiliary verb 'be' is in the present tense, the main verb must be nominalized with a nonfuture nominalizer, and the combination indicates a continuing action in the present. The meaning is similar to that of the simple present tense discussed in §2.2.2.5, except that it has the force of an assumed evidential. Notice the examples in (204), in which explicit use of evidentials in the present tense is compared with the use of the auxiliary verb 'be'.

(204) a. *bue-jɨ-bE*   *ĩ*
     study-NFUT^MS^NMLZ-be^3s 3ms

     He is studying. (i.e., the speaker sees the person studying)

   b. *bue-jɨ*   *'bA-I-bI*   *ĩ*
     study-NFUT^MS^NMLZ be-STV-3ms 3ms

     He is studying. (assumed; the speaker does not see the person studying)

   c. *bue-jɨ-bEbu*   *ĩ*
     study-NFUT^MS^NMLZ-be^PROB 3ms
     He is probably studying.

d. *bue-jɨ-bE-jA* ɨ̃
   study-NFUT^MS^NMLZ-be^3ms-REP 3ms
   He is reportedly studying.

This combination of a nonfuture nominalization with the present tense auxiliary verb *'bA-* is commonly used with the irrealis form of the auxiliary verb *'bA-*, as in (205). In this example, the nominalized verb is itself an auxiliary verb, the verb *ja-* 'do'. (This auxiliary verb construction is discussed in §2.4.)

(205) *jɨ du-A-Rɨ̃   ja-bE-kɨ   'bA-xɨ-wɨ jɨ bɨ̃-RE*
      1s remove-CAUS-GER do-NEG-NFUT^MS^NMLZ be-IRR-NON3 1s 2s-OBJ

   'xãkɨ bãxã jɨ a-I-kakɨ   'jo-pe
   INTNT 1pinc 1s say-STV-N/H^1ms this-SIM
   "Maybe I am not the one who causes to remove from you (what is causing your illness)," we, that is I, say like this.

If the auxiliary verb is in the future tense, the main verb is nominalized with a nonfuture nominalizer, and the result indicates continuing action in the future, as seen in (206).

(206) *bue-jɨ   bA-kɨ'jɨ-bẽ   obedi-ɨxɨ-A*
      study-NFUT^MS^NMLZ be-FUT^MS^NMLZ-FUT^3s many-CLS:year-PL

   xɨo-I-põẽ-kɨ   te-kɨjɨ
   cure-STV-AG^NMLZ-MS become-FUT^MS^NMLZ
   He will be studying many years (in order) to become a doctor.

2.3.2 Continued action aspect

The continued action aspect is used to express continued or prolonged action. In this, it resembles several other aspects. The continued action aspect, however, focuses on the continuation of the action, and can therefore be glossed 'he keeps on Xing'.

The continued action construction is formed by adding the object suffix *-RE* to the main verb, and following this by an inflected form of a motion verb such as *ku-* 'walk' or *dɨ̃-* 'go'. The main verb may be causativized, but all inflectional morphemes are attached to the auxiliary verb.

(207) di-E　　　　　xẽ-Ij-E　　　　　kɨ-bE-Rɨbɨ-RE
　　　this-IN^PL^NMLZ hang-STV-IN^PL^NMLZ exist-NEG-CLS:time-OBJ

　　　kai-Rõ　　　wo-RE　　ku-Ij-Abẽ　　　ĩ　　xoe-we
　　　all-CLS:place seek-OBJ walk-STV-N/H^3ms 3ms toucan-CLS:flat
　　　During the time when there aren't any of these fruits, the toucan
　　　keeps on looking everywhere (for something to eat).

(208) dã ˈbãrẽ ã-RE　　ku-I-wɨ　　　ij-E　　　　　xẽ-Ij-E
　　　3p also eat-OBJ walk-STV-NON3 this-IN^PL^NMLZ hang-STV-IN^PL^NMLZ

　　　ij-E　　　　　xurekɨboba　xẽ-Ij-E-RE
　　　this-IN^PL^NMLZ kind^of^tree hang-STV-IN^PL^NMLZ-OBJ

　　　ã-jA-Ibã　　　　dã　xoe-we-wA
　　　eat-STV-N/H^3p 3p toucan-CLS:flat-PL
　　　They also are ones that keep on eating these fruits; this kind of tree
　　　fruit, the toucans eat.

(209) aru ke　te-Rĩ　ˈjɨ-ka-wɨ-RE　　　ˈbã-I　　dĩ-RE　dĩ-Iwɨ-RE
　　　and thus do-GER 1s-PART-PL-OBJ trail-LOC go-OBJ go-NFUT^PL^NMLZ-OBJ

　　　a-kakɨ　　　jɨ　ˈjɨ-ka-wɨ-RE
　　　say-N/H^1ms 1s 1s-PART-PL-OBJ
　　　And then I said to my companions, the ones who kept on going
　　　along on the trail...

(210) kopai-Rĩ　ˈxã-RE　da-I-Rõ　　　　　ˈbA-wɨ　di-E-RE
　　　return-GER see-OBJ come-STV-IN^SG^NMLZ be-NON3 this-IN^PL^NMLZ-OBJ

　　　ˈkari. aipi-Iwɨ　　　　ã-Iwɨ-RE
　　　BT　how^many-NFUT^PL^NMLZ eat-NFUT^PL^NMLZ-OBJ

　　　di-E　　　　　obe-Rõ-pe　　　　　　ˈxã-RE
　　　this-IN^PL^NMLZ be^many-IN^SG^NMLZ^SIM see-OBJ

    da-jɨ-apa   *ʹkari*
    come-NFUT^MS^NMLZ-EMPH BT

Returning, they keep on being watched. He keeps on looking at how many are eating so many of those.

In (211), notice that one of the main verb roots (*ku-* 'walk') and the auxiliary verb root are identical. (The expected tense suffix is omitted from the main verb *eda-* 'arrive', a not infrequent occurrence before the emphatic suffix (or clitic) *-apa.*)

(211) *aru dɨ-Rĩ   ea-Rĩ   ku-RE   ku-Rĩ   kopai-Rĩ   eda-I-apa*
     and go-GER arrive-GER walk-OBJ walk-GER return-GER arrive-STV-EMPH
     And going, arriving, continuing to walk, returning he arrived.

2.3.3 Independent purpose clause

The independent purpose clause indicates motion with the purpose of performing the action of the main verb. (Cubeo also has a more general dependent purpose clause construction, discussed in §6.4.3.)

The independent purpose clause construction is formed by nominalizing the main verb, and encliticizing to this a conjugated form of a motion verb, which functions as the auxiliary verb. The nominalizer suffixes agree in gender and number with the subject of the main verb. For masculine singular and feminine singular subjects, the nonfuture nominalizers *-kɨ* 'masculine singular' and *-ko* 'feminine singular' are used with both dynamic and stative verbs. With plural subjects, the nominalizer *-Rã* 'plural' is used. (This suffix normally serves as a plural suffix on nouns.)

Examples of the usage of the independent purpose clause construction are given in (212)–(218).

(212) *oko-kobe-I   ĩ-ko-Rĩ-bĩko   oko-RE*
     water-CLS:hole-LOC get-NFUT^FS^NMLZ-go-3fs water-OBJ
     She recently went to get water at the well.

(213) *aru ʹkari ʹxãkɨ ʹjobekɨ-RI-xãrãwɨ-A   ʹjobo-I*
     and BT   INTNT three-NMLZ-CLS:day-PL after-LOC

     ʹxã-Rã-Ra-xA-Rã   a-RExa-Abẽ-jA
     see-PL^NMLZ-come-IMP-IMP^AN^PL say-HPAST-N/H^3ms-REP
     And three days later, "You all come to see," he reportedly said.

(214) ke   te-Ij-E   baxu-RE   'xākɨ 'wārĩ-wA 'kari
      thus   do-STV-IN^PL^NMLZ   same-OBJ INTNT pig-PL   BT

      ea-Rã-Rĩ-Ibã-jA   'ĩ-RE   'kari
      arrive-PL^NMLZ-go-N/H^3p-REP   3ms-OBJ BT

      While he was doing this very thing, the pigs reportedly went in order to get to where he was.

(215) 'xākɨ   jĩxã   'bārē   ūkū-Rã-eko-karã   dẽ   jeba-I
      INTNT   1pexc also   drink-PL^NMLZ-enter-N/H^1pexc   3p^POS   beside-LOC
      We also entered their place in order to drink.

(216) aru   di-Rɨ̃bĩ̃   'kari dāĩ'dū baxi   boa-'Rã-Rĩ-I-Rõ
      and this-CLS:time BT   late   right^at   kill-PL^NMLZ-go-STV-IN^SG^NMLZ

      'bA-wɨ
      be-NON3
      And then, right at evening, some have habitually gone in order to hunt.

(217) a. kuja-Rã-Rĩ-Iwɨ-bU   jĩxã
         bathe-PL^NMLZ-go-NFUT^PL^NMLZ-be   1pexc
         We are going in order to bathe.

      b. aru ãĩbã   boa-'kɨjɨ-Rĩ-RExa-kakɨ   jɨ
         and animal kill-FUT^MSG^NMLZ-go-HPAST-N/H^1ms 1s
         And I went in order to hunt.

(218) jãbĩ-I   ape-Rõ-I-ta   ape-Rõ
      night-LOC other-CLS:place-LOC-GOAL   other-CLS:place

      ĩbã-Rõ-I-ta   kɨ-kɨjɨ-ea-Rĩ
      town-CLS:place-LOC-GOAL   exist-FUT^MS^NMLZ-arrive-GER

      'xã-RE   ku-Rĩ   eda-Rĩ   kopai-Rĩ   da-I-wɨ   jɨ
      see-OBJ walk-GER   arrive-GER   return-GER   come-STV-NON3   1s
      Arriving at night in order to be in another place, in another village, watching (lit., continuing to see), arriving, returning, I have come back.

Verbs

An exception to the regular forms of the independent purpose clause occurs with the particular auxiliary verb *dɨ̃-* 'go' in the singular present tense forms. (The plural forms and the nonpresent tense forms with this auxiliary verb are regular.) The auxiliary verb's stem is deleted (although its nasalization remains, having spread onto the suffixes to its right); its suffixes are cliticized onto the main verb. The resulting fused suffixes are shown in the table in (219).

(219) Irregular forms of the independent purpose clause construction

Person/gender	Gender marker	(Verb root 'go')	Nominal-izer	Clitic 'be'
1, 2 feminine singular	-ko	∅	-jõ	-bU
3 feminine singular	-ko	∅	-jõ	-bE
1, 2 masculine singular	-kɨ	∅	-j̃ɨ	-bU
3 masculine singular	-kɨ	∅	-j̃ɨ	-bE

The examples in (220) is the expected but nonexisting form compared with the irregular existing form.

(220) a. *kuja-kɨ-Rɨ̃-j̃ɨ-bU
bathe-NFUT^MS^NMLZ-go-NFUT^MS^NMLZ-be

b. kuja-kɨ-j̃ɨ-bU
bathe-NFUT^MS^NMLZ-NFUT^MS^NMLZ-be
I am going in order to bathe.

The irregular forms shown above suggest that the future nominalizers (shown in the table in (159) on page 49) derive historically from something similar to the independent purpose clause construction.

2.3.4 Compound causative

In addition to the morphological causative discussed in §2.2.3, there is a causative marked by a compound verb construction.

Unlike the morphological causative, the compound verb causative is fully productive. It is formed by attaching the object suffix -RE to the main verb, and following this by a conjugated form of the auxiliary verb ja- 'do, make', which bears any inflectional affixes. Example (221) is from the Cubeo legend of the sandman, and examples (222) and (223) are from prayers.

(221) ɨ̃ kɨ-kɨ bɨ̃xã-RE jaɨ-bEũbẽ kɨ-RE
3ms exist-NFUT^MS^NMLZ 2^PL-OBJ be^quick-NEG soul live-OBJ

ja-kɨjɨ-bẽ 'a-wa-I-bI xede
make-FUT^MS^NMLZ-FUT^3s say-ACST-STV-3ms okay

"When he is around, he will cause you to not have any energy (lit., to live with a slow soul)," he has said, so there!

(222) aru ke te-Rĩ jɨ̃xẽ ã-Ij-E-RE 'bãrẽ bɨkɨ-RE
and thus do-GER 1pexc^POS eat-STV-IN^PL^NMLZ-OBJ also grow-OBJ

ja-xA-kɨ jɨ̃xã-RE 'bixa-bE-kijepe aru 'xu-wA
make-IMP-MS 1pexc-OBJ get^ruined-NEG-PUR^DS and insect-PL

ã-bE-Rãxijepe
eat-NEG-PUR^DS

And doing thus, also cause our food to grow in order that it not be ruined on us, and in order that insects not eat it.

(223) bĩ kɨ-E boxe bĩ apɨ-'E boxe
2s^POS exist-IN^PL^NMLZ payment 2s^POS be^alive-IN^PL^NMLZ payment

bĩ 'jãxã-Ij-E boxe jɨ̃xã-RE boxe bĩ
2s^POS suffer-STV-IN^PL^NMLZ payment 1pexc-OBJ payment 2s^POS

'dapia-RE ja-Ij-E boxe xipoka-te-xA-kɨ
think-OBJ make-STV-IN^PL^NMLZ payment before-become-IMP-MS

bĩ Jesucristo
2s Jesus^Christ

Because you exist, because you are alive, because you have suffered on our behalf, because you cause us to think, guide us, Jesus Christ.

2.4 Gerundive complements

Some verbs, such as *kōbāxi-* 'be accustomed to' and *bāxi-* 'be able to', select subjectless gerundive verbs (i.e., verbs with the gerundive suffix *-Rĩ*) as complements. Such gerundive complements normally precede the verb selecting them as in (224) and (225). While a verb's complements normally appear adjacent to the verb (most often before the verb, as discussed in chapter 5), in (225) the object of the verb 'speak' has been moved to a focus position at the end of the sentence.

(224) *i-Rã   pṍẽ-wA   da-Rĩ   kōbāxi-Iwɨ-bU*
  this-PL people-PL come-GER be^accustomed^to-NFUT^PL^NMLZ-be
  These people are accustomed to coming...

(225) *ĩ   'jawa-Rĩ   bāxi-bE-RExa-Abē-jA   'dã-RE*
  3ms speak-GER be^able-NEG-HPAST-N/H^3ms-REP 3p-OBJ
  He wasn't able to speak to them, reportedly.

Another verb selecting gerundive complements is *'xã-* 'see'. The meaning of this construction is to begin to do the action expressed by the gerund(s), or to do that action (or those actions) in a restricted or limited way: *xēdĩ'ā-Rĩ 'xã-* (petition-GER see) 'ask (a) question(s)', *ūkū-Rĩ 'xã-* (drink-GER see) 'taste liquids', *ā-Rĩ 'xã-* (eat-GER see) 'taste food', and *do-A-Rĩ 'xã-* (put^on-CAUS-GER see) 'touch'.

Gerundive verbs are also used in subordinate clauses to mark a verb the action of which occurs immediately prior to that of the main verb (see §6.4.1). We consider that usage of gerunds to be a case of clause chaining, rather than of complementation, since the chaining construction can be formed with any pair of semantically appropriate verbs.

2.5 Clausal complements

Apart from quotatives (discussed in §5.3), Cubeo avoids what would be clausal complements in other languages, substituting instead several other constructions. This section briefly describes those substitutions; the constructions are discussed in more detail in other sections.

Certain verbs, such as *ɨ-* 'want', *'xã-* 'see', and *daxoka-* 'stop', may take nominalized clauses as complements. Such nominalized clauses are actually noun phrases, with the nominalized verb acting as head of the noun phrase, and, therefore, case marked. Hence, the syntax is identical to that of a verb with a noun phrase complement, although the semantic effect is similar to that of clausal complements in other languages.

(226) [Juan ɨ̃-I   dɨ̃-ij-E-RE]   ɨ-wɨ   jɨ
      Juan 3ms-POS go-STV-IN^PL^NMLZ-OBJ want-NON3 1s
      I want Juan to go.

(227) [Juan ɨ̃-I   eta-ij-E-RE]   'xã-wɨ jɨ
      Juan 3ms-POS leave-STV-IN^PL^NMLZ-OBJ see-NON3 1s
      I saw Juan leave.

Another clausal complement-like construction is often used with verbs such as *'dapi-* 'think'. This construction consists of subordinating what would be the main verb in other languages with the suffix *-RU* 'if' (see §2.2.2.5); what would otherwise be the embedded clause is instead a main clause in Cubeo.

(228) a. xi   'dapia-RU   Juan dɨ̃-kɨjɨ-bẽ
         1s^POS think-IF   Juan go-FUT^MS^NMLZ-FUT^3s
         I think that Juan will go.

      b. xi   'dapia-RU   Juan dɨ̃-bE-kɨjɨ-bE
         1s^POS think-IF   Juan go-NEG-FUT^MS^NMLZ-FUT^3s^DUB
         I don't think that Juan will go.

2.6 Object incorporation

The direct object of a verb may be incorporated into the verb. The incorporated noun appears in its generic form, i.e., without a gender/number suffix or the object suffix.

(229) a. kõpɨ̃-xoa-Rɨ̃
         teeth-wash-GER
         teeth brushing

      b. ãɨ̃bã-boa-Rɨ̃
         animal-kill-GER
         hunting

      c. xoro-xoa-Rɨ̃
         dishes-wash-GER
         dish washing

d. *ā́ū́rṍ-tu-Rĩ*
cassava-squeeze-GER
manioc squeezing

While the incorporated noun does not carry any inflectional affixes, it may bear a derivational affix such as a classifier in (230).

(230) *kui'tote-kaxe-du-Rĩ*
cotton-CLS:cover-remove-GER
undressing

Object incorporation is most commonly used when the speaker is focusing on the activity denoted by the verb plus its object, as in (231).

(231) *bõã-boa-Rĩ*
fish^PL-kill-GER
fishing

If the speaker is instead focusing on a particular event, the object will not be incorporated, as in (232).

(232) a. *bõã-RE   boa-'Rĩ*
fish^PL-OBJ kill-GER
catching fish

b. *bõã-kɨ-RE   boa-'Rĩ*
fish^PL-MS-OBJ kill-GER
catching a (particular) fish

Object incorporation occurs with both stative and dynamic verbs. Examples (229)–(232) show incorporation with dynamic verbs; the examples in (233) show incorporation with stative verbs.

(233) a. *j̃a-doba-bI*
bench-sit-3ms
He's sitting on a bench.

b. *boro-kɨ-kɨ-bE*
news-exist-NFUT^MS^NMLZ-be^3s
He's a gossip.

In (234), the noun *kɨrābɨ́* 'house' is incorporated in the verb, but it also appears in a full noun phrase following comma intonation (but lacking a case suffix, perhaps because it is outside the bounds of the clause).

(234) koe-'Rī   bɨoxa-Rī   kɨrābī-ja-RExa-kebā-wɨ   pābī-kɨrābī
chop^down-GER finish-GER house-make-HPAST-ASM-PERS Indian-house
Felling trees, they made a longhouse.

The dynamic verb *ja-* 'do, make' is one that frequently incorporates its object as in (235).

(235) a. 'põ-bɨ-jA-Rī
burrow-CLS:oblong-make-GER
burrow making

b. xua-I-bo-jA-Rī
nest-STV-CLS:round-make-GER
nest making

c. 'koro-jA-Rī
liquid-make-GER
juice making

d. kai-dī-bɨ-jA-Rī
all-STV-CLS:oblong-make-GER
all kinds of (fish trap) making

A number of verbs are also formed by incorporating the object of the stative verb *kɨ-* 'be, exist': *dōbī-kɨ-* (woman-exist-) 'be married (of a man)', *ɨbɨ́-kɨ-* (man-exist-) 'be married (of a woman)', *xia-kɨ-* (flesh-exist-) 'be fat', *xia-kɨ-bE-* (flesh-exist-NEG-) 'be skinny, thin', *bẽju-kɨ-* (lies-exist-) 'be devious, deceitful'.

Similar to object incorporation are certain idiomatic noun-verb combinations in which an argument other than the direct object is incorporated: *ūbẽ-da-Ij-E* (soul-come-STV-IN^PL^NMLZ) 'recovering from an illness' (in the Cubeo belief system, the cause of sickness is that one's soul has left or has been taken); and *õpõ-boa-Ij-E* (explosion-kill-STV-IN^PL^NMLZ) 'shooting (a gun)'. This construction is not productive.

3
Nouns

3.1 Noun classes

Cubeo nouns may be categorized as inanimate or animate. The inanimate nouns may be further classified as primitive (underived), deverbal concrete, or deverbal abstract. Animate nouns may be subdivided into human and nonhuman nouns.

3.1.1 Inanimate nouns

Inanimate nouns may be classified as nonderived class 1 nouns (chiefly mass nouns and generic terms), class 2 nouns (concrete nouns, which may appear alone as well as serve as classifiers), deverbal concrete nouns, and deverbal abstract nouns.

Cubeo has a highly developed classifier system. Classifiers denote the form and/or the function of the object they refer to. They are suffixed to inanimate nouns of class 1, to verb roots, and to certain animate nouns (discussed in §3.1.2). In all cases, the resulting form is a noun. This system enables a Cubeo who sees an unfamiliar object for the first time to give it a Cubeo name.

The classifiers of Cubeo form a continuum, with one-syllable bound morphemes (such as *-jo* 'slender, pointed, cylindrical') at one extreme and multisyllable nonbound morphemes, which have independent stress, at the other extreme. These classifiers tend to form a continuum from the more general reference of the one- syllable suffixes to the more specific reference of class 2 nouns.

3.1.1.1 Classifiers. There are at least 150 classifiers in Cubeo, including the class 2 nouns, which may function as classifiers. Classifiers generally denote the form, but sometimes the function, of the object named by the word with which they occur. A verb root or a class 1 noun takes a classifier to form an inanimate concrete noun.

A typical general classifier suffix is *-jo* 'slender, pointed, cylindrical'. With this classifier such words as the following are formed: *toiwa-I-jo* (write-STV-CLS) 'pencil, chalk, pen', *pēõ-I-jo* (shine(vb)-STV-CLS) 'candle', and *tāū-jo* (metal-CLS) 'nail'. An even less specific classifier *-Ri* 'small, three dimensional' is used to form well over 100 words, including very different sorts of objects such as *kui'tote-Ri* (cotton-CLS) 'spool of thread', *tārē-Ri* (wipe-STV-CLS) 'eraser', *jaxu-I-Ri* (play-STV-CLS) 'ball', *xē-I-Ri* (hang-STV-CLS) 'various types of fruit', and *pēwā-I-Ri* (pound-STV-CLS) 'hammer'.

At the other end of the continuum are class 2 nouns, which serve as specific classifiers. An example is *joka* 'leaf', used with generic names of plants or trees to refer to their leaves, e.g., *'ōrē-joka* (banana/plantain-leaf) 'banana or plantain leaf'. *joka* is also added to the noun for paper to form *papera-joka* 'sheet of paper, page'. These more specific classifiers are less tightly bound to the class 1 noun or verb root that precedes them, in effect forming a compound noun. Class 2 nouns can also function as separate words, as described in §3.1.1.

It is not unusual for two or more classifiers to attach to a noun, with the second modifying the sense of the first: *xia-jo-kũ* (river-CLS:slender^pointed^cylindrical-CLS:hump^shaped) 'canoe', *xia-jo-we* (river-CLS:slender^pointed^cylindrical-CLS:flat^thin) 'canoe paddle'. Some place names are formed in this way: *dūbā-ja-kipori* (water^plant-CLS:river-CLS:mouth) 'mouth of seaweedlike plant creek', *popo-ja-kipori* (dry(vb)-CLS:river-CLS:mouth) 'mouth of dry creek', *wārī-bū-tākū-we* (kind^of^plant-CLS:vinelike-CLS:rapids-CLS:flat^thin) 'rapids with a kind of plant'. Occasionally, another morpheme will intervene between two classifiers, e.g., the partitive clitic *-ka:* *bēā-pūrāwi-ka-pūrāwi* (right-CLS:side-PART-CLS:side) 'right-hand side'.

The plurals of classifiers are formed in the same way as the plurals of class 2 nouns: the plural suffix *-A* may be added to any classifier. For example, the plural of the classifier *-jabe* 'seed-like' is *-jabe-'A*. When a classifier ends in /a/, the two *a*'s coalesce, so that the plural form is identical to the singular, as in (236).

(236) *pāū-boka(-A)*   *pika-boka(-A)*
    hammock-CLS:rope-PL   two-CLS:rope-PL
    two hammock ropes

A 'generic' plural of an inanimate noun can also be formed which lacks the classifier. Such generic plurals focus on the collection of objects denoted by the plural (and in that sense resemble mass nouns), rather than on the form of the individual objects (which from this point of view resemble count nouns). For instance, *kōpi-jo-A*, the plural containing the classifier *-jo* 'slender, pointed, cylindrical', denotes loose or unconnected teeth, such as those taken from a dead animal. Because they are unconnected, the form of each individual tooth is relevant. On the other hand, *kōpi-'A* is the generic plural, and denotes the teeth in a living being's mouth, which are connected by the gums to form a collective object which is itself neither slender, pointed, nor cylindrical. The form containing the classifier is also used in counting individual teeth, even though they may still be attached to the gums, since the individual teeth are again in focus. Similarly, *kōrī'ā-jo-A* denotes blades of grass, while *kōrī'ā(-A)* denotes grass in general (e.g., an area of grass); *poja-jo* denotes a strand of hair, while *poja(-A)* denotes hair in general (e.g., a head of hair).

The diminutive suffix *-xī* (discussed in §3.3.2) precedes a classifier, e.g., *tāū-xī-we* (metal-DIM-CLS:flat^thin) 'small knife'.

3.1.1.2 Class 1 nouns. Class 1 nouns are those nouns to which classifiers may be suffixed. Some nouns of class 1, particularly mass nouns, may occur either with or without a classifier: *jukira* 'salt' and *jukira-jabe* (salt-CLS:seedlike) 'grain of salt'; *oko* 'water' and *oko-rɨ* (water-CLS:small-3D) 'drop of water'; *xokɨ* 'wood', *xokɨ-kɨ* (wood-CLS:tree) 'tree', and *xokɨ-we* (wood-CLS:flat^thin) 'board'; *dēī* 'mirití palm', *dēī-jɨ* 'mirití palm tree', *dēī-Rɨ* 'mirití palm fruit', *dēī-kū* 'a bunch of mirití palm fruit', *dēī-jabe* 'mirití palm seeds', and *dēī-'porɨ* 'frond of the mirití palm'.

Other class 1 nouns never occur without classifiers, e.g., *kɨbo-* 'foot' in *kɨbo-ba* (foot-CLS:broad^flat) 'foot', *kɨbo-jo* (foot-CLS:slender^pointed^cylindrical) 'toe', *kɨbo-tʃɨā-Rɨ* (foot-CLS:base/support-CLS:small^3D) 'heel', and *kɨbo-kūā-Rɨ* (foot-bone-CLS:small^3D) 'ankle bone'.

Many class 1 nouns combine productively with a variety of classifiers. For example, the noun *tāū* 'metal, glass' appears in *tāū-tɨra-wa* (metal-CLS:circular-CLS:table) 'coin or other round metal object', *tāū-bē* (metal-CLS: threadlike) 'chain, wire', *tāū-jo* (metal-CLS:slender^pointed^cylindrical) 'nail', *tāū-kū* (metal-CLS:hump^shaped) 'motorboat', *tāū-bɨ* (glass/metal-CLS:oblong) 'bottle, jar, can', *tāū-we* (metal-CLS:flat^thin) 'knife', *tāū-xī-we* (metal-DIM-CLS:flat^thin) 'small knife', and *tāū-jako-Rɨ* (glass-eye-CLS:small^3D) 'glasses'.

Some class 1 nouns take two classifiers at the same time, e.g., *xia-jo-kū* (river-CLS:slender^pointed^cylindrical-CLS:hump^shaped) 'canoe', *xia-jo-we* (river-CLS:slender^pointed^cylindrical-CLS:flat^thin) 'paddle', and *kɨbo-tʃɨā-Rɨ* (foot-CLS:base/support-CLS:small^3D) 'heel'. Additionally, two class 1 nouns may form a compound noun, which is then followed by a classifier; for example, *kɨbo-kūā-Rɨ* (foot-bone-CLS:small^3D) 'ankle bone'.

Class 1 nouns may also undergo object incorporation, i.e., attachment to a following verb root, without a classifier or object marker suffix. The verb root, as usual, may be conjugated as a verb or serve as the base from which to derive a noun. Class 1 nouns used in this way are usually the semantic patient of the verb root, but are understood as indefinite or highly nonindividuated. For example, *ãıbã-boa-* (animal-kill-) means 'hunt'. By contrast, if a specific animal or animals were hunted, the construction would be *ãıbã-kɨ-RE boa-* (animal-MS-OBJ kill-) or *ãıbã-Rã-RE boa-* (animal-PL-OBJ kill-). (For more examples of incorporation, see page 110.)

3.1.1.3 Class 2 nouns. A class 2 noun may either occur without a classifier, or it may act as a classifier itself, in a compound noun construction. For example, the noun *pɨe* 'carrying basket made by women' serves as a classifier, as in *bia-pɨe* (hot^pepper-CLS:basket) 'basket for storing hot peppers'. Another example is the noun *kobe* 'hole', which serves as a classifier in *kɨrã-kobe* (rock-CLS:hole) 'cave' and *xedewa-kobe* (outside-CLS:hole) 'doorway, entrance'.

A class 2 noun may also follow a stative verb stem or a nominalized adjective stem. In these constructions, we analyze the verb or adjective plus classifier as a single word, principally because verb and adjective stems do not otherwise appear as words without additional suffixes.

(237) a. *xõbẽ-I-kobe*
stir-STV-CLS:hole
whirlpool

    b. *ɨbɨxɨ-RI-kobe*
deep-NMLZ-CLS:hole
deep hole

(238) a. *tʃuri   bɨo-I-kaxe*
wound tie-STV-CLS:cover
bandage

    b. *oko   ta-I-kaxe*
water cover-STV-CLS:cover
raincoat, poncho

(239) a. *xabɨ-'OwA-I-xãrãwɨ*
wait-CAUS-STV-CLS:day
day of rest

b. *oko   xārāwɨ   jēbī-RI-xārāwɨ*
   water day   black-NMLZ-CLS:day
   dark rainy day

Whereas bare nouns of class 1 lack plural forms, class 2 nouns form plurals in the same way nouns with classifiers do. That is, plurals are formed by the addition of *-A* (plural), unless the noun or classifier ends in *a*, in which case the plural form is identical to the singular. For example, the plural of *xārāwɨ* 'day' is *xārāwɨ-A* 'days', but the plural of *kajawa* 'rack' is *kajawa* 'racks'.

3.1.2 Animate nouns

Human nouns. The most common noun gender/number suffixes (which may also be analyzed as classifier suffixes) used on human nouns are: *-kɨ* 'masculine singular', *-ko* 'feminine singular', and *-wA* 'plural'. In addition, the plural of *dōbī'ō* 'woman' is used as a suffix (*-Rōbī-wA*) when referring to a totally female group.

(240) a. *pōē-Rōbī-wA*
       person-woman-PL
       people (all female)

   b. *xɨejo-Rōbī-wA*
       child-woman-PL
       girls

Kinship terms are obligatorily possessed. In the singular, most take the same suffixes that other singular human nouns take: *-kɨ* 'masculine singular' and *-ko* 'feminine singular'.

(241) a. *bī-bābī-kɨ*
       2s^POS-older^sibling-MS
       your older brother

   b. *bī-bābī-ko*
       2s^POS-older^sibling-FS
       your older sister

c. *xi-pa-ko*
    1s︵POS-parent-FS
    my mother

Most of these kinship terms replace the singular suffix with the animate plural suffix *-Rã* for their plural form, but some take the animate plural suffix *-wA* instead.

(242) a. *bĩ-bābĩ-Rã*
    2s︵POS-older︵sibling-PL
    your older brothers and sisters

b. *ĩ-I   biki-wA*
    3ms︵POS adult-PL
    his parents

A few kinship terms take gender suffixes which are homophonous with the passive nominalizers, viz., *-bĩ* 'masculine singular passive nominalizer' and *-bõ* 'feminine singular passive nominalizer'. (Gender and number marking of nominalizations are discussed in §3.1.4.3.) The plural forms of these kinship terms usually add the animate plural classifier *-wA* to the singular form, a pluralizing strategy not normally used for human nouns where normally a plural suffix replaces the corresponding singular suffix.

(243) a. *xi-parĩ-bõ*
    1s︵POS-cross︵sibling︵of︵parent-FS
    my cross aunt

b. *xi-parĩ-bõ-wA*
    1s︵POS-cross︵sibling︵of︵parent-FS-PL
    my cross aunts

A few exceptional kinship terms do not employ these gender/number suffixes as in (244).

(244) *xi-parĩ-jO*
    1s︵POS-cross︵sibling︵of︵parent-MS
    my cross uncle

Nouns 79

Other human nouns include those for people of certain ethnic groups, and these take the same gender/number suffixes used for kinship terms. For example, a neighboring indigenous group to the Cubeos are the Cacuas. *boro-kɨ* is a Cacua man, *boro-ko* is a Cacua woman, and *boro-wA* are Cacua people. People in general are *põẽ-wA* (person-PL). This has a feminine singular form *põẽ-ko*, a masculine singular form *põẽ-kɨ*, and an all feminine plural form *põẽ-Rõbĩ-wA*.

The nouns *ĩbĩ* 'man' and *dõbĩ'õ* 'woman' do not have a gender/number suffix in the singular.

3.1.2.2 Nonhuman animate nouns. Some names of animals, birds, insects, and fish take a classifier, for example *kũĩ-bo* (turtle-CLS:small^round) 'turtle'. Such names are considered masculine for purposes of gender agreement on adjectives. Some of these names take after the classifier either the feminine suffix *-ko*, to mark the animal as specifically being feminine, or the plural suffix *-wA*: *xɨxɨ-we* 'opossum (masculine)' (*-we* is a classifier for flat thin objects), *xɨxɨ-we-ko* 'opossum (feminine)', *xɨxɨ-we-wA* 'opossums'.

Other animal names taking classifiers drop the classifier in the plural: *jupari-Rɨ* (rabo^colorado-CLS:3D) '*rabo colorado* (species of fish, singular)' and *jupari-wA* (rabo^colorado-PL) '*rabo colorado* (plural)'.

Other names of animals take animate gender/number suffixes in place of the classifier: *bĩbĩ-jo* 'hummingbird (masculine)', *bĩbĩ-ko* 'hummingbird (feminine)', and *bĩbĩ-wA* 'hummingbirds'. A few names of animals which do not take classifiers add a feminine or plural suffix after what appears to be a masculine suffix: *we-kɨ* 'tapir (masculine)', *we-kɨ-ko* 'tapir (feminine)', and *we-kɨ-wA* 'tapirs'. Certain nouns, such as *jawɨbĩ* 'dog', take no suffixes in the masculine singular, but take the usual feminine singular suffix *-ko* and the plural suffix *-wA*: *jawɨbĩ-ko* 'dog (feminine)', and *jawɨbĩ-wA* 'dogs'.

The default gender for an animal name, that is, the gender used when the actual gender is either unknown or irrelevant, is apparently arbitrary. Most animals are by default masculine, but *jãbã-ko* 'deer (SG)', *jãbã* 'deer (PL)' are by default feminine. A few animals simply lack masculine genders (toads: singular *bɨbɨ-ko*, plural *bɨbɨ-wA*).

Substitution of a suitable classifier or class 2 noun for the more usual gender/number suffix or classifier forms an inanimate noun from the animate noun: *kũĩ xia-Rɨ* (turtle flesh-CLS:small^3D) 'turtle meat', *jãbã xia-Rɨ* (deer flesh-CLS:small^3D) 'deer meat'.

Finally, some nonhuman animate nouns are derived from verbs by adding active or passive nominalizers. As with deverbal human nouns, no further gender/number or classifier suffixes are added, as in (245).

(245) a. xokɨ-kɨ-I   tuba-kɨ
         wood-CLS:tree-LOC perch-NFUT^MS^NMLZ
         male bird/animal sitting/perching in a tree

   b. José-I   tuba-bĩ
      José-POS mount-PSV^MS^NMLZ
      male animal on which José is mounted

Other animate nouns. In accordance with traditional Cubeo beliefs in the animacy of celestial bodies, the nouns *awi'a* 'sun, clock, month', *awi'a xārāwɨ-ka-kɨ* (sun day-PART-MS) 'sun' (lit., the sun belonging to the day), *awi'a jābī-ka-kɨ* (sun night-PART-MS) 'moon' (lit., the sun belonging to the night), and *abi'ako-Rɨ* 'star' are grammatically animate and masculine. Adjective and verbal agreement is with masculine suffixes, seen in (246).

(246) toiwa-I-jo   jeba-I   tuba-bI   awi'a
      write-STV-CLS:cone beside-LOC perch-3ms clock
      The clock is beside the pencil.

3.1.3 Pronouns

3.1.3.1 Personal pronouns. The personal subject pronouns are listed in the table in (247).

(247) Personal subject pronouns

Person	Singular	Plural
1 exclusive		jĩxā
	jɨ	
inclusive		bãxā
2	bĩ	bĩxā
3 masculine	ĩ	
		dã
feminine	õ	

The object pronouns consist of the corresponding subject pronouns plus the direct object suffix -*RE*. With the exception of the third-person object pronouns, in which the first syllable is stressed (*'ĩ-RE* 'him', *'õ-RE*

Nouns

'her', and *'dā-RE* 'them') the second syllable of these object pronouns is stressed, as expected.

3.1.3.2 Reflexive pronouns. Reflexive pronouns are formed from the possessive adjectives (see §4.1.5), followed by the word *baxu* 'self, selves'. The suffix *-bā* or *-bīā* 'identical individual' (see §3.3.7) is often attached to *baxu*, as in (248).

(248) *ke   te-Rī   koji-karā   jīxē   baxu-bīā   ī   'jo-pe   a-I-bI*
 thus do-GER talk-N/H ̂1pexc 1pexc ̂POS self-IDENT 3ms this-SIM say-STV-3ms

 bāxē   tāū-tɨra-RE   kɨ-wA-bE   boxe   a-karā
 1pinc ̂POS metal-CLS:circle-OBJ exist-CAUS-NEG payment say-N/H ̂1pexc
 Then we talked among ourselves/to each other: "He is saying like this because we don't have money," we said.

Reflexive pronouns are generally coreferential with the subject, as in (248); alternatively, they can appear in apposition with a coreferential noun phrase, with emphatic meaning.

(249) *aru   di-xura-wɨ   baxu-bā-ta   bɨkɨ-Ij-Awī*
 and this-cocoon-CLS:tube self-IDENT-FOC grow-STV-N/H ̂3IN
 And that cocoon all by itself habitually grows.

Plural reflexives also do the duty of reciprocals, as in (250).

(250) *kaja-te-Iwɨ-bU   dē   baxu*
 help-do-NFUT ̂PL ̂NMLZ-be 3p ̂POS self
 They are helping each other.

3.1.3.3 Possessive pronouns. The stems of the possessive pronouns are shown in the table in (251). They are clearly related to the corresponding personal pronouns, but there are differences, particularly in the form of the first and second persons in the singular.

(251) Possessive pronoun stems

Person	Singular	Plural
1 exclusive	ʼxɨ-	jɨ̃xẽ
inclusive		bãxẽ
2	ʼbɨ̃-	bɨ̃xẽ
3	(ɨ̃) xɨ-	dẽ

The stem is marked for the gender and number of the possessor, as shown; the first-person plural further distinguishes inclusive and exclusive forms. In the third-person singular form, the parenthesized word is the third-person masculine singular pronoun 'he', representing the possessor. The third-person feminine pronoun õ or a noun may be substituted, for instance: *Pedro xɨ-kū* (Pedro POS-CLS:humpˆshaped) 'Pedro's hump-shaped object' (such as a canoe).

In most cases, a suffix agreeing with the referent of the possessed item is added to the appropriate stem from the chart in (150) on page 46. When the possessed item is animate, this agreeing suffix is one of the gender/number suffixes: *-kɨ* 'masculine singular', *-ko* 'feminine singular', *-Rã* 'animate plural' (used with animals), or *-wɨ* 'animate plural nominalizer' (used with humans); for example, *ʼxɨ-kɨ* (my-MS) 'my male one' (referring to a close male relative), *ʼxɨ-Rã* (my-PLˆNMLZ) 'my animate ones' (i.e., my animals). Similarly, when the referent of the pronoun is an inanimate object, and the possessor is singular, the agreeing suffix (the inanimate singular nominalizer *-Rõ*, the inanimate plural nominalizer *-jE*, or a classifier) is added to one of the stems from the chart, for instance *ʼxɨ-Rõ* (my-INˆSGˆNMLZ) 'my object (of unspecified kind)', *ʼxɨ-we* (my-CLS:flatˆthin) 'my flat, thin object'.

When the possessor is plural and the possessed object is inanimate, however, the agreeing suffix (inanimate nominalizer or classifier) is instead attached to the stem *xɨ-*, which follows the possessive pronoun proper: *dẽ xɨ-Rõ* (their thing-INˆSGˆNMLZ) 'their thing (of unspecified kind)'.

3.3.1.4 Demonstrative pronouns. The demonstrative pronouns of Cubeo are, in most cases, formed from the demonstrative prefixes discussed in §3.3.1, plus gender/number suffixes. The gender/number suffixes appear to come from various paradigms. In some cases they are cognate with the dynamic form of the nonfuture nominalizers, in another case with the stative form of that nominalizer, and in still another case

Nouns

with a plural animate noun suffix. The demonstrative pronouns for animate referents are shown in (252).

(252) Demonstrative pronouns for animate referents

	Proximate 'this, these'	Distal 'that, those'
Masculine singular	jãĩ	ã-j̃ĩ
Feminine singular	i-ko	ã-jõ
Animate plural	i-Rã	ãdɨ-Rã

For inanimate referents, there are both deictic and anaphoric demonstrative pronouns, as shown in (253). In the case of a classifier ending in *a*, the singular and plural will be homophonous, since a sequence of two *a*'s is reduced to one; see §1.4.4.

(253) Demonstrative pronouns for inanimate referents

	'this/these' (near)	'that/those' (far)	'this/these' (anaphoric)
Singular	jo	dõ	(none)
	i- + CLS	ãdɨ- + CLS	di- + CLS
Mass or plural	ij-E	ãdɨ-'E	di-E
	i- + CLS + -A	ãdɨ- + CLS + -A	di- + CLS + -A
Abstract idea	ij-E	ãdɨ-'E	di-E

As seen in (253), many of the inanimate demonstrative pronouns are formed with classifiers, e.g., *di-bẽ* (this-CLS:threadlike) 'this (previously referred to) threadlike object', *ãdɨ-jãbĩ* (that-CLS:building) 'that building (over there)', *i-boxɨ-A* (this-CLS:bundlelike-PL) 'these brooms'.

Demonstrative pronouns may serve as heads of noun phrases themselves, or they may precede the head noun of a noun phrase, in that case functioning as a demonstrative adjective. Examples (254) and (255) illustrate these two uses.

(254) ɨra-Rõ   'koro kɨ-wA-bã   i-Rã
    big-IN^SG^NMLZ liquid exist-CAUS-3p this-PL
    These animate ones (i.e., bees) have a lot of liquid (understood from the context to be honey).

(255) 'dō-pe   'bA-Abẽ   jāī   pābūrɨ
that-SIM be-N/H^3ms this^MS armadillo
That's what the armadillo is like.

The demonstrative prefix *ape-* 'other, another', when combined with a gender/number suffix or a classifier, also forms a demonstrative pronoun referring to another object of the type specified by the classifier: *ape-ko* (other-FS) 'another female one', *ape-kɨ* (other-MS) 'another male one', and *ape-Rõ* (other-IN^SG^NMLZ) 'another thing'. In the animate plural, it takes the *-wɨ* suffix *ape-wɨ* (other-PL) 'others'. (This plural suffix is also used with the quantifier *kai-* 'all, every', discussed in §4.2, and with partitives, discussed in §3.3.8.) An example of the use of this demonstrative pronoun is given in (256).

(256) ke   te-Rī   'kari ape-wɨ   eda-RExa-kebã-wɨ
thus do-GER BT other-PL arrive-HPAST-ASM-PERS
Then others evidently arrived a long time ago.

As discussed in "*-RE* as locative/temporal suffix" on page 113, the demonstrative inanimate pronouns may also be used as locatives by attaching the *-RE* object/locative suffix: *dō-RE* 'there'.

3.1.3.5 Interrogative pronouns. *aipe* 'what?', *'ārī* 'where?', and *jābẽ* 'who?' are invariant forms of the interrogative pronouns, except that the suffix *-xã* 'and those with him/her' can be added to *jābẽ* to form *jābẽ-xã* 'who (plural)?'.

(257) aipe   ja-jɨ-Rī̄   bī̄
what do-NFUT^MS^NMLZ-INTR 2s
What are you doing?

The pronoun *je* 'what?' is another interrogative pronoun. In (258), *je* takes the interrogative form of the clitic *-bU* 'be'.

(258) 'je-bA   i-we
what-be^INTR this-CLS:flat
What is this (flat, thin object)?

For animate beings, gender/number suffixes are added to *je* to form *'je-kɨ* 'what (masculine)?', *'je-ko* 'what (feminine)?', and *'je-Rã* 'what (plural)?'.

Nouns 85

(259) ¹je-kɨ-bA   jãĩ
    what-MS-beˆINTR thisˆMS
    What is this (animate MS being)?

(260) ¹je-Rã   ābɨ́-kɨ-RI   dã
    what-PL   name-exist-INTR 3p
    What are their names?

Any classifier or gender suffix can be added to ¹a- 'which?' to form an interrogative pronoun.

(261) ¹a-kɨ-bA   ɨra-kɨ
    which-MS-beˆINTR big-MS
    Which (animate) one is big?

3.1.4 Deverbal nouns

As discussed in chapter 2, both stative and dynamic verbs can be nominalized with active nonfuture nominalizers (see page 45), passive nominalizers (see page 55), and future nominalizers (see page 48). In addition, verbs may also be nominalized with classifiers or class 2 nouns, and with the noun põẽ 'person'. The morphology of these various nominalizations is discussed in more detail in the subsections below.

The affixes of propositional attitude -ijɨ 'desiderative' and -Rĩ-du 'frustrative, counterexpectation', the negative -bE, the tense/aspect suffixes -xE 'conditional' and -xɨro 'present irrealis' (this allomorph of the present irrealis is used before the nominalizers in place of the usual -xɨ), and the derivational suffixes -wA 'causative', -ka 'benefactive', and -Ikõxẽ 'authoritative', can all be added to the verb before it is nominalized.

In addition to their use in several tenses, nominalized verbs may be used as heads of noun phrases and relative clauses. In practice, the latter two usages are often indistinguishable; as is explained in §6.3, relative clauses often appear in noun phrases without an overt head noun, and when they do modify an overt noun, they could be considered to be appositives (see §3.2.3).

Where helpful, the nominalized verb in the examples of the following subsections are bolded.

3.1.4.1 Deverbal concrete nouns. A stative verb root plus the suffix -RI, or a dynamic verb root plus the stativizer suffix -I, followed by a classifier becomes a deverbal concrete noun. For example, the nouns in (262) and (263) are derived with the stative verb kɨ- 'be, live, exist'. The word for 'houseboat', a concept which is not native to the culture, illustrates the productivity of this process.

(262) kṹɨ̃-bo-I   kɨ-RI-tõkũ
turtle-CLS:round-POS live-NMLZ-CLS:box
turtle shell (lit., box a turtle lives in)

(263) kɨ̃rãbĩ kɨ-RI-kũ
house live-NMLZ-CLS:hump
houseboat

The nouns in (264) and (265) are derived from the dynamic verb root *xātūrū-* 'roll'.

(264) xātūrū-I-kū
roll-STV-CLS:hump
car, truck, bus

(265) xātūrū-I-Rɨ
roll-STV-CLS:3D
tire

Since class 2 nouns are, in effect, classifiers, nouns may also be derived from verbs by attaching a class 2 noun root after the verb and the *-I* or *-RI* suffix.

(266) xidoxa-RI-xãrãwɨ
be^scary-NMLZ-day
a scary day

Nouns derived from verbs with classifiers or class 2 nouns freely enter into compound noun constructions.

(267) a. oko   bexa-I-Rõ
water descend-STV-IN^SG^NMLZ
ditch

   b. oko   xaro-I-kobe
water send-STV-CLS:hole
well (with a pump)

Nouns 87

Note that in (267a), the nominalized verb is intransitive. Since only direct objects can be incorporated into verbs, this rules out an analysis in which the noun *oko* 'water' is first incorporated into the verb before the verb is nominalized.

3.1.4.2 Deverbal abstract nouns. Deverbal abstract nouns are formed by adding the abstract specific nominalizer suffix *-Rõ* (glossed 'IN^SG^NMLZ', since it also functions as the inanimate singular nominalizer) or the abstract general nominalizer suffix *-E* (glossed 'IN^PL^NMLZ', since it also functions as the inanimate plural nominalizer) to a stative verb stem. Examples include *xɨo-Ij-E* (cure-STV-IN^PL^NMLZ) 'medicine' and *ã-Ij-E* (eat-STV-IN^PL^NMLZ) 'food', the latter illustrated in (268).

(268) *aru jɨ dõ-I di-E-RE 'xã-Rĩ tʃĩõ-kakɨ ke*
and 1s that-LOC this-IN^PL^NMLZ-OBJ see-GER be^sad-N/H^1ms thus

ãrõxã-xE-ta-bã-tʃĩã bãxẽ ã-Ij-E a-Rĩ
be^like-COND-FOC-3p-FOC 1pinc^POS eat-STV-IN^PL^NMLZ say-GER

'dapia-kakɨ
think-N/H^1ms

And I was sad, seeing that there: "Would our food be like that? Good grief!" I thought.

The difference in meaning of the nominalizers *-Rõ* and *-E* is difficult to define. Salser and Salser (1979) analyzed the suffixes *-Rõ* as singular and *-E* as plural, and in the present tense construction (see page 45), these suffixes have precisely that meaning. However, in the context of nominalizations used as nouns (as opposed to their participial use in the present tense construction), we have analyzed *-Rõ* as a count or specific nominalizer and *-E* as a mass or general nominalizer. For instance, the nominalizations in (269) and (270) refer to sports in general versus a particular game or match, and to life in general versus the particular place one lives.

(269) a. *jaxu-Ij-E*
play-STV-IN^PL^NMLZ
sports

b. *jaxu-I-Rõ*
play-STV-IN^SG^NMLZ
game or match

(270) a. *kɨ-E*
    live-IN^PL^NMLZ
    life

  b. *kɨ-Rõ*
    live-IN^SG^NMLZ
    fact that something exists; place of being or living

Because the nominalizer *-Rõ* also has the sense of 'place, location', the last noun in (270) can also mean 'village, town'. Note that this nominalizer is also homophonous with the demonstrative pronoun *dõ* 'that', which is often used with the object/locative suffix *-RE* to mean 'there'.

The count or specific nominalizer *-Rõ* can also be attached after the negative suffix *-bE*, for instance *oka-bE-Rõ* (rain-NEG-IN^SG^NMLZ) 'place with no rain, desert'. A similar construction is formed by suffixing *-bE* and *-Rõ* to a noun: *xokɨ-bE-Rõ* (wood-NEG-IN^SG^NMLZ) 'place with no trees'.

3.1.4.3 Deverbal animate nouns. Deverbal animate nouns may be formed with the animate nonfuture active nominalizers (given in (150) on page 46) or with the passive nominalizers (given in (179) on page 55). (No further gender/number suffixes are added.)

(271) a. *bue-jɨ*
    teach-NFUT^MS^NMLZ
    man teacher

  b. *bue-I-bɨ̃*
    teach-STV-PSV^MS^NMLZ
    male student

  c. *bue-jO*
    teach-NFUT^FS^NMLZ
    woman teacher

  d. *bue-I-bõ*
    teach-STV-PSV^FS^NMLZ
    female student

e. *bue-Iwɨ*
   teach-NFUT^PL^NMLZ
   teachers

f. *bue-I-bārā*
   teach-STV-PSV^PL^NMLZ
   students

(272) a. *kore-jɨ*
   take^care^of-NFUT^MS^NMLZ
   male who takes care of (e.g., guard, guardian, watchdog)

b. *kore-I-bɨ̃*
   take^care^of-STV-PSV^MS^NMLZ
   male who is taken care of

(273) a. *kojɨ-jO*
   tell-NFUT^FS^NMLZ
   female who tells (female narrator)

b. *kojɨ-I-bõ*
   tell-STV-PSV^FS^NMLZ
   female who is told about

Example (274) illustrates the use of such a nominalization in a text.

(274) *aru bɨ̃xã di-Rɨ̃bɨ̃   põẽ-wA-RE   'xã-Iwɨ*
   and 2p this-CLS:time person-PL-OBJ watch-NFUT^PL^NMLZ

   te-xA-Rã   bɨ̃xã a-Rɨ̃   'kari 'dã-RE i-Rã-RE
   become-IMP-IMP^AN^PL 2p say-GER BT 3p-OBJ this-PL-OBJ

   põẽ-wA-ka-wɨ   'bA-Rɨ̃-du-I-wI   'kari jawɨbɨ̃-wA
   person-PL-PART-PL be-GER-FRUS-STV-NON3 BT dog-PL

   'bA-Rãxɨwɨ-RE   'kari 'xãkɨ 'kari xɨ̃bẽ-RI-xɨ̃-kɨ
   be-FUT^PL^NMLZ-OBJ BT INTNT BT blue/green-NMLZ-DIM-MS

'dã-RE xebẽ   dabɨbo-Abẽ-jA
3p-OBJ tongue   pull-N/H^3ms-REP

And (God) saying to them, to these who had been people, who were to become dogs, "Then become watchdogs (lit., people watchers)," and reportedly God pulled their tongues.

The animate noun *põẽ-* 'person' plus a gender/number suffix may also be suffixed to a verb, forming an agentive deverbal noun meaning 'one who does X'. In this use, we gloss *põẽ-* as (AG^NMLZ) 'agentive nominalizer'. For example: *bue-I-põẽ-wA* (teach-STV-AG^NMLZ-PL) 'teachers', *bēbẽ-I-põẽ-wA* (work-STV-AG^NMLZ-PL) 'workers', *ã-Ij-E-RE tota-I-põẽ-kɨ* (eat-STV-IN^PL^NMLZ-OBJ pierce-STV-AG^NMLZ-MS) 'one who pierces his food' (referring to a bird that kills its prey by sticking it with his beak). Note in the latter example that the nominalization is actually a full relative clause, since the object is not incorporated into the verb. The example in (275) of an agentive nominalization is from a text.

(275) xipo-bɨ   'pa-I-Rõ   ixi-Rõ-RE
      head-CLS:oblong be^similar-STV-IN^SG^NMLZ hurt-IN^SG^NMLZ-OBJ

pɨ   ke   'bA-xɨ-wɨ   baxu bãxã-RE
as^far^as thus be-IRR-NON3 self 1pinc-OBJ

kore-'OwA-I-põẽ-kɨ   a-I-Rõ
take^care^of-CAUS-STV-AG^NMLZ-MS   say-STV-IN^SG^NMLZ

'bA-Awɨ-RA   dõ
be-N/H^IN^3-UNIQUE   that

"Even like a headache, thus perhaps it is," that is what is said to us by a very knowing person. (The verb stem *kore-'OwA-*, the causative of the verb meaning 'to take care of, guard, wait for', means 'to know, realize'.)

3.2 Noun phrases

A noun phrase consists minimally of a head noun (or occasionally a quantifier, see §4.2). It may be modified by possessive noun phrases, adjectival and quantifier modifiers, relative clauses, and other noun phrases in apposition. These modifiers are discussed in the following subsections.

Nouns

3.2.1 Possessives

As is typical of OV languages, the possessor noun phrase generally precedes the noun phrase indicating the thing possessed. Nonpronominal possessor noun phrases are case marked with a possessive suffix (see page 118).

(276) pĩpĩ-bo-I   'papi-kɨ
      spider-CLS:round-POS net-CLS:tree
      spider's web

Alternatively, the possessor noun phrase may lack a possessive suffix, with its relationship to the following possessed noun phrase being shown by an intervening possessive adjective (see §4.1.5).

(277) a. Pedro ĩ-I   xia-jo-kũ
         Pedro 3ms-POS river-CLS:cone-CLS:hump
         Pedro's canoe

      b. Pedro ĩ-I   jawibĩ-ko
         Pedro 3ms-POS dog-FS
         Pedro's female dog

(278) arutʃu-RE dẽ   kɨõ-I-Rõ
      rice-OBJ   3p^POS   grind-STV-IN^SG^NMLZ
      their rice mill

3.2.2 Adjective and quantifier modification

Nouns can be modified by adjectives, quantifiers, and nominalized verbs. Modification by means of nominalized verbs, although it appears to be similar to adjectival modification, can in fact be analyzed as modification by means of a reduced relative clause. Relative clauses are postnominal or, more commonly, appear in a noun phrase without an overt head noun. This is treated with greater detail in §6.3.

While adjectives and quantifiers normally precede a head noun, the order is sometimes reversed, as in (279)–(280).

(279) a. jĩxẽ   ku-Ij-E-RE   pɨka-Rã   ɨbĩ-wA
         1pexc^POS walk-STV-IN^PL^NMLZ-OBJ   two-PL   man-PL

    bāka-Rõ-I   bābã-Rɨ̃bɨ̃   dɨ̃-karã
    jungle-CLS:place-LOC first-CLS:time go-N/H^1pexc
    When we two men were walking in the jungle, first we went...

b. bũxã-joka-wA   pɨka-Rã aru kõbĩ'õwãĩ-wA pɨka-Rã boa-'wɨ
   palometa-CLS:leaf-PL two-PL and sardine-PL   two-PL kill-NON3

   jɨ̃
   1s

I caught two *palometas* and two sardines.

(280) a. peka-xɨ̃-jo-A   'kɨ̃-xɨ̃-jo-A-ke   aru 'jobo
      firewood-DIM-CLS:cone-PL small-DIM-CLS:cone-PL-INST and after

     ɨra-we-A-ke   peka-we-A-ke   bɨoxa-Rɨ̃
     big-CLS:flat-PL-INST firewood-CLS:flat-PL-INST finish-GER

    kõãĩ-jɨ-RE   tɨ-O-Rɨ̃   dakuwa-jO-bU
    pot-CLS:funnel-OBJ place-CAUS-GER start^a^fire-NFUT^FS^NMLZ-be

With small sticks and later finishing with big pieces of split firewood, placing the pot (balanced on the three hourglass-shaped clay supports), I light the fire.

  b. aru bābã-Rɨ̃bɨ̃   'kɨ̃-xɨ̃-kɨ   wɨ-O-kɨ
    and first-CLS:time small-DIM-MS be^sleepy-CAUS-NFUT^MS^NMLZ

    eda-Ij-Abẽ-jA
    arrive-STV-N/H^3ms-REP

And first, the little one who causes (people) to be sleepy reportedly habitually comes.

Postnominal modification by adjectives and quantifiers appears to be controlled by discourse factors. Specifically, when the modifier represents new information to the hearers, it is more likely to occur postnominally.

A demonstrative pronoun modifying a head noun almost always precedes that head noun, as in (281)–(286).

(281) jãĩ   kui'tote-bɨ̃bɨ̃-jo
     this^MS gray^breasted^sabrewing-hummingbird-CLS:cone

      kɨ-Abẽ   kai-Rõ
      live-N/H^3ms all-CLS:place
      The gray-breasted sabrewing hummingbird lives everywhere.

(282) aru i-Rã   ape-wɨ   būbĩ-wA xobo-Rõ-ka-wɨ
      and this-PL other-PL bee-PL   ground-CLS:place-PART-PL^NMLZ

      te-I-bārã   ãbẽ-Rã dã põẽ-wA-RE
      become-STV-PSV^PL^NMLZ bad-PL 3p person-PL-OBJ

      ixi-RIwɨ-ta-bU
      hurt-NFUT^PL^NMLZ-FOC-bẹ
      And others of these bees that live in the ground becoming bad ones really hurt people.

(283) 'dõ-pe bA-te-'Awĩ   di-jābĩ   kĩrābĩ
      that-SIM be-DYN-N/H^IN^3 this-CLS:building house
      That house was like that.

(284) aru di-bɨ   kobo-bɨ   korika-I
      and this-CLS:oblong kind^of^fish^trap-CLS:oblong middle-LOC
      And in the middle of that fish trap...

(285) ape-jābĩ   herramienta para-I-jābĩ
      other-CLS:building tool   lie^down-STV-CLS:building
      Another building, the tool house...

(286) di-jābĩ   'planta   para-I-jābĩ
      this-CLS:building generator lie^down-STV-CLS:building
      That building, the one where the generator is kept...

    The reverse order, such as *põẽ-kɨ jāĩ* (person-MS this^MS) is emphatic: 'this man!'.

    In over 100 texts we have examined, the maximum number of modifiers found with a single noun is three. As discussed in §3.2.3, when the speaker wishes to use multiple adjectives, a common strategy is to use two noun phrases in apposition, apportioning the adjective modifiers between the two noun phrases. A description of the habits of the oriole exemplifies this. The author of the text uses two noun phrases in apposition (bracketed in

(287)). The head noun of each noun phrase is marked by the object suffix -RE, and each noun phrase has one modifier.

(287) [kai-xĩ-E   jai-xĩ-bẽ-A-RE]   [beto-jĩ
      all-DIM-IN^PL^NMLZ vine-DIM-CLS:thread-PL-OBJ cumare^palm-CLS:funnel

       xipokoro-ka-xĩ-bẽ-A-RE]   ĩ-Rĩ   pẽpẽ-jA-Ibã
       new^shoots-PART-DIM-CLS:thread-PL-OBJ get-GER mold-STV-N/H^3p

       dã dẽ   xua-I-bo-A   ja-Iwɨ
       3p 3p^POS nest-STV-CLS:round-PL make-NFUT^PL^NMLZ
All kinds of little vines, little new shoots of *cumare* palm vines, getting (them), they mold (them), making their (the orioles') nests.

Another author, writing about a small, round object used in a shaman's curing ceremony, uses a different strategy to break up multiple modifiers: the verb separates the adjectives from the head noun in (288).

(288) ape-bo   pidi-pe   'pa-I-bo   di-bo
      other-CLS:round charm-SIM   be^similar-STV-CLS:round this-CLS:round

       'bA-Awɨ̃ bẽ   kai'wa-I-bo
       be-N/H^3 well cure-STV-CLS:round
Another small round one which is like a charm, this is one that cures well.

3.2.3 Noun phrases in apposition

Perhaps in order to avoid a large number of modifiers for a given head noun, noun phrases in apposition are a commonly used strategy for giving additional information about the referent; multiple modifiers are attached to the appositive noun. Appositive noun phrases are signalled in speech by pauses, indicated in (289) and (290) with slashes.

(289) kũĩ'dã-ko dōbĩ'õ/ dẽ   xabo-ko/ 'dã-RE
      one-FS   woman   3p^POS boss-FS   3p-OBJ

       kore-jO
       be^in^charge^of-NFUT^FS^NMLZ
A woman, their boss, being in charge of them...

Nouns

(290) ke   te-Rī   ˈkari ape-wɨ bue-I-pōē-wA/   bākapōē-wA/
      thus do-GER BT   other-PL teach-STV-AG^NMLZ-PL Curripaco-PL

      eda-RExa-Ibã
      arrive-HPAST-N/H^3p
      Then other teachers, Curripacos, arrived a long time ago.

A common strategy to emphasize a participant in a discourse consists of juxtaposing a personal or demonstrative pronoun and a noun, usually in that order, and usually following the verb, as in (291)–(293).

(291) bo   xipoka da-jɨ-bE   ĩ   u
      heat before come-NFUT^MS^NMLZ-be^3s 3ms sloth
      Before the hot weather (summer) he comes, the sloth.

(292) ɨra-kɨ ˈbA-Abē   ĩ   jāpā-bo
      big-MS be-N/H^3ms 3ms pavón^fish-CLS:round
      He, the *pavón* fish, is big.

(293) xapu-wɨ jɨ ˈdā-RE ākɨrīōbē-wA-RE
      blow-NON3 1s 3p-OBJ type^of^army^ant-PL-OBJ
      I recently sprayed them, the army ants.

A pronoun and a noun in apposition sometimes precede the verb, as in (294).

(294) aru ĩ   bɨkɨ-kɨ   da-Ij-Abē-jA
      and 3ms adult-MS come-STV-N/H^3ms-REP
      And he, the old man, reportedly habitually comes.

Example (295) shows a demonstrative pronoun and a noun phrase in apposition, as indicated by the fact that both the demonstrative and the noun 'bees' are marked by the object suffix.

(295) aru ˈkowɨ-A ˈpo-I-Rɨbɨ-A-RE   bāxā pōē-wA ˈbārē
      and flower-PL bloom-STV-CLS:time-PL-OBJ 1pinc person-PL also

      wo-Ij-Awĩ   i-Rā-RE   būbɨ-wA-RE dē   ˈkoro-RE
      seek-STV-N/H^1pinc this-PL-OBJ bee-PL-OBJ 3p^POS liquid-OBJ

ĩ-Rãxɨwɨ
get-PUR^SS

And when the flowers bloom, we people also habitually look for them, the bees, in order to get their honey.

3.3 Noun affixes and clitics

In this section, we discuss nominal affixes and clitics: the demonstrative prefixes, the diminutive, associative, certainty, similarity, separation, and identity suffixes, the partitive clitic, and the case marking suffixes.

3.3.1 Demonstrative prefixes

The demonstrative prefixes are: *i-* 'this, these, (definite, nearby)', *ãdĩ-* 'that, those (definite, farther away)', *di-* 'this, that, these, those (anaphoric, i.e., previously referred to)', *jo-* 'this (indefinite)', *dõ-* 'that (indefinite, nearby)', *ãdõ-* 'that (indefinite, farther away)', and *ape-* 'other, another'. There is also a rare demonstrative *dĩ-xĩ-* used with nouns that take the diminutive *-xĩ*, and which means 'this, that, these, those (anaphoric)'. The demonstrative pronouns discussed in §3.1.3.4 are, for the most part, based on these demonstrative prefixes.

The anaphoric demonstrative is illustrated in (296).

(296) a. *dĩ-xĩ-kuru-xĩ-bɨ*
this-DIM-CLS:bag-DIM-CLS:oblong
this (previously referred to) little bag

b. *di-kuru-bɨ*
this-CLS:bag-CLS:oblong
this (previously referred to) bag

3.3.2 *-xɨ* diminutive

The suffix *-xĩ* 'diminutive' means 'small', and may carry additional implications of 'insignificant, unimportant' or of 'loved, appreciated'. It is attached to a noun before the classifier or the gender/number marker: *xɨejo-xĩ-kɨ* (child-DIM-MS) 'little boy', *peka-xĩ-jo* (firewood-DIM-CLS:cone) 'a piece of firewood'. It may also be attached to a stative verb the subject of which (if explicit) also bears the diminutive suffix, either following the *-RI* nominalizer, or directly; in the latter case, *-xĩ* itself nominalizes the verb. In effect, this constitutes agreement in diminutive marking between the subject and the nominalized verb as shown in (297).

(297) a. *xobo-Rō-I   kɨ-RI-xĩ-Rã*
    ground-CLS:place-LOC live-NMLZ-DIM-PL
    little ones (grubs) that live in the ground

 b. *pẽõ-xĩ-jo*
    shine-DIM-CLS:cone
    small candle

 c. *jaɨ-bE-xĩ-Rã*
    be^quick-NEG-DIM-PL
    ones (birds) that aren't very speedy

(298) a. *xɨejo-xĩ-ko o-I-xĩ-ko   bõ-I-bõ-bE*
    child-DIM-FS cry-STV-DIM-FS have^fever-STV-PSV^FS^NMLZ-be^3s
    The little girl who is crying has a fever.

 b. *bĩbĩ-xĩ-jo   wɨ-I-xĩ-kɨ-RE   'xã-wɨ jɨ*
    hummingbird-DIM-CLS:cone fly-STV-DIM-MS-OBJ see-NON3 1s
    I saw a small hummingbird flying.

The diminutive suffix is occasionally duplicated, particularly with the *dĩ-* 'this' prefix: *dĩ-xĩ-kuru-xĩ-bɨ* (this-DIM-CLS:bag-DIM-CLS:oblong) 'this (previously referred to) little bag', *dĩ-xĩ-tuku-xĩ-bɨ* (this-DIM-CLS:room-DIM-CLS:oblong) 'this little room'.

All diminutive nouns take *-Rã* as the animate plural suffix, regardless of their plural forms in the absence of the diminutive suffix, as seen in (299)-(301).

(299) a. *xɨejo-wA*
    child-PL
    children

 b. *xɨejo-xĩ-Rã*
    child-DIM-PL
    little children

(300) a. *kai-wɨ*
    all-PL
    all

   b. *kai-xĩ-Rã*
    all-DIM-PL
    all

(301) a. *bɨkɨ-wA*
    adult-PL
    adults, old people, parents

   b. *bɨkɨ-xĩ-Rã*
    adult-DIM-PL
    little old people

The examples in (302) and (303) from texts show uses of the suffix -*xĩ* 'diminutive'. In (302) the meanings are physical smallness and nearness; in (303) the meaning is insignificance or unimportance.

(302) *ke   te-Rĩ   ēbĩ-xĩ-Rã-RE-bā   ēkã-xĩ-Rɨ-I*
    thus do-GER sardine-DIM-PL-OBJ-IDENT edge-DIM-CLS:3D-LOC

    da-I-xĩ-Rã-RE   tota-Rĩ
    come-STV-DIM-PL-OBJ pierce-GER

    'bã-wa-RI-xĩ-E
    ascend^from^the^port-ACST-NMLZ-DIM-IN^PL^NMLZ

    xãrɨ-'O-Ij-Abẽ   ɨ̃
    swallow-CAUS-STV-N/H^3ms 3ms

   Then, habitually spearing (with his beak) right while going up from the port, he (the river trumpeter bird) swallows the very same little sardines that come to the very edge of the shore.

(303) *ɨ-bE-Rĩ   kɨ-RI-xĩ-Rã   bãxã 'xãkɨ bãxẽ*
    want-NEG-GER exist-NMLZ-DIM-PL 1pinc INTNT 1pinc^POS

kɨ-Rõ-ka-kɨ   eda-RU   'ke-RA   tūrã-Rĩ
exist-IN^SG^NMLZ-PART-MS arrive-IF thus-UNIQUE roll^up-GER

dũ-I-apa   'kari
suck-STV-EMPH BT

But we insignificant/unimportant ones who just exist, if a man from our place/town arrives, only just rolling up (cigars) we smoke.

3.3.3 -xã associative

The suffix -xã 'associative' is used on animate nouns to mean 'this one and those associated with him or her': *Gregorio-xã* 'Gregorio and those with him'. In general, this would refer to the people who live in his house, or, since he is a village headman, it could refer to all the people in his village. In a different context, it could refer to the people who traveled with Gregorio, including non-Cubeos. The suffix -xã follows all other noncase suffixes.

(304) *jãbẽ-xã-ke   da-Rã-Rĩ   bɨ̃xã*
      who-ASC-INST come-PL-INTR 2p
      With whom (all) did you (all) come?

(305) *Timoteo-xã   kopai-da-Rãxɨ-itʃɨ-bã   dãĩ'dũ*
      Timoteo-ASC return-come-NRFUT^PL-IRR-3p late
      Timoteo and those with him perhaps will return later/in the evening.

3.3.4 -REka certainty

The suffix -REka means 'exactly' or 'certainty' and is demonstrated in (306) and (307).

(306) *dõ-pe-REka   jA-xA-kɨ*
      that-SIM-CERT do-IMP-MS
      Do it exactly like that.

(307) *ɨ̃-I   kojɨ-Ij-E-pe-REka   kojɨ-jɨ-bU   bɨ̃xã-RE*
      3ms-POS tell-STV-IN^PL^NMLZ-SIM-CERT tell-NFUT^MS^NMLZ-be 2p-OBJ
      I'm telling you exactly what he has said.

The example in (308) is from a text about the origin of one of the Cubeo sibs. The morpheme *-REka* is a clitic, not limited to appearing on nouns; in (308), it appears on the conjunction *aru*. Finally, (309) is from a prayer for safety on a trip, and (310) is from a folktale.

(308) aru-REka di-kobe-A   ki-wA-wɨ   dẽ
and-CERT this-CLS:hole-PL exist-CAUS-NON3 3p^POS

    põẽ-te-I-kobe-A   'bA-ke
    person-become-STV-CLS:hole-PL be-NFUT^IN^PL^NMLZ
And certainly we have those holes where they were born.

(309) apɨ-kɨ   xipoka-te-jɨ   'bɨ-REka
be^alive-NFUT^MS^NMLZ before-do-NFUT^MS^NMLZ 2s-CERT

    'bA-xA-kɨ jĩxā-RE xipoka-te-jɨ   jĩxẽ
    be-IMP-MS 1pexc-OBJ before-do-NFUT^MS^NMLZ 1pexc^POS

    ea-Rãxijepe   jĩxẽ   dɨ-I-Rõ-I
    arrive-PUR^DS 1pexc^POS go-STV-IN^SG^NMLZ-LOC
Exactly you who are alive and who certainly leads/guides us, be our guide in order that we arrive at the place we are going to.

(310) xɨ̃xõ-Rɨ   'bārẽ xawe'a-ka-kɨ-REka   bA-te-'Abẽ-jA
squirrel-CLS:3D also already-PART-MS-CERT be-DYN-N/H^3ms-REP

    xɨ̃xõ-Rɨ
    squirrel-CLS:3D
The squirrel also was reportedly one of the very ones who lived in ancient times.

3.3.5 *-pe* similarity

The noun suffix *-pe* means 'like, similar to'. It is frequently used in conjunction with the stative verb *ārōxã-* or the dynamic verb *'pa-*, both of which mean 'be like, similar to'.

(311) jawi-pe   ārōxā-ki   ku-Ij-Abẽ   xārāwɨ-RE
    jaguar-SIM be^like-NFUT^MS^NMLZ walk-STV-N/H^3ms day-OBJ
    Like a jaguar he (the *coati mundi*) roams around during the day.

(312) dã 'bA-Ibã 'bɨ̃-xɨ̃-Rã jaɨ-bE-xɨ̃-Rã-pe
3p be-N/H^3p bird-DIM-PL be^quick-NEG-DIM-PL-SIM

    ãrõxã-RIwɨ
    be^similar-NFUT^PL^NMLZ

They (the *pipira*, similar to a dove) are small birds which are like ones that aren't very speedy.

(313) tʃiai-Rɨ-pe ãrõxã-Abẽ ɨ̃
cicada-CLS:3D-SIM be^similar-N/H^3ms 3ms

He (the lion ant) is similar to the cicada.

(314) xɨejo-kɨ-wA-bIko kũĩ'dã-ko kai-pɨka-pɨrɨ-'A-pe
child-exist-CAUS-3FS one-FS all-two-hand-PL-SIM

    'pa-Iwɨ baxu
    be^similar-NFUT^PL^NMLZ exactly

One (female rabbit) even has ten (lit., like two hands) babies!

(315) ke bA-RU kũĩ'dã-pɨrɨ-pe 'pa-I-ɨxɨ-A 'jobo-I
thus be-IF one-hand-SIM be^similar-STV-CLS:year-PL after-LOC

    bue-I-Rõ ɨra-Rõ kɨ-bE-te-wI
    teach-STV-IN^SG^NMLZ big-IN^SG^NMLZ exist-NEG-DYN-NON3

    xi kɨ-Rõ-RE
    1s^POS live-IN^SG^NMLZ-OBJ

Thus being, after five (lit., like one hand) years there wasn't a lot of teaching in my village.

The suffix *-pe* can also appear with other verbs, as seen in (316)–(320).

(316) di-E bA-ki'je-RE 'jo-pe a-Rĩ
this-IN^PL^NMLZ be-FUT^IN^PL^NMLZ-OBJ this-SIM say-GER

    daro-RExa-Ibã-jA bɨ̃xã-RE xi 'a-wa-Rõ-pe
    send-HPAST-N/H^3p-REP 2p-OBJ 1s^POS say-ACST-IN^SG^NMLZ-SIM

    a-jɨ   *a-RExa-Abẽ*
    say-NFUT^MS^NMLZ say-HPAST-N/H^3ms
"About that which will be, like this saying, reportedly they sent (a message) to you (all) a long time ago, I'm saying just like I say," he said.

(317) *'dõ-pe ja-xA-kɨ jɨ̃xã-RE*
   that-SIM do-IMP-MS 1pexc-OBJ
   Do like that for us.

(318) *'xãkɨ tataro-ko koapa 'jo-pe 'bA-Ako aru ape-Rõ*
   INTNT butterfly-FS every this-SIM be-N/H^3fs and other-IN^SG^NMLZ

   'xãkɨ 'jo-pe 'bA-Abẽ butʃi-kɨ
   INTNT this-SIM be-N/H^3ms slug-MS
   Every butterfly is like this. And another thing, the slug is like this.

  The example in (321) is from a text in which a man describes how a terrible wind storm knocked down trees in the jungle, and even twisted and broke them up.

(319) *kũĩ'dã xio kɨo-I-Rõ-pe   dɨ̃-I-wɨ kaij-E*
   one garden grind-STV-IN^SG^NMLZ-SIM go-STV-NON3 all-IN^PL^NMLZ
   All (the trees) are like a garden going through a grinder.

  The suffix *-pe* occurs in combination with the suffix *-REka* (discussed in the preceding section) to form *-pe-REka* 'exactly like', as shown in (320).

(320) *pɨ ɨxɨ-Rɨ̃bɨ̃ da-Ij-E-pe-REka   'xãkɨ*
   until season-CLS:time come-STV-IN^PL^NMLZ-SIM-CERT INTNT

   ɨxɨ xipoka jo kaxedo xãrãwɨ-bo 'jobo-I 'kari
   season before this caterpillar day-CLS:round after-LOC BT

   'xãkɨ kaxedo xãrãwɨ-bo eko-Rɨ̃-buru 'jobo-I 'xãkɨ
   INTNT caterpillar day-CLS:round enter-GER-AFTER after-LOC INTNT

   ã-I-kɨ-I   'koro dẽ a-I-Rõ   'kari
   eat-STV-NFUT^MS^NMLZ-POS liquid 3p^POS say-STV-IN^SG^NMLZ BT

Nouns

    xiwa-I   *'koro oka-Ij-Abẽ-RA*   *ĩ*
    upstream-LOC liquid rain-STV-N/H^3ms-UNIQUE 3ms

Until right when summer (the dry season) comes, before that dry season, after a certain caterpillar's hatching-out day, the anaconda's (lit., the eater's) liquid, they say, he rains his liquid upstream, I'm telling you.

(321) *xura-te-Rĩ*   *ĩ*   *'bãrẽ tataro-ko*
       cocoon-make-GER 3ms also butterfly-FS

        põẽ-te-Ij-E-pe-REka
        person-become-STV-IN^PL^NMLZ-SIM-CERT

        põẽ-te-Ij-Abẽ
        person-become-STV-N/H^3ms

He also (the slug), being metamorphosed, is born just like the butterfly is born.

3.3.6 -wa separation

The suffix *-wa* (separation) means 'separately, individually, alone'.

(322) *di-E-RE*   *ja-jɨ-wa*   *bɨoxa-I-Rõ*
       this-IN^PL^NMLZ-OBJ make-NFUT^MS^NMLZ-SEP finish-STV-IN^SG^NMLZ

        'bA-Awĩ   *'kari*
        be-N/H^IN^3 BT

…each one separately/individually making this, it gets finished.

(323) *ke   te-Iwɨ-RE*   *'xã-Rĩ põẽ-wA   ĩ-jA-Ibã*
       thus do-NFUT^PL^NMLZ-OBJ see-GER person-PL get-STV-N/H^3p

        dẽ   *'bĩ-xĩ-Rã-wa*
        3p^POS bird-DIM-PL-SEP

When people see them (birds) doing thus, they get their own individual ones (birds) (for pets).

When *-wa* occurs on a negative nominalized verb root, it means 'without'.

(324) ke   te-Rī   ˈa-Ako   jɨ-RE aru   ˈkū-boa-I-jabe-A-RE
      thus do-GER   say-N/Hˆ3fs 1s-OBJ and worm-kill-STV-CLS:seed-PL-OBJ

   ūkū-xA-kɨ   xawe-xɨ̄-Rā   ā-bE-kɨ-wa
   drink-IMP-MS already-DIM-LOC eat-NEG-NFUTˆMSˆNMLZ-SEP
   Doing that, she said to me, "And take parasite purging pills early in the morning without eating."

In §6.4.3.4, the dependent concessive clause, marked by -wakari, is discussed. This same suffix occurs on nouns in the nominative case (i.e., subjects), with the meaning 'emphatically separated from others, emphatically alone, by oneself'. Invariably, the noun phrase marked by this suffix is the first element of the independent clause. The suffix -wakari may be a fusing of the suffix -wa 'individually' with ˈkari 'backbone tag'. (The 'backbone tag', glossed BT in the examples, is a discourse particle; see Salser and Salser 1979.)

(325) ˈjɨ-wakari ˈxā-wɨ   ˈdā-RE
      1s-SELF   see-NON3 3p-OBJ
      I myself saw them.

(326) jawibī-wA-wakari ˈɨ̄-RE   kuxu-Rī   boa-ˈRā-bā
      dog-PL-SELF   3ms-OBJ chase-GER kill-R/DˆPLˆASM-3p
      The dogs themselves chasing (caught and) killed him (a small rodent).

The suffix -REka (discussed above) follows the noun suffix -wa (separation), resulting in the meaning 'that person him/herself'.

(327) xipoka-te-Abẽ   ˈɨ̄-wa-REka Sergio-wa ˈkari
      before-do-N/Hˆ3ms 3ms-SEP-CERT Serge-SEP BT
      He himself, Serge himself, guided us (on the tour).

3.3.7 -bɨ̃ã and -bã identity

The suffixes -bɨ̃ã and -bã mean 'identical to, the same as'. While these two suffixes often seem to have more or less the same meaning, they may be distinguished, for instance, when they are suffixed to the the emphatic word baxu 'self, same, very' (lit., 'body'): baxu-bɨ̃ã means 'together, among themselves', while baxu-bã means 'individually, to or by oneself'.

(328) boa-'Rĩ xarɨwa-Rã-xA-RE-wɨ   a-Rĩ   ĩ-RE
      kill-GER get^rid^of-IMP^AN^PL-IMP-OBJ-PL say-GER 3ms-OBJ

   'dapia-Iwɨ   'bA-te-Ibã-jA   dẽ   baxu-bã
   think-NFUT^PL^NMLZ be-DYN-N/H^3p-REP 3p^POS self-IDENT
   "Let's killing, get rid of (him)", saying they reportedly thought about him to themselves.

(329) ke   te-Rĩ   kojɨ-karã   jɨ̃xẽ   baxu-bĩã   ĩ   'jo-pe
      then do-GER talk-N/H^1pexc 1pexc^POS self-IDENT 3ms this-SIM

   a-I-bI   bãxẽ   tãũ-tɨra-RE   kɨ-wA-bE
   say-STV-3ms 1pinc^POS metal-CLS:circle-OBJ exist-CAUS-NEG

   boxe   a-karã
   payment say-N/H^1pexc
   Then we talked among ourselves/to each other, "He is saying like this because we don't have money," we said.

(330) aru di-xura-wɨ   baxu-bã-ta   bɨkɨ-Ij-Awĩ
      and this-cocoon-CLS:tube self-IDENT-FOC grow-STV-N/H^IN^3
      And that cocoon all by itself habitually grows.

(331) aru ke te-Rĩ   ape-Rõ   bẽbẽ-I-Rõ   jɨ̃xẽ
      and then do-GER other-IN^SG^NMLZ work-STV-IN^SG^NMLZ 1pexc^POS

   baxu-bĩã ja-jA-wɨ   jɨ̃xẽ   di-E-RE
   self-IDENT do-STV-NON3 1pexc^POS this-IN^PL^NMLZ-OBJ

   bẽbẽ-Ij-E-RE   ote-Ij-E-RE   jɨ̃xẽ
   work-STV-IN^PL^NMLZ-OBJ plant-STV-IN^PL^NMLZ-OBJ 1pexc^POS

   baxu-bĩã ja-jA-wɨ   kɨi-ba-RE
   self-IDENT do-STV-NON3 bitter^manioc-CLS:broad-OBJ

   ote-Ij-E-RE   'õrẽ-RE   ote-Rĩ
   plant-STV-IN^PL^NMLZ-OBJ plantain-OBJ plant^seed-GER

kawabēdē-RE   ote-Rĩ   kaij-E   ã-Ij-E
sugar^cane-OBJ plant-GER all-IN^PL^NMLZ eat-STV-IN^PL^NMLZ

koapa
every^individually

And then we ourselves are doing another job together. Our working at that, we ourselves together are doing planting, planting manioc, planting plantains, planting sugar cane, all our various kinds of food.

(332) aru   dō-I   pista-RE   bēbē-Ibã-ikɨ   'bãrē
      and that-LOC airstrip-OBJ work-N/H^3p-NARR^FOC also

   ape-xĩ-E-RE   da-wA-Rĩ   kaij-E
   other-DIM-IN^PL^NMLZ-OBJ come-CAUS-GER all-IN^PL^NMLZ

   ã-Ij-E-RE   da-wA-Rãxɨ-Rō
   eat-STV-IN^PL^NMLZ-OBJ come-CAUS-NRFUT^PL-IN^SG^NMLZ

   ɨ-E-ɨ-Rĩ   wɨ-I-kũ-RE   'orexa-Rãxɨwɨ
   want-IN^PL^NMLZ-fall-GER fly-STV-CLS:hump-OBJ call-FUT^PL^NMLZ

   'kari kai-wɨ pābɨ-wA jĩxē   baxu-bĩā jãbē kōxē-bE-bã
   BT   all-PL Cubeo-PL 1pexc^POS self-IDENT who order-NEG-3p

And there they worked on the airstrip, I say, also. Bringing various things, all the food they would bring, getting tired (lit., wanting to fall), ones who would call an airplane, all the Cubeos, we ourselves, nobody (lit., who) orders (us) around.

In addition to their use on *baxu* 'self, selves', both -*bĩā* and -*bã* attach to subject, object, locative, and temporal nouns, as shown in (333) and (334). (See also (302) on page 98.)

(333) jeba-RE   ēbē-bE-Abē   xokɨ-kɨ-A-bĩā-ta
      low^down-OBJ descend-NEG-N/H^3ms wood-CLS:tree-PL-IDENT-FOC

   kɨ-Abē
   live-N/H^3ms

He (the howler monkey) does not come down low. Right among the trees is where he lives.

(334) *jeba-xī-E   baxi   dī-Ij-Abē   ʹke-RA   ʹxāki*
low^down-DIM-IN^PL^NMLZ right^at go-STV-N/H^3ms thus-UNIQUE INTNT

jeba-xī-E-bā-ta   kā-Ij-Abē
low^down-DIM-IN^PL^NMLZ-IDENT-FOC   sleep-STV-N/H^3ms

xoe-we
toucan-CLS:flat

Exactly way down low he only goes...It is in the same way-down-low place that the toucan sleeps.

When used with temporal nouns, the primary meaning of *-bīā* and *-bā* is 'even', as in (335) and (336).

(335) *kopai-da-kɨjɨ-bū   bīxē   kojɨ-Rī buba-Rāxije*
return-come-FUT^MS^NMLZ-FUT^NON3 2p^POS tell-GER finish-BEFORE^PL

xipoka-bīā   xi   ʹjawa-Ij-E-RE   kai-Rõ-A
before-IDENT 1s^POS speak-STV-IN^PL^NMLZ-OBJ all-CLS:place-PL

bāxē   ībā-Rõ-A-I
1pinc^POS town-CLS:place-PL-LOC

I will return even obviously before you finish telling my news in all our towns.

(336) *di-Rɨbɨ-bīā-REka   wo-Rī   dī-RExa-wɨ-jA   kawa-Rõ*
this-CLS:time-IDENT-CERT open-GER go-HPAST-NON3-REP buzzard-CLS:place

bēā-Rõ   xɨbE-RI-xī-kɨ-I   kɨ-Rõ
be^good-IN^SG^NMLZ blue/green-NMLZ-DIM-MS-POS exist-IN^SG^NMLZ

Certainly, even right during that very time, heaven (lit., good sky God's place) was reportedly opened up. (Matthew 3:16b)

The suffixes *-bīā* and *-bā* combine with the suffix *-REka* 'exact' to form *-bīā-REka* 'exactly together, externally identical' and *-bā-REka* 'exactly individually, internally identical', as in (337) and (338).

(337) *koeda-Rī   xɨejo-xī-kɨ-RE   ʹxi-pa-ko-RE   ʹbārē*
wake^up-GER child-DIM-MS-OBJ POS-parent-FS-OBJ also

dɨ-wA-RExa-Abẽ-jA   José di-jābɨ̄-bā-REka   Egipto
  go-CAUS-HPAST-N/H^3ms-REP José this-CLS:night-IDENT-CERT Egypt

  ābɨ̄-kɨ-RI-xobo-Rõ-I-ta   dupi-Rɨ̄
  name-exist-NMLZ-land-CLS:place-LOC-GOAL hide-GER

  dɨ̄-RExa-Ibā-jA   dā
  go-HPAST-N/H^3p-REP 3p

A long time ago, reportedly José, waking up, took the small child and his mother also. Exactly on that very same night, escaping, they went to the land called Egypt. (Matthew 2:14)

(338) ɨ-bE-Rɨ̄-ta   di-jābɨ̄-bɨ̄ā-REka   kūɨ̄'dā-kɨ
      want-NEG-GER-FOC   this-CLS:night-IDENT-CERT one-MS

      xɨ̄bẽ-RI-xɨ̄-kɨ-I   daro-I-bɨ̄   'āxere ea-Rɨ̄
      blue/green-NMLZ-DIM-MS-POS send-STV-PSV^MS^NMLZ angel arrive-GER

      dẽ   jeba-I   wo-A-ka-Rɨ̄   'dā-RE di-jābɨ̄
      3p^POS beside-LOC open-CAUS-BEN-GER 3p-OBJ this-CLS:building

      xedewa-kobe-RE   xipoka-te-RExa-Abẽ-jA   'dā-RE dō-RE
      outside-CLS:hole-OBJ before-do-HPAST-N/H^3ms-REP 3p-OBJ that-OBJ

      xoka-Rɨ̄
      leave^behind-GER

But on that exact same night, reportedly one of God's sent ones, an angel, arriving beside them, causing to open for their benefit the door of that building, he led them away from there. (Acts 5:19)

The suffix *-bɨ̄ā* (identity) has the allomorph *-bɨ̄* when it appears before the suffix *-ka* (doubt): *-bɨ̄-ka* (doubtfully/possibly identical).

(339) ke   te-Rɨ̄ bedi'owa jo-bɨ̄-ka   da-kɨjɨ-bū
      thus do-GER again   this-IDENT-DUB come-FUT^MS^NMLZ-FUT^NON3
      Then, once again I will come (possibly) right here...

(340) 'pōbɨ-ja-Rɨ̄   kɨ-Ibā   dā aru dō-bɨ̄-ka
      burrow-make-GER live-N/H^3p 3p and that-IDENT-DUB

'xĩ-xūã-Rĩ
egg-put^on^the^ground-GER
They live making burrows. And laying eggs (possibly) right there...

(341) pɨ   'xākɨ xia-jo-bE-do-bĩ-ka
      as^far^as INTNT river-CLS:cone-NEG-CLS:broad-IDENT-DUB

      kopedɨ-kɨ-Ra-jɨ-apa
      turn^around-NFUT^MS^NMLZ-come-NFUT^MS^NMLZ-EMPH
      He definitely comes (in order) to turn around (possibly) right at
      the mouth of the river.

(342) dõ-bĩ-ka   dɨ̃-karã
      that-IDENT-DUB   go-N/H^1pexc
      We went (possibly) to that same place.

(343) 'xākɨ 'ke-Rõ-bĩã   jɨ-RE xi   ābū-jo-I
      INTNT thus-IN^SG^NMLZ-IDENT 1s-OBJ 1s^POS arm-CLS:cone-LOC

      do-A-Ako
      penetrate-CAUS-N/H^3fs
      Just like that she obviously stuck me in my finger.

3.3.8 -ka partitive

The clitic -ka 'partitive' means 'part of, pertaining to X', where X refers to the noun -ka cliticizes to. The noun to which -ka cliticizes is unmarked for case, while the clitic -ka is inflected for gender and number (as well as case): -ka-kɨ (PART-MS) 'he who pertains to, I/you (masculine singular) who pertain to', -ka-ko (PART-FS) 'she who pertains to, I/you (feminine singular) who pertain to', -ka-wɨ (PART-PL) 'they/we/you who pertain to', -ka-Rõ or -ka plus a classifier 'it/this/that which pertains to', and the irregular form -'ke (PART-PL; the expected form would be *-ka-E). These forms are illustrated in (344)–(347).

(344) xawabo-bɨ-ka-ko-bE
      Tapurucuara-CLS:oblong-PART-FS-be^3s
      She pertains to (the town of) Tapurucuara. (The literal meaning of
      xawabo is 'submerged tree trunk'.)

(345) i-Rā   būbɨ-wA   xokɨ-kɨ-ka-wɨ
      this-PL bee-PL   wood-CLS:tree-PART-PL
      These bees that live in (lit., pertain to) trees...

(346) jɨ bōā-RE   boa-'wɨ   bāka-xita-bɨ-ka-wɨ-RE
      1s fish^PL-OBJ kill-NON3 jungle-pool-CLS:oblong-PART-PL-OBJ
      I recently caught some fish, ones that live in (lit., pertain to) the lake.

(347) ke   te-Rĩ   ĩ   'kari kū-Abē   'jɨ-ka-kɨ-RE
      thus do-GER 3ms BT   bite-N/H^3ms   1s-PART-MS-OBJ
      Then he (a snake) bit my companion (lit., a man who pertains to me).

3.3.9 Case marking suffixes

Cubeo has five case marking suffixes that can be attached to pronouns and nouns. (The subject case is unmarked.)

3.3.9.1 The -RE suffix. The suffix *-RE* is used to mark both direct and indirect objects, as well as certain locative and temporal nouns. These two uses are discussed in the following subsections.

-RE as object marker. *-RE* is by far the predominant marker for direct objects, alternating only occasionally with the absence of any marker. In (348), *tɨbĩ-RE* 'otter' is the direct object of the verb.

(348) 'xā-bI   tɨbĩ-RE
      see-3ms otter-OBJ
      He recently saw an otter.

-RE also marks indirect objects. In (349), *xɨejo-kɨ-RE* 'boy' is the indirect object.

(349) aru ape-kɨ   jārādawi-xɨejo-kɨ-RE   'xɨ-wɨ   jɨ tres
      and other-MS   white^person-child-MS-OBJ   give-NON3 1s three
      And I gave three to another little white boy.

-RE is obligatory on the indirect object, and the majority of direct objects (apart from the object incorporation construction, see §2.6) are also marked with *-RE*. The factors influencing when *-RE* may be omitted

Nouns   111

from a (nonincorporated) direct object, leaving it without an overt case marker, are the inanimacy of the object, introducing an animate object, and in lists. These will now be explained in more detail.

Inanimacy of object. In most cases where *-RE* is omitted, the object is inanimate (and the focus is on the activity), as in (350)–(352).

(350) kui'tote-kaxe-A   xoa-Rĩ
      cotton-CLS:cover-PL wash-GER
      clothes washing

(351) oko   kaju'a   ūkū-Rĩ
      water stir^food drink-GER
      drinking *mingao* (a hot tapioca drink)

(352) 'ke-Rō-RA   'kari bue-I-jābĩ-A
      thus-IN^SG^NMLZ-UNIQUE BT   teach-STV-CLS:building-PL

      ja-RExa-Ibã
      make-HPAST-N/H^3p
      Well then, a long time ago they built school buildings.

It is rare to find an animate direct object without *-RE*; exceptions are given under the second and third factors. Personal pronouns, being highest in animacy, are always marked with *-RE* when they are objects.

Introducing an animate object. The *-RE* suffix may be omitted from an animate object if the object is sentence-final and is being newly introduced into the discourse. Usually the referent of such a noun phrase serves as the subject of the next sentence, as in (353) and (354).

(353) dō-I   ea-karã   kũĩ'dā-kɨ ājã   ke   te-Rĩ   ĩ   'kari
      that-LOC find-N/H^1pexc one-MS   snake thus do-GER 3ms BT

      kũ-Abẽ   'jɨ-ka-kɨ-RE
      bite-N/H^3ms 1s-PART-MS-OBJ
      There we found a snake. Then he bit my companion.

(354) ĩ   boa-'bI wekoro-Rɨ   wekoro-Rɨ   kɨ-Abẽ
      3ms kill-3ms talking^catfish-CLS:3D talking^catfish-CLS:3D exist-N/H^3ms

ĩ   ēpā-kũ-I   wekoro-Rɨ   'bãrẽ
3ms sand-CLS:hump-LOC   talking^catfish-CLS:3D also

ko-Ij-Abẽ   kobo-bɨ-RE   'bãrẽ
enter-STV-N/H^3ms kind^of^fish^trap-CLS:oblong-OBJ also

He caught a talking catfish. The talking catfish lives in the sand. Also the talking catfish enters a certain fish trap.

Lists. In lists of (noncoordinate) noun phrases, all of which function as the direct object of a single verb, the *-RE* suffix may be omitted on all but the first such noun phrase. A list of names of fish is given in (355); *-RE* occurs on only the first of these names. The main verb *boa-* 'kill' occurs both before and after the list, both times referring to the same event. (See §5.1 on such repetition.)

(355) boa-'bI jupari-Rɨ-RE   ape-ko   dẽɨdokɨ-ko warĩ-ko
      kill-3ms rabo^colorado-CLS:3D-OBJ other-FS ñacundá-FS jacha-FS

      pidubā-ko   boa-'bI   ĩ   bɨkɨ-kɨ
      tucunaré-FS kill-3ms 3ms old-MS

The old man recently caught a *rabo colorado*, also a *ñacundá*, a *jacha*, and a *tucunaré* [or *pavón*].

Similarly, while in the first sentence of (356), *bõã* 'fish (plural)' has the object suffix, as does its modifier *bāka-xita-bɨ-ka-wɨ* (jungle-pool-CLS:oblong-PART-PL) 'of the lake variety', in the second sentence the object marker is omitted because *bõã* appears in a list.

(356) jɨ bõã-RE   boa-'wɨ   bāka-xita-bɨ-ka-wɨ-RE
      1s fish^PL-OBJ kill-NON3 jungle-pool-CLS:oblong-PART-PL-OBJ

      būxā-joka-wA   pɨka-Rã aru   kōbĩ'õwāĩ-wA   pɨka-Rã
      palometa-CLS:leaf-PL two-PL and kind^of^sardine-PL two-PL

      boa-'wɨ   jɨ
      kill-NON3 1s

I caught fish, fish from the lake. I killed two *palometa* and two sardines.

Nouns

When a multiword noun phrase is marked by -*RE*, the last word of the phrase is always marked by -*RE*; preceding words in the phrase may or may not be so marked. The direct objects are bracketed in (357)–(360).

(357) *[põẽ-wA bãxi-Rɨwɨ-RE]*   '*dõ-pe   a-Ibã-jA*
       person-PL know-NFUT^PL^NMLZ-OBJ that-SIM say-N/H^3p-REP
       They reportedly said that to knowledgeable people.

(358) *[jawi-RE   ɨra-kɨ-RE] dõ-I   ea-RExa-kakɨ   [jawi-RE*
       jaguar-OBJ big-MS-OBJ that-LOC find-HPAST-N/H^1ms jaguar-OBJ

       ɨra-kɨ-RE]
       big-MS-OBJ
       A big jaguar I found there, a big jaguar.

(359) *[ɨra-kɨ 'je-kɨ   'pa-jɨ-RE*
       big-MS what-MS be^similar-NFUT^MS^NMLZ-OBJ

       xidoxa-kɨ-RE]   '*xã-wɨ   jɨ*
       be^scary-NFUT^MS^NMLZ-OBJ   see-NON3 1s
       A big something-or-other, like a frightening thing, I saw.

(360) *ɨ-bE-Rĩ-ta*   '*xã-I-wɨ*   *jɨ [ɨra-kɨ ãĩbã-kɨ-RE]   dõ-I*
       want-NEG-GER-FOC   see-STV-NON3 1s big-MS animal-MS-OBJ that-LOC
       But (lit., not wanting), I've seen a big animal there.

-*RE as locative/temporal suffix.* In addition to its use as an accusative and dative case marker, -*RE* is found fairly frequently on temporal noun phrases and occasionally on locative noun phrases also. Rather than pointing to a particular position in space or time, as does the case marker -*I* 'locative, temporal' (discussed in §3.3.9.2), -*RE* marks a time or place as the general setting for some event.

We first consider the temporal use of the suffix -*RE*. In this usage, it is always attached to an inherently temporal noun such as *kari-* 'today', or to a noun suffixed with a temporal suffix such as the classifier -*Rɨbɨ̃* 'time'.

(361) *xãrãwɨ-RE*   *jãbĩ-RE*
       day-OBJ   night-OBJ
       by day, during the day   by night, during the night

(362) kari-RE   xawe-xī-Rã-RE
today-OBJ   already-DIM-LOC-OBJ
today, now   during the early morning
        (xawe-Rã- 'tomorrow')

(363) bābā-Rɨ̃bɨ̃-RE   oko-Rɨ̃bɨ̃-A-RE
first-CLS:time-OBJ   water-CLS:time-PL-OBJ
at first, in the beginning   in the rainy seasons

(364) ˈkowɨ-A   po-I-Rɨ̃bɨ̃-A-RE
flower-PL   bloom-STV-CLS:time-PL-OBJ
during the flower-blooming seasons

In its locative use, -RE is found on a limited range of demonstrative pronouns, most often *jo* 'this' and *dō* 'that', forming *jo-RE* 'here' and *dō-RE* 'there'. It also appears on place names, both proper names such as *Mitú-RE* 'in (at) Mitú' and *xawabobɨ-RE* 'in (at) Tapurucuara', and common names such as *kɨrābɨ-RE* 'in (at) the house' and *xɨo-I-jābɨ-RE* (cure-STV-CLS:building-OBJ) 'in (at) the clinic/hospital'. -RE usually appears on place names after the place has been introduced with the locative case marker -I.

As discussed in §3.3.9.2, a locative marked with -I generally indicates a shift to a new scene, whereas a place marked with -RE does not. In (365), the place *xio* 'garden' is introduced with the case marker -I 'locative' in the first sentence and referred to as *dō-RE* (that-LOC) 'there' in the second sentence.

(365) xio-I   dɨ̃-jO-bU   jɨ   dō-RE   kɨi-jA-Rɨ̃
garden-STV go-NFUT^FS^NMLZ-be 1s that-OBJ bitter^manioc-make-GER

kopai-da-Rɨ̃
return-come-GER
I go to the garden. There cultivating manioc, coming returning...

The excerpts in (366)–(368) are from a text about a tour of a town. The first sentence shows a shift in location to a rice mill and uses -I.

(366) dɨ̃-karã   bedi'owa   ku-Rā-Rɨ̃-Iwɨ   arutʃu-RE
go-N/H^1pexc again   walk-PL^NMLZ-go-NFUT^PL^NMLZ rice-OBJ

kɨ̃õ-I-Rõ-I-ta　　　　　　　Puerto Llera-I
grind-STV-IN^SG^NMLZ-LOC-GOAL Puerto Lleras-LOC
We went (in order) to visit a rice mill in Puerto Lleras.

The scene having been set, dõ-RE 'there' occurs in the rest of the text.

(367) ˈkɨ-te-Ibã　　dõ-RE　bẽbẽ-I-põẽ-wA　　kũĩˈdã-pɨrɨ-pe
exist-DYN-N/H^3p that-OBJ work-STV-AG^NMLZ-PL one-hand-SIM

ˈpa-Iwɨ
be^similar-NFUT^PL^NMLZ
There were five workers there.

At the end of the description of the rice mill, the author tells how they walked along the river bank and then introduces the next place they visited with the -I (locative) suffix.

(368) dõ-I　　ˈxã-karã　　jɨxã dẽ　　wekɨ-wA-RE　dẽ
that-LOC see-N/H^1pexc 1pexc 3p^POS COW-PL-OBJ 3p^POS

boa-I-Rõ-RE
kill-STV-IN^SG^NMLZ-OBJ
There we saw their slaughter house for their cows.

Rarely, -RE is found on a postpositional.

(369) aru xia pɨedõ-RE　ˈbãrẽ wɨ-Ij-Ako　　õ
and river above-OBJ also fly-STV-N/H^3fs 3fs
And also she (a bird) flies above the river.

-RE also marks source, i.e., the place from which the subject moves. The examples (370)–(372) illustrate this use of -RE.

(370) ke　te-Rɨ̃　di-jãbɨ̃-RE　　eta-Rɨ̃　dɨ̃-Rɨ̃
thus do-GER this-CLS:building-OBJ leave-GER go-GER

eko-karã　　koxedeka
enter-N/H^1pexc again
Then leaving this building, we entered again (another building we had been in before).

(371) jɨ da-kakɨ   xi   kɨrābɨ̃-RE
      1s come-N/H^1ms 1s^POS house-OBJ
      I came from my house.

(372) pare dāɨ'dū eta-wɨ   jɨxā̃ Mitú-RE xoka-Rɨ̃
      very late leave-NON3 1pexc Mitú-OBJ leave^behind-GER
      We recently left Mitú very late.

The gerundive verb *xoka-Rɨ̃* 'leaving behind' in (372) means 'away from'. An alternative analysis is that *xoka-Rɨ̃* is a postposition which selects the object case on its noun phrase complement. The same meaning 'away from' is conveyed in a more emphatic way using the gerundive verb *xarɨwa-Rɨ̃* 'getting rid of, throwing out'.

(373) eta-xA-Rā   'koxixi-I-jābɨ̃-RE   xarɨwa-Rɨ̃
      leave-IMP-IMP^AN^PL meet-STV-CLS:building-OBJ get^rid^of-GER
      Get out of the meeting house!

3.3.9.2 The -*I* suffix. The suffix -*I* has two general uses: as a general locative and temporal case marker and as a genitive case marker.

General locative and temporal. The suffix -*I* 'locative, temporal' is used to indicate position in space and time, or direction. We gloss it as LOC (locative) in both usages. It is by far the most common case marker indicating location. With stative verbs it indicates location 'in, on, at', as in (374)–(377).

(374) doba-ko-bU   jɨ kuja-I-kajawa-I
      sit-NFUT^FS^NMLZ-be 1s bathe-STV-CLS:rack-LOC
      I am sitting on the dock.

(375) xawabo-bɨ-I   kɨ-wɨ   jɨ
      Tapurucuara-CLS:oblong-LOC live-NON3 1s
      I live in Tapurucuara.

(376) aru ɨ̃ kɨ-Abē   kɨrā-kū-I
      and 3ms live-N/H^3ms rock-CLS:hump-LOC
      And he lives on a hill.

Nouns

(377) dɨ́-wɨ́　　　jɨ̀　wɨ-I-kū　　　　ēbẽ-I-Rõ-I
　　　go-NON3　1s　fly-STV-CLS:hump　descend-STV-IN^SG^NMLZ-LOC

　　　bēbẽ-kɨjɨ̃
　　　work-FUT^MS^NMLZ
　　　I went (in order) to work on the airstrip.

With motion verbs, -I (locative) often marks goal 'into, at' or direction 'to' as in (378).

(378) ke　　te-Rĩ-ta　　xatu-karã　　　xātūrū-I-kū-I
　　　thus　do-GER-FOC　board-N/H^1pexc　roll-STV-CLS:hump-LOC
　　　Then we got into the car.

It can also show where the motion is taking place ('along'), for example, going along a river bank or a trail.

(379) ke　　te-Rĩ　kopai-da-Rĩ　　　xia　ēkã-Rɨ-I　　　　ku-Rã-Rɨ-Rĩ
　　　thus　do-GER　return-come-GER　river　edge-CLS:3D-LOC　walk-PL-go-GER

　　　bexa-karã　　　　　　jɨ̃xã
　　　go^downstream-N/H^1pexc　1pexc
　　　So returning, coming along the river bank we kept on going downstream.

-I also occurs on temporal noun phrases, but less frequently than on locative noun phrases. An example is given in (380).

(380) ke　　te-Rĩ　ape-xārāwɨ-I　　dɨ́-karã
　　　thus　do-GER　other-CLS:day-LOC　go-N/H^1pexc
　　　So on another day we went...

-I also occurs on almost all locative and temporal postpositions some of which are shown in (381)–(383).

(381) tɨ-O-I-wa　　　　piedõ-I
　　　place-CAUS-STV-CLS:table　over-LOC
　　　on the table

(382) dõ 'jobo-I
    that after-LOC
    after that

(383) í-I   jai-kije   xipoka-I
    3ms-POS die-FUT^IN^PL^NMLZ before-LOC
    before his death

Possessive. The suffix *-I* 'genitive' also marks animate possessive noun phrases, as in (384)–(386).

(384) i-ko-I   'bã-ko
    this-FS-POS child-FS
    this (female) one's daughter

(385) Vícto-I   kɨrãbĩ
    Víctor-POS house
    Víctor's house

(386) kai-wɨ i-Rã   bue-I-xɨejo-wA-I   papera
    all-PL this-PL teach-STV-child-PL-POS paper
    all the students' papers

The 'possession' of a part by an inanimate noun is represented by use of a classifier or by a compound noun construction, with no special case marking, as in (387) and (388).

(387) xoki-kawabɨ-A
    wood-CLS:branch-PL
    tree branches

(388) xia-jo-kũ   jɨa-we
    river-CLS:cone-CLS:hump bench-CLS:flat
    canoe thwart

3.3.9.3 *-ke* as instrument and accompaniment. The case marker for instrument and accompaniment is *-ke* 'with, by'.

(389) jĩxã da-karã   xia-jo-kũ-ke
      1pexc come-N/H^1pexc river-CLS:cone-CLS:hump-INST
      We came by canoe.

(390) ape-kɨ   ɨbɨ tota-ta-RExa-Abē   ōpō-jɨ-ke   'ɨ-RE
      other-MS man hit-ITER-HPAST-N/H^3ms explosion-CLS:funnel-INST 3ms-OBJ
      Another man hit him repeatedly with a gun.

(391) aru dõ-I   xi   kɨ-E-RE   toroxɨ-wɨ   jɨ
      and that-LOC 1s^POS exist-IN^PL^NMLZ-OBJ be^happy-NON3 1s

      'xi-bã-Rã-ke
      1s^POS-child-PL-INST
      And when I'm there, I'm happy (being) with my children.

The combination of -bã 'identity' plus the suffix -ke is sometimes used as a coordinator on the first of two singular noun phrases, resulting in a coordinate noun phrase of dual number as in (392).[6]

(392) lunes   xãrãwɨ-RE finka 'jobo-I-ta   ku-Rã-Rɨ-karã
      Monday   day-OBJ   farm behind-LOC-GOAL   walk-PL-go-N/H^1pexc

      jĩxã Saúl-bã-ke
      1pexc Saúl-IDENT-INST
      On Monday we, I with Saúl, the two of us, went (in order) to take a walk behind the farm.

3.3.9.4 -Rã as specific locative and temporal. The case suffix -Rã is used on nouns and postpositions to indicate a specific location or time: 'right at, on, in'. In its locative use, it implies physical contact. Note the contrast in (393) and (394); the first has the general locative suffix -I, while the second has the specific locative -Rã and implies physical contact. Additional examples of the use of -Rã are given in (395)–(398).

(393) 'bɨ-xɨ-kɨ   wɨ-jɨ-bE   kɨrãbɨ pɨedõ-I
      bird-DIM-MS   fly-NFUT^MS^NMLZ-be^3s   house over-LOC
      The bird is flying over the house.

---

[6] The conjunction aru is also used to conjoin noun phrases; see §4.5.

(394) 'bɨ-xɨ-kɨ   tuba-kɨ-bE   kɨ̄rābɨ̄ pɨedō-Rā
      bird-DIM-MS perch-NFUT^MS^NMLZ-be^3s house over-LOC
      The bird is perching on top of the house.

(395) dɨ-kɨ-Rā   'koxɨ̃xẽ-Rɨ̃
      this-CLS:tree-LOC get^entangled-GER
      being entangled right on this net (spider web)

(396) aru ke   te-Ij-E-ta   ea-Rɨ̃
      and thus do-STV-IN^PL^NMLZ-FOC arrive-GER

  xobo-tākū-bɨ-Rā   tɨ-Rɨ̃
  ground-ridge-CLS:oblong-LOC fall-GER

  do-Rā-Rɨ̃-kebā-wɨ   aru dō-I-ta   ea-Rɨ̃
  penetrate-PL^NMLZ-go-ASM-PERS and that-LOC-GOAL arrive-GER

  kopedi-Rɨ̃   dɨ̃-Awɨ   dō-I-ta.   ea-Rɨ̃   eta-Rɨ̃
  turn^around-GER go-N/H^1pinc that-LOC-GOAL arrive-GER leave-GER

  dɨ̃-I-kakɨ   tɨ-kakɨ   kɨra-I-Rɨ   pɨedō-Rā
  go-STV-WHILE^SS fall-N/H^1ms step^on-STV-CLS:3D over-LOC

And when it happened thus, arriving (landing) right on top of a ridge of dirt, falling we went penetrating (into the ground). And arriving as far as there, turning around we went there. Arriving, as I was going to leave, I fell right on top of (tripped over) the wheel (of the airplane; lit., a stepping thing).

(397) bo   korika-Rā xūā-Rɨ̃   ke   ja-Rɨ̃
      heat middle-LOC place^on^the^ground-GER thus do-GER

  xɨtɨ-te-I-joka-RE   kõxɨ̄jō-Rɨ̃ toa-bo   ēkā-Rɨ
  be^sticky-become-STV-CLS:leaf-OBJ rub-GER fire-CLS:round edge-CLS:3D

  xūā-xA-Rā   'kari
  place^on^the^ground-IMP-IMP^AN^PL BT

Placing (them) on the ground right when it is sunny, thus doing, rubbing the leaves that have become sticky, place them on the ground around the edge of the fire.

(398) *ĩ   ĩ-I   pĩkõ-bũ-RE   jãĩ-RE   Bãwitʃikuri-RE*
3ms 3ms-POS tail-CLS:vine-OBJ this^MS-OBJ Mawichicuri-OBJ

jēbĩ-doba-RI-Rĩbĩ   bĩxĩ-Rĩbĩ-Rã   ʼkari   ĩ-I
black-sit-NMLZ-CLS:time   yajé-CLS:time-LOC   BT   3ms-POS

pĩkõ-bũ-RE   piaʼjo-Rĩ   daro-Rĩ   tuba-te-Abẽ-jA
tail-CLS:vine-OBJ arch-GER   send-GER   perch-DYN-N/H^3ms-REP

jo-Rã   ʼkari
this-LOC BT

At the funeral (lit., the black sitting time) of this Mawichicuri, right at the *yajé*-taking time, tossing and arching his tail, he (a squirrel) reportedly squatted right here.

3.3.9.5 -ta as goal and limit. The suffix *-ta* marks a place as a goal, or a time as a limit, and can often be translated as 'very, quite'. It follows any locative or temporal case suffix.

The locative *-ta* is used on a locative word only when it is the goal of a motion verb as is shown in (399) and (400).

(399) *doa-Rĩ   dĩ-wɨ   jĩxã   pɨ   ape-bo*
paddle-GER   go-NON3   1pexc   as^far^as other-CLS:round

ēkã-bo-I-ta
edge-CLS:round-LOC-GOAL

We recently paddled way over to the other shore.

(400) *ke   te-Rĩ   ape-ki   ĩbĩ   ʼbA-ki-RE*
thus   do-GER   other-MS man   be-NFUT^MS^NMLZ-OBJ

xaro-RExa-Ibã-jA   boa-I-Rõ-I-ta
send-HPAST-N/H^3p-REP   kill-IN^SG^NMLZ-LOC-GOAL

Then, a long time ago, they reportedly sent another man, who has since died, to that killing place.

-ta may also be used on a directional word, limiting the spatial realm in which the event takes place, as in (401) and (402).

(401) dɨ̃-Rĩ pɨ   xiwa-I-ta
     go-GER as^far^as upstream-LOC-GOAL
     Going upstream to a certain point...

(402) jeba-I-ta   kɨ-Abẽ   ĩ
     low^down-LOC-GOAL   live-N/H^3ms 3ms
     He (a bird) lives down very low (near the ground).

The limiter *-ta* is also used occasionally on temporal nouns to indicate time, with the meaning 'until'.

(403) bãũbẽ eda-bE-te-Awĩ   pɨ   dãɨ'dũ-ta eda-Awĩ
     rapidly arrive-NEG-DYN-N/H^IN^3 until late-GOAL arrive-N/H^IN^3
     It (the airplane) didn't arrive quickly. It didn't arrive until quite late in the afternoon.

(404) aru xawe-xɨ̃-Rã-RA-ta   'kaju   'orexa-kije
     and already-DIM-LOC-UNIQUE-GOAL   rooster call-FUT^IN^PL^NMLZ

     xɨpoka-I   'ĩ-RE   'xɨ-xA-Rã
     before-LOC 3ms-OBJ give-IMP-IMP^AN^PL
     And first thing in the morning before the rooster crows, give him (this medicine).

4
Other Word Classes

4.1 Adjectives

4.1.1 Adjectives versus nouns and stative verbs

In many Tucanoan languages, there is little or no difference between adjectives and verbs; nominalized verbs (in effect, reduced relative clauses) serve the function for which adjectives would be used in other languages. Cubeo, however, does have a small class of adjectives, which are distinct from both nouns and verbs. These adjectives most resemble nouns; however, nouns and adjectives may be distinguished by the classifiers that appear (or fail to appear) on each. As discussed in chapter 3, when a noun modifies another noun in a compound noun construction, usually only the second noun takes a classifier (e.g., *kɨbo-kũã-Rɨ* (foot-bone-CLS:small^three^dimensional) 'ankle bone'). But when an adjective modifies a noun, both the noun and the adjective take classifiers or gender markers. Usually, the classifiers or gender markers on the adjective and noun are identical, e.g., *tataro-ko tra-ko* (butterfly-FSG big-FSG) 'big butterfly', *tãũ-jo tra-jo* (metal-CLS:slender^pointed^cylindrical big-CLS: slender^pointed^cylindrical) 'big nail'. But sometimes they differ—*doe-we ɨra-kɨ* (coral^snake-CLS:flat big-MSG) 'big coral snake'.

A further difference between the adjectival modification of nouns on the one hand, and compound nouns on the other, is that the head noun of a compound noun follows its noun modifier(s): *bia-pɨe* (hot^pepper-CLS:basket) 'basket for storing hot peppers'. (The example in the preceding paragraph of the word for 'ankle bone' also exemplifies this pattern.) But an adjective modifier may follow the head noun, as discussed in §3.2.2. (Adjectives may also appear without an overt head noun in positions where noun phrases are expected, e.g., as the subject of a clause; we analyze this construction as a headless noun phrase.)

Adjectives differ from verbs in not needing to be nominalized in order to modify a noun, as illustrated above. Verbs must either be nominalized (in which case they may be analyzed as reduced relative clauses, cf. §3.2.2 and §6.3) or adjectivized with the *-RI* suffix (see §6.1.3). Furthermore, adjectives cannot take the inflectional affixes for verbs (discussed in §2.2.2).

4.1.2 Nonderived adjectives

The class of nonderived adjectives is small. Among the adjective roots are *ape-* 'other', *bɨkɨ-* 'old (of animate nouns)', *kai-* 'entire, all', *pedẽ-* 'dry', *xaɨxĩ-* 'curly', *xaweka-* 'old (of inanimate nouns)', *'kĩxĩ-* 'small', and *ɨra-* 'big, wide, fat'.

4.1.3 Derived adjectives

We have analyzed the suffix *-RI* as a nominalizing suffix (see §3.1.4.1). However, the resulting word also exhibits characteristics of adjectives, such as bearing the same classifier as the noun that it modifies. The number 'three' is an example; at least historically, it may be derived from a verb *'jo-bE-kɨ-* (accompany-NEG-be-) 'three'. (Since its meaning is more or less noncompositional, we have glossed this number elsewhere without breaking it down into these constituent morphemes: *'jobekɨ-* 'three'.) When it modifies a noun, this number often takes the *-RI* adjective suffix followed by a classifier. Note the classifier agreement in example (405).

(405) *dɨ-Rɨ*   *'xiwɨ-I*   *'jobekɨ-RI-tɨkarɨ-A*
this-CLS:3D inside-LOC three-NMLZ-CLS:cylinder-PL

    pẽõ-I-tɨkarɨ-A   *epe-Ij-E*   *xaɨ-wɨ*
    shine-STV-CLS:cylinder-PL put-STV-INˆPLˆNMLZ beˆnecessary-NON3
It is necessary to put three batteries in the (flashlight).

4.1.4 Indefinite adjectives

The indefinite terms 'whoever', 'whichever', 'wherever', 'whenever', etc., are expressed in Cubeo by the adjective root *'a-* 'which' followed by a classifier, a gender/number suffix, or by a nominalizer. Like other adjectives, indefinite adjectives bearing a classifier or gender/number marker must be followed by an agreeing noun: *'a-kɨ põẽ-kɨ* (which-MS person-MS) 'whichever man, whoever', *'a-ko põẽ-ko* (which-FS person-FS) 'whichever woman'.

(406) *'a-kɨ   põẽ-kɨ   bõā   boa-'jɨ̃   toroxɨ-bɨ̃*
which-ms person-ms fish-PL kill-NPUT^MS^NMLZ be happy-3ms
Whoever catches fish is happy.

However, these indefinite adjectives are homophonous with the interrogative pronouns discussed in §3.1.3. But when *'a-* is followed by a nominalizer, it has the meaning 'wherever', and the resulting derived indefinite pronoun does not require an additional noun.

(407) *'a-Rõ   bɨ̃   dɨ̃-kirõ-RE   dɨ̃-kixɨ-wɨ̃*
which-IN^SG^NMLZ 2s^POS go-FUT^IN^SG^NMLZ-OBJ go-NRFUT^MS-NON3

'bɨ̃-ke
2s-INST
Wherever you will go, I am going to go with you.

4.1.5 Possessive adjectives

The set of personal possessive adjectives is given in the table in (408); the set is similar to, but not identical to, the possessive pronoun stems given in the table in (251).

(408) Possessive adjectives

Person		Singular	Plural
1	exclusive	*xɨ*	*jɨ̃xẽ*
	inclusive		*bãxẽ*
2		*bɨ̃*	*bɨ̃xẽ*
3	masculine	*ɨ̃-I*	*dẽ*
	feminine	*õ-I*	

Possessive adjectives precede the noun they modify, as in (409) and (410).

(409) xi   pāū-kɨ
   1s^POS hammock-CLS:tree
   my hammock

(410) ɨ́-I   ābī'ā
   3ms-POS name
   his name

All kinship terms are obligatorily possessed, either by possessive adjectives (which are procliticized to the kinship nouns) or by noun phrases marked in the genitive case (see page 118). Most kinship terms take the possessive adjectives shown in the table in (408), but a few take the possessive prefix ′xi- 'his, her' in the third-person singular. This third-person singular possessive differs from the first-person singular possessive adjective xi- only in that the third-person possessive prefix is stressed.

(411) a. *xi-pako*
   1s^POS-mother
   my mother

b. *′xi-pako*
   POS-mother
   his/her mother

4.1.6 Adjective inflection

Adjectives may also take the diminutive suffix -*xī* (also used on nouns; see §3.3.2). This suffix is attached after the nominalizer -*RI* adjective suffix: *ībɨ́xɨ-bE-xī-jo* (long-NEG-DIM-CLS:slender^pointed^cylindrical) 'short, little, slender pointed cylindrical object', *kīrā-xī-bo bo-RI-xā-bo* (stone-DIM-CLS:small^round be^white-NMLZ-DIM-CLS:small^round) 'small white stone'.

Adjectives are inflected to agree in gender or classifier and number with the noun they modify (even if that noun is not overt). The suffixes used to mark agreement follow the diminutive if present and are discussed in the following subsections.

4.1.6.1 Adjectival agreement with animate nouns. Adjectives modifying singular animate nouns take -*ko* 'feminine singular' or -*kɨ* 'masculine singular'. These suffixes are also used on nouns (see §3.1.2).

Other Word Classes   127

(412) a. *dōbī'ō   ɨra-ko*
       woman big-FS
       big woman

   b. *xɨejo-xɨ̄-kɨ   'kɨ̄-xɨ̄-kɨ*
      child-DIM-MS little-DIM-MS
      little boy

As discussed in §3.1.2.2, the gender of certain animate nouns is grammatical, not semantic; adjectives modifying such nouns agree with this grammatical gender, as seen in the examples in (413).

(413) a. *tataro-ko   ɨra-ko*
         butterfly-FS big-FS
         big butterfly

   b. *jawɨbĩ   ɨra-kɨ*
      dog   big-MS
      big dog

   c. *'bɨ̄xɨ̄-kɨ   ɨra-kɨ*
      bird-MS   big-MS
      big bird

When an adjective modifies a nonhuman animate noun which takes a classifier in the singular, the adjective takes an adjectival gender suffix, rather than a classifier. Unless the gender of the animal is known and in focus, the adjective is marked with the masculine gender, as in (421).

(414) *doe-we   ɨra-kɨ*
      coral^snake-CLS:flat big-MS
      big coral snake

All adjectives modifying plural animate nouns may take the feminine plural suffix *-Rōbĩwā*. For nonfeminine plurals, there is a wide variety of plural suffixes: the plural animate suffix *-Rā*, the plural animate suffix *-wA*, the plural animate active nominalizer *-wɨ*, and the plural animate nonfuture nominalizer *-RIwɨ*. The adjectives *bābā-* 'young', *pɨka-* 'two', and *'kɨ̄xɨ-* 'small' fall into the first set, taking *-Rā*; *bɨkɨ-* 'old' and *jārādawɨ-*

'rich' take *-wA*; *ape-* 'other' and *kai-* 'entire, all' take *-wɨ*; and *pedē-* 'dry' and *dūrī-* 'right, truthful, correct' take *-RIwɨ*.

4.1.6.2 Adjectival agreement with inanimate nouns. As has been mentioned, when an adjective modifies an inanimate noun that has a classifier, the adjective takes the same classifier.

(415) a. *tāū-jo*   *ɨra-jo*
metal-CLS:cone big-CLS:cone
big nail

b. *papera-joka*   *ɨra-joka*
paper-CLS:leaf big-CLS:leaf
big sheet of paper

Adjectives may also be procliticized to a class 2 noun; in this construction, they do not take gender/number suffixes (see §3.1.1.3).

(416) *koeda-wɨ*   *oko-xārāwɨ*   *jēbī-RI-xārāwɨ*
wake^up-NON3 water-CLS:day black-NMLZ-CLS:day

xidoxa-RI-xārāwɨ-RE   *'xā-wɨ*
be^scary-NMLZ-CLS:day-OBJ see-NON3
When we woke up we saw (it was) a dark, scary, rainy day.

When an adjective modifies a class 1 noun which does not have a classifier, i.e., a mass noun, the adjective takes the abstract nominalizing suffix, *-Rō* 'abstract specific nominalizer'. Although these adjectives usually follow the noun they modify, they precede mass nouns.

(417) *ɨra-Rō*   *xiwe*
big-IN^SG^NMLZ blood
lots of blood

4.1.7 Comparison of adjectives

Comparisons involving adjectives may be expressed by means of coordinated clauses or a gerundive construction, although neither construction is very common in spoken or written Cubeo.

In the coordinate construction, the adjective expressing the quality of comparison appears in the first clause, modified by a comparative word, generally *pɨedõ* 'more' (lit., 'above, over'), but sometimes *kãtʃĩdõ* 'less' (lit., 'under, beneath'). The standard of comparison appears in the second clause, optionally modified by an antonymous or negated adjective. (418) illustrates this construction, comparing the size of the dog *Brinco* (the quality of comparison) to that of *pitʃadã* 'cat' (the standard of comparison). The standard of comparison follows the quality of comparison, as is typical of OV languages.

(418) *Brinco pɨedõ   ɨra-kɨ-bE   aru pitʃadã ˈkĩ-xĩ-kɨ-bE*
Brinco above/over big-MS-beˆ3s and cat   small-DIM-MS-beˆ3s
Brinco is bigger than the cat.

The other construction used to express a comparison also uses *pɨedõ* 'over' or *kãtʃĩdõ* 'under' modifying the quality of comparison, and a gerundive form of *xarɨwa-Rĩ* (throwˆout-GER) 'getting rid of, throwing away, throwing out' serving as a postposition to the noun phrase which is the standard of comparison.

(419) *ˈɨ-ta-bE   xɨo-Ij-E   pɨedõ   bãxɨ-kɨ*
3ms-FOC-beˆ3s cure-STV-INˆPLˆNMLZ above/over know-NFUTˆMSˆNMLZ

ape-wɨ-RE   xarɨwa-Rĩ
other-PL-OBJ getˆridˆof-GER
He certainly is more knowledgeable about medicine than other people are.

4.2 Quantifiers

Quantifiers in Cubeo can be considered a subclass of adjectives, but they show some diversity. The quantifier *ɨre* 'many', for example, is invariable (i.e., it takes no suffixes): *ɨre põẽ-wA* (many person-PL) 'manyˆpeople', *ɨre kɨ-we* (many be-CLS:flatˆthin) 'many flat, thin things'. (This word can be derived historically from *ɨra-* 'big' + *-E* 'inanimate plural nominalizer', although it is now used with both animate and inanimate referents.)

The quantifier *kai-* 'all, every' is unusual in that when it modifies a noun with a classifier, *kai-* usually takes a nominalizing suffix rather than a classifier. Thus, the (a) forms in (420) and (421) are more common than the (b) forms.

(420) a. *kaij-E*   *xokɨ-kɨ-A*
       all/every-IN^PL^NMLZ wood-CLS:tree-PL
       all the trees, every tree

   b. *kai-kɨ-A*   *xokɨ-kɨ-A*
      all/every-CLS:tree-PL wood-CLS:tree-PL
      all the trees, every tree

(421) a. *kaij-E*   *karo-we-A*
       all/every-IN^PL^NMLZ machete-CLS:flat-PL
       all the machetes, every machete

   b. *kai-we-A*   *karo-we-A*
      all/every-CLS:flat-PL machete-CLS:flat-PL
      all the machetes, every machete

When modifying a class 2 noun (a noun that acts as a classifier), however, *kai-* 'all, every' is procliticized to the noun, rather than taking a nominalizing suffix as shown in the examples in (422).

(422) a. *kai-xãrãwɨ*
       all-CLS:day
       all day

   b. *kai-xãrãwɨ-A*
      all-CLS:day-PL
      every day

   c. *kai-baxu*
      all-CLS:body
      (the) entire body

When modifying an animate noun, the quantifier *kai-* takes one of the usual gender/number suffixes, namely *-kɨ* 'masculine singular', *-ko* 'feminine singular', or *-wɨ* 'plural': *kai-wɨ xabo-wA* (all-PL^NMLZ chief-PL) 'all the chiefs, every chief'.

The interrogative quantifiers 'how many?' and 'how much?' are formed from the root *aipi* 'how much, how many' plus an appropriate nominalizer or classifier (with the inanimate singular nominalizer *-Rõ* used both for objects in general and for mass nouns).

(423) aipi-wɨ   bɨ̄-bābɨ̄-Rā   kɨ-ko-Rɨ̃   bɨ̄
how^many-PL 2s^POS-older^sibling-PL exist-NFUT^FS^NMLZ-INTR 2s
How many older sisters and brothers do you have?

(424) aipi-Rõ   boxe   kɨ-RI   i-we
how^much-IN^SG^NMLZ payment exist-INTR this-CLS:flat

  tāũ-xɨ̄-we
  metal-DIM-CLS:flat
  How much does this knife cost?

(425) aipi-we-A   xia-jo-we-A   kɨ-RI   dõ-RE
how^many-CLS:flat-PL river-CLS:cone-CLS:flat-PL exist-INTR that-OBJ
How many canoe paddles are there over there?

The interrogative determiner *'a-* 'which', while not strictly speaking a quantifier, behaves similarly to the interrogative quantifiers *aipi-wɨ* 'how many' and *aipi-Rõ* 'how much'. It is followed by a classifier (optionally pluralized), as in (426).

(426) *'a-tukubɨ-bA*
which-CLS:room-be^INTR
Which room is it?

4.3 Adverbs

The Cubeo language includes locative, temporal, and manner adverbs, as well as adverbs which modify adjectives.

4.3.1 Nonderived adverbs

Some of the nonderived adverbs are: *xawe* 'already', *kārēxā* 'still, yet', *pare* 'very, a lot', *xãwē* 'truly, really', *ke* 'thus', *bẽ* 'well', and *ābẽ* 'badly'.

(427) *toroxɨ-RExa-Ibā*   pare
be^happy-HPAST-N/H^3p very
They were very happy.

(428) xatɨ-'O-kixi-wɨ   kãrẽxã a-Rɨ̃   'da-Abẽ-jA
      cross-CAUS-NRFUT^MS-NON3 still   say-GER come-N/H^3ms-REP
      "I'm still going to cause (you) to cross soon," he reportedly came saying.

These adverbs may either precede or follow the adjective, verb, or adverb they modify.

(429) a. 'xã-xA-kɨ jãĩ   ãĩbã-kɨ   ɨra-kɨ pare
         see-IMP-MS this^MS animal-MS big-MS very
         Look at this very big animal!

      b. 'xã-xA-kɨ jãĩ   ãĩbã-kɨ   pare ɨra-kɨ
         see-IMP-MS this^MS animal-MS very big-MS
         Look at this very big animal!

4.3.2 Derived adverbs

Adverbs can be derived from pronouns, nouns, and adjectives. In addition, adverbial clauses are based on nominalized verbs or gerunds; these are discussed in §6.4.

The case marker -*I* 'locative/temporal' causes a noun to function as a locative or temporal adverb: *kɨ̃rã-kũ-I* (rock-CLS:hump-LOC) 'on the hill', *Jũã-I kɨ-Rõ-I* (Juan-POS live-IN^SG^NMLZ-LOC) 'in/at Juan's place', and *martes xãrãwɨ-I* (Tuesday day-LOC) 'on Tuesday' (lit., 'on Tuesday day'). Such words are adverbial in the sense that unlike nominative or accusative nouns, they may be added to any clause where semantically appropriate, regardless of the argument structure of the verb. They remain nouns with regard to their morphology.

Some adverbs of time are formed by an adjective root or a class 1 noun—a mass noun or generic term—plus the classifier -*Rɨ̃bɨ̃* (time). Some examples are *bãbã-Rɨ̃bɨ̃* (new/first-CLS:time) 'at first, in the beginning, first of all', *bɨ̃xɨ̃-Rɨ̃bɨ̃* (Banisteriopsis^capi-CLS:time) 'a mythological time when people first took the hallucinogenic drug *Banisteriopsis capi*', and *ape-Rɨ̃bɨ̃* (other-CLS:time) 'sometime, another time'. Since the result is a noun with respect to its morphology, it can be further suffixed with the -*I* locative suffix or the -*RE* object case suffix, both in their adverbial sense; the former allows a focus on the specific time, while the latter implies a focus on the duration.

From the pronouns *jo* 'this' and *dõ* 'that' are derived such adverbs as *jo-RE* (this-OBJ) 'here', *dõ-RE* (that-OBJ) 'there', '*jo-pe* (this-SIM) 'like this, thus' (cataphoric reference), '*dõ-pe* (that-SIM) 'like that, thus' (anaphoric reference), *jo-bɨ̄-ka* (this-IDENT-DUB) 'right here', *dō-bɨ̄-ka* (that-IDENT-DUB) 'right there', *jo-bɨ̄'ā-REka* (this-IDENT-DUB) 'exactly right here', and *dō-bɨ̄'ā-REka* (that-IDENT-DUB) 'exactly right there'.

(430) *aipi-we-A   xia-jo-we-A   kɨ-RI   dō-RE*
how^many-CLS:flat-PL river-CLS:cone-CLS:flat-PL exist-INTR that-OBJ
How many canoe paddles are there over there?

(431) *'dō-pe ja-xA-kɨ j̃xā-RE*
that-SIM do-IMP-MS 1pexc-OBJ
Do like that for us.

Some adverbs appear to have been derived historically from roots which have since been lost. An example is *koxedeka* 'again', where the ending appears to be the suffix *-REka* (see §3.3.4). Similarly, the ending on *bedi'owa* 'once more, again' could have originally been the noun suffix *-wa* (separation) (see §3.3.6). However, now it seems that *bedi'o-* and *koxe-* are fused to these suffixes and no longer have independent meaning.

Likewise, the following five related forms all mean something like 'rapidly': *baū-bE, baū-bE-RA, baū-bE-xī-E, baū-bE-xī-E-REka,* and *baū-bE-REka*. They would appear to be derived from a verb root **baū-* 'move slowly' plus *-bE* (negative). But there is no such verb root in modern Cubeo (although there is a noun root *baū-* meaning 'enemy'). Also, the following three forms all mean something like 'slowly': *dɨiba-xī-E, dɨiba-REka,* and *dɨiba-xī-E-REku,* but there is no present-day verb root **dɨiba-*. Other adverbs of this type include *kaja-xī-E* 'close, nearby' and *kaja-xī-E-REka* 'immediately, at once', which may be related to the verb *kaja-te-* (help-do-) 'help' (which may be derived historically from a verb root **kaja-* plus the dynamicizer suffix *te-*).

The etymology of the adverbs 'down low' and 'up high' is also uncertain. *jeba-I* is also a postposition meaning 'beside, next to' (see the next section). *ībɨ̄-I* may be related to the adjective *ībīxɨ-* 'tall, high, long, deep'. This adjective may consist of two morphemes, *ībɨ̄-* 'high' and a nonproductive verbalizing morpheme *-xɨ*. These adverbs also appear in the data with various additional suffixes, including *ībɨ̄-I-ta* (up^high-LOC-GOAL) 'as far as up high', *jeba-I-ta* (down^low-LOC-GOAL) 'as far as down low', *jeba-xī-E-I-ta* (down^low-DIM-IN^PL^NMLZ-LOC-GOAL) 'as far as really down low', and *jeba-xī-E* (down^low-DIM-IN^PL^NMLZ) 'the quality, state, or condition of being down low'.

A noun phrase plus a postposition bearing the locative suffix *-I* functions as an adverbial locative phrase, e.g., *kīrābī 'xɨwɨ-I* (house inside-LOC) 'inside the house'.

4.3.3 Adverb inflection

The adverbs *ābẽ* 'badly' and *bẽ* 'well' may be intensified by attaching the suffix *-I*, as in (432).

(432) bɨ̃-RE dū-RU, ābẽ-I   ixi-xE-bU   bɨ̃-RE
      2s-OBJ suck-IF badly-INTNS hurt-COND-be 2s-OBJ
      If he (a horsefly) were to bite you, it would hurt very badly.

Most adverbs take certain discourse suffixes, e.g., *pare-ta* (very-FOC) 'very much', *bẽ-RA* (well-UNIQUE) 'extremely well', and *'ke-REka* (thus-CERT) 'exactly thus'.

4.3.4 Comparison of adverbs

Cubeo has a comparative construction with adverbial force, used to compare the degree to which two subjects perform the action of a verb. This construction is formed by modifying the verb with a postpositional phrase, the latter consisting of one of the postpostions *pɨedõ* 'over' to mean 'more' or *kātʃɨdõ* 'under' to mean 'less', plus the noun phrase which is the standard of comparison in its possessive form. This construction, exemplified in (433)–(435), is uncommon.

(433) xi-bābɨ̃-kɨ   xi   pɨedõ   'kuja-jI-bE
      1s^POS-older^sibling-MS 1s^POS over/above run-NFUT^MS^NMLZ-be^3s
      My older brother runs faster than I do.

(434) jɨ-RE   xēdī'ā-Rī   'xā-bE-xA-kɨ   bī   kātʃɨdõ   bãxi-wɨ   jɨ
      1s-OBJ ask-GER   see-NEG-IMP-MS 2s^POS under/beneath know-NON3 1s
      Don't ask me, I know less than you.

(435) 'xɨ-pa-kɨ   ɨ̃-I   pɨedõ   xawi'o-I-bI
      3s^POS-parent-MS 3s-POS over/above weave-STV-3ms
      His father weaves better than he does.

4.4 Postpositions

As is common in languages of the OV type, Cubeo has postpositions rather than prepositions. These postpositions are of two classes: uninflected and inflected. Inflected postpositions take noun phrases as their

Other Word Classes

objects, while uninflected postpositions take inflected postpositional phrases as their objects.

4.4.1 Uninflected postpositions

Uninflected postpositions may appear following inflected postpositional phrases or adverbials (i.e., locative or temporal nouns, or adverbs). The uninflected postpositions of Cubeo are *baxi* 'right at', *baxu* 'truly, exactly', and *koapa* 'every one individually'. When serving as complements to these uninflected postpositions, inflected postpositions or adverbs are in the unmarked nominative case as shown in (436)–(445).

(436) *eda-wɨ   xãrãwɨ korika baxi*
arrive-NON3 day   middle right^at
I arrived right at noon.

(437) *deõ   kũɨ-karã   Urania baxi*
gasoline run^out-N/H^1pexc Urania right^at
We ran out of gas right at Urania.

(438) *otfo   baxi   bue-Rã-xA-RE*
eight right^at teach-IMP^AN^PL-IMP-OBJ
Let's start class (lit., let's teach) at 8:00 on the dot.

(439) *jeba-xĩ-E   baxi   dɨ-Ij-Abẽ   'ke-RA*
low^down-DIM-IN^PL^NMLZ right^at go-STV-N/H^3ms thus-UNIQUE
He (a bird) habitually only goes down low.

(440) *kai-Rɨbɨ-A   baxu*
all-CLS:time-PL exactly
just all the time...

(441) *kore-karã   tres 'ora baxu*
wait^for-N/H^1pexc three hour exactly
We waited for exactly three hours.

(442) *awi'a do-RE dɨ-Ij-E   baxu-RE   dɨ-Ij-Abẽ   'kari*
sun   set-OBJ go-STV-IN^PL^NMLZ exactly-OBJ go-STV-N/H^3ms BT
He goes exactly when the sun is setting.

(443) xãrãwɨ-A koapa
      day-PL   every^individually
      day by day, each day

(444) põē-wA   xia   koapa
      person-PL river every^individually
      people on various rivers

(445) ij-E   koapa
      this-IN^PL^NMLZ   every^individually
      each one of these

The uninflected postposition *baxu* takes an optional -*REka* 'certainty', -*RE* 'object', or -*ta* 'focus' suffix, but *baxi* only takes -*ta*, and *koapa* appears not to take any affixes at all.

4.4.2 Inflected postpositions

Cubeo has three inflected postpositions that indicate order in both time and space: '*jobo* 'after, behind', *korika* 'in the middle, midpoint in position or time', and *xipoka* 'before, in front of, ahead of'. '*jobo* and *xipoka* function at clause level to introduce dependent temporal clauses (see §6.4.1) and at phrase level as postpositions to indicating time or location: *xãrãwɨ korika baxi* (day middle right^at) 'noon' and *kɨrãbĩ korika-I* (house middle-LOC) 'in the middle of the house'. The other inflected postpositions are: *pɨedõ* 'above, on top of, over', *kãtʃɨdõ* 'below, beneath, under', '*xiwɨ* 'inside, in', *xedewa* 'outside', *xẽdẽbo* 'between, among', *jeba* 'next to', and *pidĩdɨ* 'at the end of'.

The noun phrase object of an inflected postposition is in the (unmarked) nominative case. If a personal pronoun is the object of an inflected postposition, however, the possessive adjective form is used: *Juan jeba-I* (Juan beside-LOC) 'beside Juan', but *ĩ-I jeba-I* (3ms-POS beside-LOC) 'beside him', *õ-I pɨedõ-I* (3fs-POS on^top^of-LOC) 'on her', or *xi xipoka-I* (1s^POS IN^front^of-LOC) 'in front of me'.

The postposition may take the locative suffix -*I*, forming an adverbial phrase, e.g., *kɨrãbĩ 'jobo-I* (house behind-LOC) 'behind the house'; or it may be the object of an uninflected postposition, as described in the previous section.

(446) dẽ   korika-I   doba-bIko   bibi-ko
3p^POS middle-LOC sit-3fs   toad-FS
The toad is sitting between them.

4.5 Conjunctions

The conjunction *aru* 'and' is used to join noun phrases. In a list of items, sometimes *aru* occurs before each item except the first one, sometimes it only occurs before the last one, and sometimes it occurs between the first two items and before the last one. Sometimes ꞌ*barẽ* 'also' is also used following the last of the conjoined noun phrases.

(447) kawabẽdẽ-RE   jãbū-RE,   puju-RE   aru   japi-RE
sugar^cane-OBJ ñame-OBJ   chonque-OBJ and sweet^potato-OBJ

ki-wA-bã
exist-CAUS-3PL

They have sugar cane, *ñame*, *chonque* (two kinds of tubers), and sweet potatoes.

(448) ꞌōrẽ-RE   aru kii-ba-RE   aru   wea-RE
plantain-OBJ and bitter^manioc-CLS:broad-OBJ and corn-OBJ

aru ixi-RE   ote-jA-Ibã
and pineapple-OBJ plant-STV-N/H^3p

They habitually plant plantains, and bitter manioc plants, and corn, and pineapple.

(449) dō-I   ꞌki-te-bã   ēbū-wA   aru
that-LOC exist-DYN-3p red^howler^monkey-PL and

xixi-wA   ꞌbãrẽ aru bōã   ꞌbãrẽ
capuchin^monkey-PL also   and fish^PL also

Over there were red howler monkeys and capuchin monkeys and fish.

(450) kai-wɨ ɨbɨ-wA i-xia-ka-wɨ   ja-Ij-E
      all-PL man-PL this-river-PART-PL make-STV-IN^PL^NMLZ

   bãxi-RIwɨ-bU   xia-jo-kū-RE   aru
   know-NFUT^PL^NMLZ-be   river-CLS:cone-CLS:hump-OBJ and

   pie-bi-A-RE   jūka-RE   aru 'papi-kɨ-RE
   basket-CLS:oblong-PL-OBJ palm^fiber-OBJ and net-CLS:tree-OBJ

   'bãrẽ
   also

All the men of the Vaupés know how to make a canoe, and tall square baskets, thread from palm fiber, and a fishing net also.

aru is also used to conjoin clauses; in this use, it often has the meaning 'and then'.

(451) eda-Rĩ   'kɨ-te-karã   aru wɨ-I-kū-RE
      arrive-GER exist-DYN-N/H^1pexc and fly-STV-CLS:hump-OBJ

   kore-karã   tres   'ora   baxu
   wait^for-N/H^1pexc three hour exact

Arriving, we were there and (then) we waited for the plane for exactly three hours.

In addition to the use of conjunctions, independent clauses are frequently linked by repeating the main verb of the preceding independent clause in the gerundive form (see §6.4.1.2). Alternatively, the second clause may begin with the word *ke* 'thus' followed by the verbs *te-* 'do' or *ja-* 'do', with the gerund suffix *-Rĩ*, or the dependent clause conditional suffix *-RU*, or one of the nonfuture nominalizers. The focus of such a clause is determined by the choice among these suffixes. For example, if a clause begins with *ke te-jɨ* (thus do-NFUT^MS^NMLZ) 'he doing thus', the focus is on the participant. If a clause begins with *ke te-Rĩ* (thus do-GER) 'thus doing', the focus is on the action (Salser and Salser 1979.)

Another frequent link between independent clauses is the term which introduces a reason clause, *ke ba-RU* (thus be-IF) 'so, therefore'.

Independent clauses can also be linked by expressions involving the suffix *-pe* 'like, similar to', e.g., *'dõ-pe ja-Rĩ* (that-SIM do-GER) 'like that doing'. The conjunction *i-bE-Rĩ-ta* (want-NEG-GER-FOC) 'lit., not wanting' expresses the idea of 'but, however'.

(452) ɨ-bE-Rɨ̃-ta   'xaro-bE-bI   ɨ̃
    want-NEG-GER-FOC appear-NEG-3ms 3ms
    But (lit., not wanting), he doesn't appear.

4.6 Interjections

Cubeo has a wide variety of interjections, including onomatopoetic words and phrases which employ much reduplication to express the calls of animals and birds, and even the noises of insects and fish, as well as the sounds of different objects and activities. (See López and López 1986.)

The affirmative interjection is *'xɨ̃xɨ̃* 'yes' and the negative is *bi* 'no'. Among the many other interjections are: *aju*, expressing frustration, *bɨ*, indicating pain, frustration, or sadness, and *'xoxo*, an exclamation of anger. *xede* indicates relief, often because of having finished some activity.

5
Clause Structure

5.1 Word order in the clause

There is great variation in the order of the constituents of the Cubeo clause, particularly in independent clauses. The orders that occur most frequently in independent clauses are (O)VS and SV(O), but VSO and SOV orders are not uncommon. Within the verb phrase, the order OV is more common than the order VO. (The word order of quotative clauses is discussed in §5.3, and that of other subordinate clauses in chapter 6.)

The examples (453)–(456) have intransitive verbs with overt subjects. The more common order, verb-subject is shown in (453) and (454), while (455) and (456) show the less common order of subject-verb.

(453) ke   te-Rĩ   bexa-RExa-Ibã   pai-wA
thus do-GER go^downstream IIPAST N/H^3p priest-PL
Then (lit., thus doing), the priests went downstream a long time ago.

(454) ɨ-bE-Rĩ-ta   'xaro-bE-bI   ĩ
want-NEG-GER-FOC appear-NEG-3ms 3ms
But (lit., not wanting), he doesn't appear.

(455) u   da-kebã-wɨ   bābā-Rɨ̃bɨ̃-RE   San Gabriel
sloth come-ASM-PERS first-CLS:time-OBJ San Gabriel

duika-ka-pūrāwɨ-I
downstream-PART-side-LOC

The sloth first evidently came downstream on the side (of the river) pertaining to (the town of) San Gabriel.

(456) jɨ̃xã da-karã   xia-jo-kū-ke
     1pexc come-N/H^1pexc river-CLS:cone-CLS:hump-INST
     We came by canoe.

Transitive verbs are shown in (457)–(461) and present the more usual patterns in their order of frequency in the data: OVS, SVO, VSO, SOV, and (least common) VOS.

(457) ʼke-Rõ-RA   ʼdã-RE ʼkaju-wA-RE   buba-karã   jɨ̃xã
     thus-IN^SG^NMLZ-UNIQUE 3p-OBJ chicken-PL-OBJ finish-N/H^1pexc 1pexc
     That's all, we finished (with) the chickens. (OVS)

(458) ke   te-Ij-E   baxu-RE   ʼxāki   ʼwãrĩ-wA ʼkari
     thus do-STV-IN^PL^NMLZ same-OBJ INTNT pig-PL   BT

     ea-Rã-Rɨ̃-Ibã-jA   ʼɨ̃-RE   ʼkari
     arrive-PL-go-N/H^3p-REP 3ms-OBJ BT
     While he was doing this very thing, the pigs reportedly went (in order) to get to where he was. (SVO)

(459) ʼorexa-wɨ jɨ̃xã ʼdã-RE
     call-NON3 1pexc 3p-OBJ
     We called them. (VSO)

(460) kari-RE bɨ̃xã põẽ-wA-RE   ʼxã-Iwɨ   te-xA-Rã
     now-OBJ 2p person-PL-OBJ see-NFUT^PL^NMLZ become-IMP-IMP^AN^PL
     Now you (all) become people-watchers. (SOV)

(461) dɨ̃-wA-Abẽ   jɨ̃xã-RE Capitán Zander pɨ
     go-CAUS-N/H^3ms 1pexc-OBJ Captain Zander as^far^as

     Puerto-I-ta
     Puerto-LOC-GOAL
     Captain Zander took us as far as Puerto (Lleras). (VOS)

In addition to the above orders, it is not uncommon for the subject or the verb (or occasionally the object) to appear twice in the same clause. When the subject (or object) appears twice, it appears either as a noun phrase both before and after the verb, or else as a full (nonpronominal) noun phrase on one side of the verb and as a pronoun on the other side; with objects, both noun phrases (or the noun phrase and the pronoun) are case marked. Typically, the full noun phrase is separated from the rest of the sentence by a pause, indicating that it is a topicalization construction. For instance, in a Cubeo text consisting of descriptions of various fish, many of the descriptions are introduced by a clause in which the name of the fish precedes the verb, and a coreferential pronoun follows the verb. Many of these repetitions appear in short sentences, so the repetition is probably not because of a heavy information load, but rather serves for emphasis. Two examples from this text are given in (462) and (463).

(462) a. ābā-Rɨ   ˈbārẽ kɨ-Abẽ   ɨ̃
misingo-CLS:3D also   exist-N/H^3ms 3ms
This misingo (fish) also, he exists.

b. ābā-Rɨ-RE   ˈbārẽ boa-ˈwɨ jɨ̃ ˈɨ̃-RE
misingo-CLS:3D-OBJ also   kill-NON3 1s 3ms-OBJ
This misingo (fish) also, I killed.

(463) bikoe-ko ˈbārẽ kɨ-Ako   õ
calochi-FS also exist-N/H^3fs 3fs
This calochi (fish), she also exists.

When the verb is repeated, it occurs both before and after the subject. In this case, there is often a very long noun phrase present between the two repetitions; the repetition may serve to emphasize the action of the verb, as shown in (464) and (465).

(464) ˈbā-wA   ā-jA-Ibā   bēdē-kɨ
macaw-PL eat-STV-N/H^3p jungle^ice^cream-CLS:tree

     bāka-Rō-ka-kɨ-RE   ā-jA-Ibā
     jungle-CLS:place-PART-CLS:tree-OBJ eat-STV-N/H^3p
Macaws eat wild (not domesticated) 'jungle ice cream fruit', they eat it.

(465) aru ã-Ij-Abẽ   pɨ̃pɨ̃-wA-RE pɨ̃pɨ̃-bo-I
      and eat-STV-N/H^3ms spider-PL-OBJ spider-CLS:round-POS

      'papi-kɨ   kɨ-RIwɨ-RE   ã-Ij-Abẽ
      net-CLS:tree exist-NFUT^PL^NMLZ-OBJ eat-STV-N/H^3ms

And he eats spiders, ones that are in spider webs, he eats them.

5.2 Question words

Interrogative words, such as *je* 'what', *aipe* 'what, how', *aipijede* 'when', *jãbẽ* 'who', *aipidõ* 'how much', and *'ãrĩ* 'where', are fronted in their clause as in (466).

(466) 'ãrĩ   dɨ̃-jɨ̃-Rɨ̃   bɨ̃
      where go-NFUT^MS^NMLZ-INTR 2s
      Where are you going?

5.3 Quotations

Cubeo quotations are always direct quotes. A quotation is almost invariably followed by a quote margin clause, which consists of some form of the verb 'say' as in (467).

(467) 'xatɨ-'O-kixi-wɨ   kãrẽxã a-Rĩ   'da-Abẽ-jA
      cross-CAUS-NRFUT^MS-NON3 still say-GER come-N/H^3ms-REP
      "I'm still going to cause (you) to cross soon," he reportedly came saying.

Quotations are often preceded by such a quote margin clause as well, particularly if the quotation is long.

(468) a-karã   jɨ̃xã   [bɨ̃   boa-'Rɨ̃-buru]   da-wɨ   jɨ̃xã
      say-N/H^1pexc   1pexc   2s^POS kill-GER-AFTER   come-NON3   1pexc

      a-karã   jɨ̃xã   'bãrẽ
      say-N/H^1pexc   1pexc also
      We said, "After you beat us, we came," we said also.

Clause Structure

When a prolonged conversation between two people is quoted, however, the quote margins are often omitted, particularly if the exchanges between the two speakers are short. Even then, a quote margin is often included every third or fourth exchange, perhaps to orient the listener. The quote margins are more apt to occur if the speakers are of the same gender, since confusion is more likely than when the speakers are of opposite genders. The examples (467)–(471) from texts illustrate quote margins.

(469) xɨbɨka-ko   ʹbãrẽ ɨ-RE-te-Ij-A-RI-tʃɨ̃ã
golden^agouti-FS also   want-OBJ-do-STV-N/H-INTR-EMPH

    a-kakɨ   jɨ   ʹɨ̃-RE
    say-N/H^1ms 1s 3ms-OBJ

"Does the golden agouti (a burrowing rodent) also habitually get fussy/moody? Good grief!" I said to him. (VSO)

(470) jɨ a-wɨ   Eva-RE aru Luz Marina-RE ʹbãrẽ ẽbũ-wA
1s say-NON3 Eva-OBJ and Luz Marina-OBJ also kind^of^ant-PL

    obe-RIwɨ   ʹkɨ-te-bã
    be^many-NFUT^PL^NMLZ exist-DYN-3p

I said to Eva and Luz Marina, "There were a lot of ants!" (SVO)

(471) aru [bɨ̃xẽ boxe-ja-Rɨ̃   bɨoxa-Ij-ERE]   dɨ̃-Rã-xA-RE
and 2p^POS payment-make-GER finish-STV-WHEN^DS go-IMP^AN^PL-IMP-OBJ

    a-kakɨ   jɨ   ʹjɨ-ka-wɨ-RE
    say-N/H^1ms 1s 1s-PART-PL-OBJ

"And when you finish shopping, let's go," I said to my companions. (VSO)

6
Subordination

In this chapter, we discuss relative clauses and adverbial clauses. The two constructions are very similar; most adverbial clauses have exactly the structure of a headless relative clause. A similar construction (a nominalized clause) is used with clausal complements to verbs (see §2.5).

Most subordinate clauses are formed by nominalizing the verb. In the case of relative clauses, the nominalizing suffix agrees in gender and number with the verbal argument being relativized. In the case of adverbial clauses, the nominalizing suffix is usually an inanimate nominalizer, since the nominalization refers to the action of the subordinate verb (cf. the use of the inanimate nominalizers to form nouns referring to the action of the verb root, as discussed in §3.1.4.2). However, some adverbial clauses are formed with nominalizing suffixes which agree with the subject of the clause.

6.1 Argument structure of subordinate clauses

Word order in subordinate clauses is normally SVO, although SOV order also occurs. Quotations embedded under subordinate clauses usually precede the dependent verb, as in (472).

(472) ūbā-I-āībā-kɨ-RE   wo-xA-Rā   jɨ-RE ɨ-I
carry-STV-animal-MS-OBJ seek-IMP-IMP^AN^PL 1s-OBJ 3ms-POS

a-Ij-E   boxe   jāī   ūbā-I-āībā-kɨ-RE
say-STV-IN^PL^NMLZ payment this^MS carry-STV-animal-MS-OBJ

    wo-Rĩ   ea-Rĩ   da-wA-Ibã-jA
    seek-GER find-GER come-CAUS-N/N^3PL-REP

Because of his saying, "Look for a mount for me," they reportedly seeking, finding, brought him a mount.

Case marking in subordinate clauses is the same as in independent clauses, with the exception of the subject. As discussed in more detail below, if the subject of the relative clause is the relativized argument, it does not appear in the relative clause. If the object of the relative clause is relativized, the verb is passivized so that the underlying object is the new subject; the underlying subject is usually present, but marked with the possessive case marker.

In adverbial clauses, if the subject of the adverbial clause is the same as the subject of the independent clause, it does not appear in the subordinate clause. If the subject of an adverbial clause is different from that of the independent clause, the adverbial clause subject generally appears as a possessive noun phrase, unless it is inanimate, in which case it appears in the nominative case.

The use of overt subjects and their case marking is thus parallel in adverbial clauses and relative clauses.

6.2 Tense marking in subordinate clauses

In this section we describe the marking of relative tense in typical subordinate clauses. For a few subordinate clause constructions, particularly gerundive clauses, there is no relative tense marking, while in certain other subordinate clauses, particularly temporal adverbial clauses, relative tense marking is done in a different manner; these special cases are discussed in the sections in which those constructions are introduced.

When the time of action of the verb in a subordinate clause is the same as that of the verb of the independent clause, the verb of the subordinate clause is unmarked for tense.

(473) 'dõ-bU [xi   koji-I-Rõ]
      that-be 1s^POS tell-STV-IN^SG^NMLZ
      That is what I've told/I have to say.

(474) [dẽ   ea-I-bãrã-RE]   da-wA-bã   dã
      3p^POS find-STV-PSV^PL^NMLZ-OBJ come-CAUS-3PL 3p
      They brought the ones (fish) they found.

If the time of action of the relative clause is prior to or after that of the independent clause, a compound verb construction is used. The main verb of the relative clause is nominalized, and it is followed by a nominalized form of the auxiliary verb ʼbA- 'be'. The nominalizer agrees with the gender and number of the (derived) subject of the relative clause. When the action of the relative clause is prior to that of the independent clause, a nonfuture nominalizer is used. When the action of the relative clause is subsequent to that of the independent clause, a future nominalizer is used. These are the same nominalizers that are used for the indefinite future tense (see the table in (159) on page 49), except that the nominalizer -Rãxiwɨ, which indicates doubt in the indefinite future, is always used, rather than the suffix -Rãxãrã. When the action of the relative clause is prior to that of the independent clause, one of the nominalizers given in the table in (475) is used. No distinction is made in subordinate clauses between recent and nonrecent past. The nominalizers in (475) may be derived from a -ka suffix plus the nonfuture nominalizers used in the present tense (see the table in (150) on page 46); in the inanimate plural form, -ka plus -E becomes -ke. This -ka suffix also appears in many of the nonrecent past tense suffixes used in main clauses, shown in the table in (140) on page 42. However, the masculine and feminine singular forms show dialectal variation between a form which includes this -ka, and a form which lacks it. In the dialect which lacks -ka, an -A may have been present historically (such a suffix also appears in many of the nonrecent past tense suffixes), but since it always follows the the stem ʼbA-, it has coalesced with the vowel of the stem and is now phonetically null.

(475) Nonfuture nominalizers used for prior time in subordinate clauses

Masculine singular	-kɨ or -kakɨ
Feminine singular	-ko or -kako
Animate plural	-kawɨ
Inanimate singular	-karõ
Inanimate plural	-ke

Examples (476)–(478) show subordinate clauses marked for prior time; note that the nominalized verb ʼbA- 'be' is case marked, since in these examples the noun phrase containing the subordinate clause, which happens to be a relative clause, is the direct object of the independent clause.

(476) [õ-I   'ɨ-Ij-E   'bA-ke-RE]   Mitú-I
     3fs-POS get-STV-IN^PL^NMLZ be-NFUT^IN^PL^NMLZ-OBJ Mitú-LOC

     ēdōā-RE   'xā-jO-wA-I-bIko jɨxā-RE
     yesterday-OBJ see-CAUS-STV-3fs 1pexc-OBJ
     She is showing us what she got (bought) in Mitú yesterday.

(477) bāxɨ-te-kakɨ   [xi   bāxɨ-bE-Rō   'bA-karō-RE]
     learn-DYN-N/H^1ms 1s^POS know-NEG-IN^SG^NMLZ be-NFUT^IN^SG^NMLZ-OBJ
     I learned what I hadn't known before.

(478) [xi   'xā-I-Rō   'bA-karō]   'kɨ-te-Awɨ
     1s^POS see-STV-IN^SG^NMLZ be-NFUT^IN^SG^NMLZ exist-DYN-N/H^IN^3
     What I had seen (prior to telling you this) was...

A relative clause marked for subsequent time is shown in (490).

(479) ɨ-I   eda-I-Rō   bA-kɨ'rō
     3ms-POS arrive-STV-IN^SG^NMLZ be-FUT^IN^SG^NMLZ
     his (future) arrival

Alternatively, a subordinate clause in which the action takes place after the action of the independent clause may be indicated by adding a near future suffix (see the table in (156) on page 48) to the verb, then nominalizing it with the same suffixes used for subordinate clauses of simultaneous time, i.e., the nonfuture nominalizing suffixes (the table in (150) on page 46) or the passive nominalizing suffixes (the table in (179) on page 55). No auxiliary verb is used in this construction.

(480) [xɨjo-wA-Rāxɨ-I-bārā]   bābā-Rɨbɨ   kārēxā kajawa
     smoke-CAUS-NRFUT^PL-STV-PSV^PL^NMLZ first-CLS:time yet   rack

     ja-I-Rō   'bA-Awɨ
     make-STV-IN^SG^NMLZ be-N/H^IN^3
     (For) ones (fish) that will be smoked, first a rack is made.

In the case of a relative clause which is a copular construction formed with the main verb 'bA- 'be', however, that verb itself is nominalized (and there is no separate auxiliary verb).

(481) bābā-Rɨ̄bɨ̄-RE   [jawibɨ̄-wA 'bA-Rāxiwɨ]   pare
      first-CLS:time-OBJ dog-PL   be-FUT^PL^NMLZ a^lot

   boro-kɨ-te-Ibā-jA   pare bēju-kɨ-te-Ibā-jA
   news-exist-DYN-N/H^3p-REP   a^lot lies-exist-DYN-N/H^3p-REP

   [dā 'bA-Rāxiwɨ]
    3p be-FUT^PL^NMLZ
   In the beginning those who would be dogs reportedly were really gossips...They who would be (dogs) reportedly told a lot of lies.

(482) [dō bA-ki'rō]   daro-Iwɨ-ta   ij-E-RE
      that be-FUT^IN^SG^NMLZ   send-NFUT^PL^NMLZ-FOC   this-IN^PL^NMLZ-OBJ

   butʃi-RE   kɨ-E-ja-Rī   dā   [jawi-wA
   tobacco-OBJ   exist-IN^PL^NMLZ-make-GER 3p   shaman-PL

   'bA-Rāxiwɨ]   daro-kebā-wɨ
   be-FUT^PL^NMLZ   send-ASM-PERS
   They who will be shamans, creating this tobacco, evidently sent (it) to that future place.

6.3 Relative clauses

As discussed in §3.2.2, relative clauses in Cubeo are either postnominal or, more commonly, appear in a noun phrase without any overt head noun. In the latter case, they can equally well be considered as noun phrases which happen to be headed by a nominalized verb. The nominalized verb is always clause final in the relative clause, and takes any case marking imposed by the independent clause. If the noun phrase being modified by the relative clause is headed by an overt noun, both the head noun and the verb of the relative clause will then be case marked. This implies that a relative clause modifying an overt noun appears in an appositive structure (cf. §3.2.3).

A relative clause consists minimally of the nominalized verb, which may be marked for time before or after the time of the action of the verb of the independent clause (as with other subordinate clauses). Cubeo uses a gapping strategy for relative clauses: the noun phrase which is relativized (i.e., the argument of the relative clause that is coreferential with the noun phrase the relative clause is modifying) does not appear internal to the relative clause.

Subjects are relativized by attaching an active nominalizing suffix to a verb, and direct objects are relativized by attaching a passive nominalizing suffix, as shown in (483).

(483) a. relativization of the subject
      jā̆ī   *jawi*   *jābā-ko-RE boa-ˈjɨ*   *ˈbA-kɨ*
      this^MS jaguar deer-FS-OBJ kill-NFUT^MS^NMLZ be-NFUT^MS^NMLZ
      this jaguar, which killed a deer

b. relativization of the direct object
      i-ko   *jābā-ko jawi*   *ɨ̃-I*   *boa-I-bõ*   *ˈbA-ko*
      this-FS deer-FS jaguar 3ms-POS kill-STV-PSV^FS^NMLZ be-NFUT^FS^NMLZ
      this deer, which was killed by a jaguar

Since the clause is passivized when the object is relativized, the underlying subject (which is generally, but not always, overt) is in the possessive case. Other arguments of the relative clause verb appear optionally, with the same case marking as in independent clauses.

In the following sections, we discuss relativization of subjects and objects and tense marking in relative clauses. The head nouns of noun phrases containing relative clauses are bolded in the examples of this section, and relative clauses are bracketed.

6.3.1 Relativization of the subject

When the subject is relativized, it does not appear internal to the relative clause. The verb is nominalized with an active nominalizer (i.e., the nonfuture nominalizers of the table (150) on page 46, or the future nominalizers of the table (159) on page 49, or with the agentive nominalizer *-põẽ* (discussed in §3.1.4.3)). Other arguments of the verb of the relative clause appear before the verb, with their usual case marking. The noun phrase modified by the relative clause may or may not contain an overt head noun; (484)–(486) show relative clauses with overt head nouns.

(484) *ˈxāki bābā-Rɨ̄bɨ̃-RE*   *õ*   [*tɨjɨjɨ-ko*   *ˈbA-kojo*]
      INTNT first-CLS:time-OBJ 3fs kind^of^frog-FS be-FUT^FS^NMLZ

Subordination

'jo-pe   a-jO   bA-te-'Ako-jA
this-SIM say-NFUT^FS^NMLZ be-DYN-N/H^3fs-REP

In the beginning, she who would be the *tijijiko* frog was reportedly saying like this.

(485) *jãĩ*   ***põẽ-kɨ***   [*eta-jɨ*   '*bA-kɨ*]   *i-we*
this^MS person-MS leave-NFUT^MS^NMLZ be-NFUT^MS^NMLZ this-CLS:flat

karo-we-RE   *xi-Abẽ*   *jɨ-RE*
machete-CLS:flat-OBJ give-N/H^3ms 1s-OBJ

The man who left gave me this machete.

(486) *ĩ*   [*jĩxã-RE dĩ-wA-jɨ*   '*bA-kɨ*]
3ms 1pexc-OBJ go-CAUS-NFUT^MS^NMLZ be-NFUT^MS^NMLZ

kolexio-ka-kɨ   *bA-te-'Abẽ-jA*
high^school-PART-MS be-DYN-N/H^3ms-REP

He who was taking us was reportedly someone from the high school.

In (487), example of a relative clause with an overt head noun, note the presence of the -*RE* object marker on both the head noun and the verb of the relative clause. The fact that the noun *bueibārārẽ* 'students' appears in the object case, rather than the nominative case, shows that it is outside of the relative clause, i.e., that this is an externally headed relative clause.

(487) '*xã-jOwA-kebã-wɨ bĩ*   ***bue-I-bãrã-RE***
see-CAUS-ASM-PERS 2s^POS study-STV-PSV^PL^NMLZ-OBJ

[*kore-wA-bE-wɨ*   '*bA-kawɨ-RE*]
guard-CAUS-NEG-PL be-NFUT^PL^NMLZ-OBJ

You evidently showed your students, the ones who hadn't known... ('know' = 'cause to guard/wait')

A relative clause modifying a demonstrative pronoun is shown in (488); again, the object case marker is repeated on both the pronoun and the verb of the relative clause.

(488) ke   bA-te-'Awɨ̃   dõ-RE   [arutʃu-RE kɨ̃õ-I-Rõ-RE]
      thus be-DYN-N/H^IN^3 that-OBJ rice-OBJ   grind-STV-IN^SG^NMLZ-OBJ
      That's the way it was at that rice mill (lit., the thing that grinds rice).

The more common headless relative clause is illustrated by (489).

(489) *[xɨjo-wA-Rãxi-I-bãrã]*   bãbã-Rɨ̃bɨ̃   kãrẽxã kajawa
      smoke-CAUS-NRFUT^PL-STV-PSV^PL^NMLZ first-CLS:time yet   rack

      ja-I-Rõ   'bA-Awɨ̃
      make-STV-IN^SG^NMLZ be-N/H^IN^3
      (For) ones (fish) that will be smoked, first a rack is made.

Since subjects are optional, and there is no relative pronoun or other overt marker of a relative clause (apart from the nominalization of the verb), the minimal relative clause is a single word: the nominalized verb. Many stative verbs have an adjective-like meaning, so that the result of modifying a noun with a stative relative clause is a structure that overtly resembles adjectival modification of a noun.

(490) **parĩ-bõ**   [bãxi-ko]   koj+-jO-bE
      mother^in^law-FS know-NFUT^FS^NMLZ tell-NFUT^FS^NMLZ-be^3s

      õ-I   'wako-RE
      3fs-POS daughter^in^law-OBJ
      A wise mother-in-law counsels her daughter-in-law.

(491) *'wãrĩ [xia-kɨ-kɨ]*   dupi-Rĩ dĩ-kɨ-be
      pig   flesh-exist-MS hide-GER go-MS-R/D^3s^ASM
      The fat pig evidently ran away.

Examples (492)–(495) are also of headless relative clauses, and show the case marking of the nominalized verb.

(492) *'xãkɨ kɨrãbĩ-I eda-Rĩ-ta   [di-ba   bA-kɨ'rõ-RE]*
      INTNT house-LOC arrive-GER-FOC this-CLS:broad be-FUT^IN^SG^NMLZ-OBJ

Subordination

ja-Ij-Abẽ
do-STV-N/H^3ms

Arriving at the house, he makes what will be a broad flat thing (i.e., a cassava turner and fire fan).

(493) bɨoxa-Rĩ 'bɨ-Rĩ   [di-bɨ   bA-ki'rõ-RE]   da-Rĩ
     finish-GER start-GER this-CLS:oblong be-FUT^IN^SG^NMLZ-OBJ come-GER

     dākō-wA-Rĩ bɨoxa-Rĩ xawi-'O-Rĩ   aru ke te-Rĩ
     rise-CAUS-GER finish-GER weave-CAUS-GER and thus do-GER

     dārē-Rĩ bɨoxa-Rĩ   'kari epe-jɨ-bE   ĩ   'kari
     sew-GER finish-GER BT   put-NFUT^MS^NMLZ-be^3s 3ms BT

After starting what will be that oblong basket, coming after, raising, weaving, and then, after sewing, he puts (it someplace).

(494) 'dā-RE wo-Rĩ   [xokɨ-kɨ   kɨ-RIwɨ-RE]   'xā-Rĩ
      3p-OBJ seek-GER wood-CLS:tree live-NFUT^PL^NMLZ-OBJ see-GER

      di-kɨ-RE   koe-'Rĩ
      this-CLS:tree-OBJ chop^down-GER

Looking for ones who live in a tree and seeing them, chopping down the tree...

(495) ['kĩ-xĩ-tʃuri-A-RE   dokɨ 'xē-I-xɨro-E-RE]   xoa-Rĩ
      small-DIM-wound-PL-OBJ dirt grab-STV-IRR-IN^PL^NMLZ-OBJ wash-GER

      xarɨwa-Rĩ-buru   'jobo-I   'kari xūā-RI-koro-RE
      get^rid^of-GER-AFTER after-LOC BT   be^red-NMLZ-CLS:liquid-OBJ

      aja-Iwɨ-bU   bāxā   'ke-RA
      put-NFUT^PL^NMLZ-be 1pinc thus-UNIQUE

Dirt which would get into (lit., grab) small wounds, after washing, getting rid of it we put red liquid (merthiolate), that's all.

In (496) the relative clause is appositive to the clause in which a coreferential noun phrase appears. The construction is similar to that in which the subject of a clause appears both before and after the verb (see §5.1).

(496) ape-kɨ   **jawi**   ʰbA-te-jɨ-bẽ   [põẽ-wA-RE
      other-MS jaguar be-DYN-R/DˆMSˆPROB-R/Dˆ3sˆPROB person-PL-OBJ

      ã-I-põẽ-kɨ]   a-RExa-Ibã   jɨ-RE
      eat-STV-AGˆNMLZ-MS say-HPAST-N/Hˆ3p 1s-OBJ

"He probably was another jaguar, a people-eating one," they said to me.

6.3.2 Relativization of objects

In order for the object of the verb to be relativized, the clause is passivized so the underlying object becomes the new subject. The underlying subject of the relative clause is usually overt, appearing as a possessive noun phrase. As in the case of relativization of the subject, the relativized argument of the verb (the underlying object = the derived subject) may or may not be overt. If it is overt, it does not appear internal to the relative clause. Other constituents of the relative clause appear before the verb, with their usual case marking or postpositions.

The verb takes a passive nominalizer (see (179) on page 55) if the relativized object is animate, and an active nominalizer (see (150) on page 46) if the relativized object is inanimate; there is no distinction between active and passive voice in the inanimate nominalizers.

The use of animate and inanimate nominalizers is nicely illustrated by the verb *kojɨ-* 'tell', which takes two objects: one for what is told, the other for what is talked about. When the former is relativized, it takes the inanimate nominalizer, since what is told is inanimate.

(497) [ãĩbã-kɨ-RE   xi   kojɨ-Ij-E-RE]
      animal-MS-OBJ   1sˆPOS tell-STV-INˆPLˆNMLZ-OBJ
      what I'm telling/have just told about the animal

On the other hand, when the object referring to what is talked about is relativized, if it is animate it will take an animate passive nominalizer, as in (498).

(498) ãĩbã-kɨ   [xi   kojɨ-I-bĩ]
      animal-MS 1sˆPOS tell-STV-PSVˆMSˆNMLZ
      the animal, the one I'm telling/have just told about

Examples (499)–(501) show relative clauses with overt head nouns.

Subordination

(499) *i-ko* **borika-ko** *[ɨ-I boa-I-bõ 'bA-ko]*
  this-FS guaracú-FS 3ms-POS kill-STV-PSV^FS^NMLZ be-NFUT^FS^NMLZ

  ɨra-ko bA-te-'bIko
  big-FS be-DYN-3fs
  This *guaracú* fish that he caught was big.

(500) *ẽdōā-RE jāī **pōē-kɨ** [xi kojɨ-I-bɨ̃]*
  yesterday-OBJ this^MS person-MS 1s^POS tell-STV-PSV^MS^NMLZ

  eda-bI jo-RE
  arrive-3ms this-OBJ
  The man I'm talking about arrived here yesterday.

(501) *jāī **xɨejo-kɨ** [xi kojɨ-I-bɨ̃-RE] 'xi-wI jɨ*
  this^MS child-MS 1s^POS tell-STV-PSV^MS^NMLZ-OBJ give-NON3 1s

  xɨtɨra
  toasted^manioc
  I gave fariña to the boy I'm talking about.

The examples of relative clauses (502) and (503) do not have overt head nouns, but do have modifying adjectives. Although the relative clauses are the direct objects of the independent verb, they lack the object marker -RE because it is frequently omitted before *koapa* 'each, every'.

(502) *aru jɨ kojɨ-kakɨ 'ō-RE [xi ã-Ij-E*
  and 1s tell-N/H^1ms 3fs-OBJ 1s^POS eat-STV-IN^PL^NMLZ

  'bA-ke] koapa
  be-NFUT^IN^PL^NMLZ every
  And I told her (the nurse) everything I had eaten.

(503) *kaij-E [ɨ-I 'xã-Ij-E] koapa [ɨ-I*
  all-IN^PL^NMLZ 3ms-POS see-STV-IN^PL^NMLZ every 3ms-POS

bāxi-E-RE]   ā-Ij-Abẽ
know-IN^PL^NMLZ-OBJ eat-STV-N/H^3ms

He (the wild pig) eats all he sees, each and every thing he is able to (eat).

(504)–(506) are examples of the relativization of objects without overt head nouns or modifying adjectives.

(504) 'ki-te-Awĩ [xoki-we-A-RE bura-I-Rõ]
   exist-DYN-N/H^IN^3 wood-CLS:flat-PL-OBJ cut-STV-IN^SG^NMLZ

   There was a thing that cut boards.

(505) ke te-Rĩ xoe baxi [xi xidi-Rõ
   thus do-GER long^ago right^at 1s^POS be^afraid-IN^SG^NMLZ

   'bA-karõ]   wai-'RExa-Awĩ ji-RE
   be-NFUT^IN^SG^NMLZ pass-HPAST-N/H^IN^3 1s-OBJ

   Then, after a really long time, I got over what I had been afraid of (lit., my fear passed me).

(506) xi do-Ij-E-RE   xoa-jO-bU   ji
   1s^POS put^on-STV-IN^PL^NMLZ-OBJ wash-NFUT^FS^NMLZ-be 1s

   I'm washing what I have been wearing.

6.3.3 Relative clauses based on 'bA-

The copular verb 'bA- 'be' in its past or future nominalized form, i.e., as a relative clause, is used to postmodify nouns. When used in its past tense form, it means 'former', i.e., the being, place, thing, or activity existed in the past but did or does not exist at the time of the action of the main verb, and when used in its future tense form, it means 'future', i.e., the being, place, thing, or activity did or does not yet exist at the time of the action of the main verb, but was or is going to be.

A common use of this construction is to refer to a dead being as in (507)–(511).

(507) ĩ-I jẽkũ-wA ['bA-kawi]
   3ms-POS grandparent-PL be-NFUT^PL^NMLZ

   his late/deceased grandparents/ancestors

(508) **bei-bo**   *['bA-kɨ-RE]*   ā-Rī   buba-bI
      mouse-CLS:round be-NFUT^MS^NMLZ-OBJ eat-GER finish-3ms
      He (the buzzard) ate the dead mouse.

(509) **Patʃi** *['bA-kɨ]*
      Pachi be-NFUT^MS^NMLZ
      the late/deceased Pachi

(510) **xi-pa-kɨ**   *['bA-kɨ]*
      1s^POS-parent-MS be-NFUT^MS^NMLZ
      my deceased father

(511) *ape-kɨ*   **tʃurara** *['bA-kɨ]*
      other-MS soldier be-NFUT^MS^NMLZ
      the other dead soldier

Example (512) is from a folktale about dogs originally having been people, and illustrates the future tense (subsequent time) form.

(512) *bābā-Rɨ̄bɨ̄-RE*   **jawibī-wA** *['bA-Rāxiwɨ]* pare
      first-CLS:time-OBJ dog-PL   be-FUT^PL^NMLZ very

      boro-kɨ-te-Ibā-jA
      news-exist-DYN-N/H^3p-REP
      In the beginning, the ones who would be dogs reportedly were really liars.

Similarly, in a procedural text describing how to make a fire fan and cassava turner, at an early stage the author refers to 'the broad and flat object-to-be' with a future tense form of *'bA-* 'be' in (513).

(513) *'xãkɨ kɨ̄rābī-I* eda-Rī-ta   **di-ba**   *[bA-kɨ'rō-RE]*
      INTNT house-LOC arrive-GER-FOC this-CLS:broad be-FUT^IN^SG^NMLZ-OBJ

      ja-Ij-Abē
      make-STV-N/H^3ms
      Upon arriving at the house, he habitually makes what will be a fire fan and cassava turner.

6.4 Adverbial clauses

In the following subsections, we discuss adverbial (subordinate) clauses which mark temporal, locative, and logical relations. With some exceptions (described under the individual constructions), such adverbial clauses usually precede the independent clause they modify.

Most adverbial clauses are formed by nominalizing the verb of the clause; the particular relation between an adverbial clause and the independent clause is often further specified by an additional subordinating suffix attached to the nominalized verb. However, some adverbial clauses are headed by verbs bearing non-nominalizing suffixes (such as the gerundive suffix) when the subordinate clause subject is the same as the independent clause subject.

In those adverbial clauses formed by nominalizing the verb, if the subject of the adverbial clause is the same as the subject of the independent clause, it does not appear in the subordinate clause, as in (514).

(514) ′ke-Rõ-RA   [dɨ̃-I-kawɨ]   ko-RExa-Ibã-jA
      thus-IN^SG^NMLZ-UNIQUE go-STV-WHILE^SS sink-HPAST-N/H^3p-REP
      Only while they were going, they reportedly sank.

If the subject of an adverbial nominalized clause is different from that of the independent clause, the adverbial clause subject is usually overt, and appears as a possessive noun phrase (with some exceptions, discussed under individual constructions).

(515) aru xau   a-Rɨ̃   dɨ̃-Ibã-jA   [ɨ̃-I   ke   a-Ij-ERE]
      and woof say-GER go-N/H^3p-REP 3ms-POS thus say-STV-WHEN^DS
      And barking, they reportedly went when he said thus.

If the overt subject of the adverbial clause is inanimate, however, and different from the subject of the independent clause, the subject is in the nominative case, since Cubeo lacks inanimate possessives.

(516) xokɨ-kɨ   tɨ-Ij-ERE   xoa-I   ′kuja-wɨ jɨ̈
      tree-CLS:tree fall-STV-when^DS be^far-LOC run-NON3 1s
      When the tree fell, I ran away.

6.4.1 Temporal adverbial clauses

There are six temporal relations expressed by adverbial subordinate clauses:

Subordination

1. The action of the subordinate verb and the main verb occur simultaneously.

2. The action of the subordinate verb occurs immediately prior to that of the main verb, with that action possibly continuing during the occurrence of the action of the main verb.

3. The action of the subordinate verb occurs prior to that of the main verb.

4. The action of the subordinate verb occurs after that of the main verb.

5. The action of the subordinate clause marks the beginning point of the action of the independent clause.

6. The action of the subordinate clause marks the end point of the action of the independent clause.

The constructions marking these various temporal relations are discussed in the following subsections. For expository purposes, we bracket the subordinate clauses in the examples.

6.4.1.1 Simultaneous occurrence. The choice of verb suffixes to mark simultaneous occurrence of the event of the subordinate clause with that of the independent clause depends on whether the subjects of the two clauses are the same or different. When the subjects of the two verbs are different, the *-E* 'inanimate plural nominalizer', i.e., the abstract general nominalizer, is added to the stative verb stem, followed by the noun suffix *-REka* 'exact'. For simplicity, we gloss this combination of suffixes, *-EREka*, 'while, different subject'. It should be noted that the inanimate plural nominalizer is used regardless of the person and number of the subject.

The subordinate clause generally precedes the independent clause in the sentence. Examples (517)–(519) illustrate adverbial clauses with different subjects from those of the independent clauses.

(517) *aru dõ-bĩ-ka 'xĩ-xũã-Rĩ [bãxẽ*
and that-IDENT-DUB egg-put^on^the^ground-GER 1pinc^POS

'xã-bE-EREka]   põẽ-te-jA-Ibã   dã
see-NEG-WHILE^DS person-become-STV-N/H^3p 3p

And possibly right there laying eggs, while we are not looking, they (birds) habitually are born.

(518) aru ĩ   'a-Rõ   bẽbẽ-Rĩ-du-Abẽ   dõ   'bãkidã-RE
      and 3ms which-IN^SG^NMLZ work-GER-FRUS-N/H^3ms that machine-OBJ

      aru [ke te-Ij-EREka-ta]   tɨ-karã
      and thus do-STV-WHILE^DS-FOC fall-N/H^1pexc

And there he tried to work on that machine (the airplane). And certainly right while he was doing thus, we fell (crashed).

(519) 'ke-Rõ-RA   'kari pai-wA eko-RExa-Ibã   kɨrãbĩ-I
      thus-IN^SG^NMLZ-UNIQUE BT priest-PL   enter-HPAST-N/H^3p house-LOC

      eko-Rĩ   xewa-RExa-Ibã   papera-RE xewa-Rĩ
      enter-GER   collect-HPAST-N/H^3p   paper-OBJ collect-GER

      xia-jo-kũ-I   aja-RExa-Ibã   dã [ke
      river-CLS:cone-CLS:hump-LOC   put-HPAST-N/H^3p   3p thus

      te-Ij-EREka]   tʃurara õpõ-boa-RExa-Ibã   kapija-RE
      do-STV-WHILE^DS   soldier explosion-kill-HPAST-N/H^3p chapel-OBJ

Only the priests entered the house a long time ago. Entering, they gathered up the books (Bibles) a long time ago. Gathering up, they put them in (their) canoe a long time ago. While they were thus doing, the soldiers shot up the chapel a long time ago.

(520) 'xãkɨ [di-E   ũbẽ xapu-Rĩ aja-Ij-EREka]   bA-te-'kebã-wɨ
      INTNT this-IN^PL^NMLZ   soul blow-GER put-STV-WHILE^DS   be-DYN-ASM-PERS

      di-E
      this-IN^PL^NMLZ

While they (the shamans) were organizing/establishing this soul blowing, evidently there were these (activities).

Subordination

(521) *[ūbẽ-ke   oka-Ij-EREka]   jĩxā eda-karā*
wind-INST rain-STV-WHILE^DS 1pexc arrive-N/H^1pexc
While it was raining and windy, we arrived.

When the subjects of the subordinate and independent verbs are the same, simultaneous occurrence of the actions is marked by the nonfuture nominalizers used for prior time on subordinate verbs (see (475) on page 149). Unlike the construction discussed in (475), however, these suffixes are added directly to the stative form of the main verb rather than to an auxiliary verb. Inanimate forms have not been seen, perhaps for pragmatic reasons. For clarity, we gloss this usage of these suffixes as 'while, same subject'.

(522) *[dɨ̃-I-kakɨ]   xiabɨ-RE   ea-bI*
go-STV-WHILE^SS alligator-OBJ arrive-3ms
While he was going, he found an alligator.

(523) *dō-I-ta   ea-Rĩ   eta-Rĩ   [dɨ̃-I-kakɨ]   tɨ-kakɨ*
that-LOC-GOAL arrive-GER leave-GER go-STV-WHILE^SS fall-N/H^1ms

   kɨra-I-Rɨ   pɨedō-Rã
   step^on-STV-CLS:3D over-LOC
Arriving over there, leaving (the airplane), while I was going, I fell over the wheel (lit., the round thing that steps on something).

(524) *'ke-Rō-RA   [dɨ̃-I-kawɨ]   ko-RExa-Ibā-jA*
thus-IN^SG^NMLZ-UNIQUE go-STV-WHILE^SS sink-HPAST-N/H^3p-REP
Only while they were going, they reportedly sank.

(525) *a-jɨ-RE   xidɨ-Rĩ   [dɨ̃-I-kakɨ]   bĩū-Rã*
say-NFUT^MS^NMLZ-OBJ be^afraid-GER go-STV-WHILE^ss thorn^PL-LOC

   kɨra-Rĩ   xata-kɨ-Rĩ-kakɨ
   step^on-GER cross-NFUT^MS^NMLZ-go-N/H^1ms
Being afraid of the one I'm telling about, while I was going, stepping on thorns, I went in order to cross (the river).

(526) *xidɨ-Rĩ   [dɨ̃-I-kakɨ]   xia-jo-kū-RE*
be^afraid-GER go-STV-WHILE^ss river-CLS:cone-CLS:hump-OBJ

xarɨwa-Rī   [bā-I-kakɨ]
get^rid^of-GER ascend^from^the^port-STV-WHILE^ss

'bixa-kakɨ   a-kakɨ   jɨ
get^lost-N/H^1ms say-N/H^1ms   1s

"Being afraid while I was going away from the canoe, while I was going up from the port, I got lost," I said.

Alternatively, simultaneous action of the subordinate and the independent verbs may be indicated by adding a nonfuture nominalizer (see (150) on page 46) to the subordinate verb. The nominalizer agrees in gender and number with the subject of the subordinate verb. If the subject of the subordinate clause is different from that of the independent clause, the subordinate clause subject is indicated by an explicit noun phrase in the nominative (unmarked) case.

Examples (527) and (528) of this construction have the same subjects in the subordinate and independent clauses.

(527) [jɨ̃xā-RE 'xā-jOwA-jɨ   kaij-E-RE]   kojɨ-'Abẽ
      1pexc-OBJ see-CAUS-NFUT^MS^NMLZ all-IN^PL^NMLZ-OBJ tell-N/H^3ms

      dõ-I   kɨ-E-RE   ɨ̃-I   bēbẽ-Ij-E   koapa
      that-LOC exist-IN^PL^NMLZ-OBJ 3ms-POS work-STV-IN^PL^NMLZ   every

While he was showing us everything, he told about each aspect of his work which he does while he is there.

(528) ɨ-bE-Rī-ta   [ɨ̃   põẽ-wA-RE   'xā-jɨ]   kūɨ̃'dā-ta
      want-NEG-GER-FOC   3ms person-PL-OBJ see-NFUT^MS^NMLZ one-FOC

      'kuja-Ij-Abẽ
      run-STV-N/H^3ms

But (lit., not wanting) whenever he (the grouse) sees people, he immediately runs away.

(529)–(531) have different subjects in the subordinate and independent clauses.

(529) aru [jɨ̃xā ea-Iwɨ   kɨ̃rā-tākū-we-I]   aru
      and 1pexc arrive-NFUT^PL^NMLZ rock-CLS:rapids-CLS:flat-LOC and

Subordination

    jɨ xidɨ-te-kakɨ   *dõ-RE*   *pare*
    1s be^afraid-DYN-N/H^1ms that-OBJ a^lot
    And when we were getting to the rapids, hey, I was really very scared there.

(530) *aru ke te-Rĩ [kopɨ-jɨ*   *jɨ jawi-RE]*
      and thus do-GER meet^up^with-NFUT^MS^NMLZ 1s jaguar-OBJ

    'da-Abẽ   *jɨ-RE kopɨ*
    come-N/H^3ms 1s-OBJ meet^up^with
    And thus doing, when I met up with a jaguar, he came upon (attacked) me.

(531) *dõ 'jobo-I ['xã-Iwɨ*   *jĩxã 'planta-RE] pare*
      that after-LOC see-NFUT^PL^NMLZ 1pexc generator-OBJ a^lot

    bɨxi-te-Awĩ
    make^noise-DYN-N/H^IN^3
    After that, while we were looking at the generator, it made a lot of noise.

6.4.1.2 Immediately prior occurrence of the action of the subordinate verb. When the action of the subordinate verb begins just prior to the action of the independent verb (and possibly continues during the time of the action of the independent verb), and the subjects of the two clauses are different, the inanimate singular nominalizer *-Rõ*, i.e., the abstract specific nominalizer, or the inanimate plural nominalizer *-E*, i.e., the abstract general nominalizer, plus the object suffix *-RE* are attached to a stative verb stem. For simplicity, we gloss these combined suffixes, *-RõRE* and *-ERE*, as 'when'. It is not clear what governs the choice between these two suffixes. The subject of the subordinate clause is indicated by a possessive noun phrase; complements of the verb are optionally indicated with their usual case marking.

(532) *aru [bãxẽ tɨ tɨ ja-Ij-ERE] eta-Rĩ 'xã-Ij-Abẽ*
      and 1pinc^POS knock knock do-STV-WHEN^DS leave-GER see-STV-N/H^3ms

    ĩ
    3ms
    And when we knock, going out, he looks.

(533) [xi   ku-Ij-ERE]   ape-Rõ   'bã-I   dɨ̃-karã
      1sˆPOS walk-STV-WHENˆDS   other-INˆSGˆNMLZ trail-LOC   go-N/Hˆ1pexc
      When I was walking, we went on another trail.

(534) aru [bɨ̃xẽ boxe-ja-Rɨ̃   bioxa-Ij-ERE]   dɨ̃-Rã-xA-RE
      and 2pˆPOS payment-make-GER   finish-STV-WHENˆDS go-IMPˆANˆPL-IMP-OBJ

      a-kakɨ   jɨ 'jɨ-ka-wɨ-RE
      say-N/Hˆ1ms 1s 1s-PART-PL-OBJ
      "And when you finish shopping, let's go," I said to my companions.

The example in (535) is one of the few in which a temporal subordinate clause follows, rather than precedes, the independent clause.

(535) aru xau   a-Rɨ̃   dɨ̃-Ibã-jA   [ɨ̃-I   ke   a-Ij-ERE]
      and woof say-GER go-N/Hˆ3p-REP   3ms-POS thus   say-STV-WHENˆDS
      And barking, they reportedly went when he said thus.

Occasionally, the auxiliary verb 'bA- 'be' is used in a construction similar to that used with many other subordinate clauses to indicate prior time (as discussed in §6.2). The main verb takes the inanimate singular nominalizer -Rõ, while the auxiliary verb takes the suffix -ka 'past tense' before -RõRE. This construction indicates that the event of the subordinate verb preceded the event of the main clause by a greater period of time.

(536) jo   [jɨ̃xẽ   eda-I-Rõ   'bA-ka-RõRE]   jɨ̃xã
      this 1pexcˆPOS   arrive-STV-INˆSGˆNMLZ be-PST-WHENˆDS   1pexc

      doba-RIwɨ   bue-Iwɨ   xãrãwɨ-A koapa
      sit-NFUTˆPLˆNMLZ study-NFUTˆPLˆNMLZ day-PL   every

      papera-joka-RE   dɨrɨ-Rɨ̃   doba-te-kakɨ   jɨ
      paper-CLS:leaf-OBJ hold-GER sit-DYN-N/Hˆ1ms   1s
      When we had arrived, we who were sitting studying each day, holding sheets of paper I sat.

When the subjects of the subordinate verb and the independent verb are the same, the subordinate verb (or verbs, in a chain of subordinate clauses) takes the gerundive suffix -Rɨ̃, as in (537)–(540).

(537) [doa-Rɨ̃] dɨ̃-wɨ jɨ̃xã pɨ ape ẽkã-bo-I-ta
paddle-GER go-NON3 1pexc as^far^as other edge-CLS:round-LOC-GOAL
Paddling, we recently went as far as to the other shore.

(538) [ɨ̃-I kã-I-kawabɨ-RE 'xã-Rɨ̃] ['ɨ̃-RE xabɨ-Rɨ̃]
3ms-POS sleep-STV-CLS:branch-OBJ see-GER 3ms-OBJ wait^in^ambush-GER

['ɨ̃-RE pu-Rɨ̃] boa-'jA-Ibã
3ms-OBJ shoot^with^a^blowgun-GER kill-STV-N/H^3p
Seeing his sleeping branch, waiting in ambush for him, shooting him with a blowgun, they kill (him).

(539) [di-kɨ-RE koe-'Rɨ̃] [dẽ kɨ-Rõ baxi
this-CLS:tree-OBJ chop^down-GER 3p^POS exist-IN^SG^NMLZ right^at

bura-Rɨ̃] ɨ̃-Ij-Awɨ̃ bãxã dẽ 'koro-RE
cut-GER get-STV-N/H^1pinc 1pinc 3p^POS liquid-OBJ
Chopping down that tree, cutting exactly where they are, we get their honey.

(540) [eda-Rɨ̃] [kuɨ'tote-kaxe du-Rɨ̃ bɨoxa-Rɨ̃]
arrive-GER cloth-CLS:cover remove-GER finish-GER

[xatɨ-'O-I-tukubɨ-I dɨ̃-Rɨ̃] oko kaju'a-Ij-E
cook-CAUS-STV-CLS:room-LOC go-GER water mix-STV-IN^PL^NMLZ

ũkũ-wɨ jɨ
drink-NON3 1s
Arriving, taking off (my) clothes, finishing (dressing), going to the kitchen, I recently drank tapioca drink.

It is common for this construction to occur with head–tail linkage of successive sentences, with the action of the previous independent clause repeated as a gerund, as in (541).

(541) põẽ-wA eko-RExa-Ibã kɨ̃rãbɨ̃ [eko-Rɨ̃] xewa-RExa-Ibã
person-PL enter-HPAST-N/H^3p house enter-GER collect-HPAST-N/H^3p

>
> *papera-RE [xewa-Rɨ]   xia-jo-kũ-I*
> paper-OBJ collect-GER river-CLS:cone-CLS:hump-LOC
>
> *aja-RExa-Ibã   dã*
> put-HPAST-N/H^3p   3p

Long ago, people entered the house. Entering, they gathered the paper (books). Gathering, they put (them) into the canoe.

The subject is understood to be the same throughout a chain of gerundive clauses; these chains are terminated by a nongerundive verb. If such a chain is followed by another chain with a different subject, the new subject will be explicitly mentioned. This is illustrated by (542), in which there are two chains of gerundive clauses. The first is terminated by the nominalized verb *bɨoxa-Ij-E* 'when we finished'; the second chain (containing only one gerund) begins with an explicit subject, which is the same as that of the independent clause that follows it.

> (542) *aru jɨ̃xã ẽdã-Rɨ   ã-Rɨ   bɨoxa-Ij-E   baxu-RE   Nancy*
> and 1pexc arrive-GER eat-GER finish-STV-IN^PL^NMLZ same-OBJ Nancy
>
> *ea-Rɨ   otʃo   baxi   bue-Rã-xA-RE   a-bIko jɨ̃xã-RE*
> arrive-GER eight right^at study-IMP^AN^PL-IMP-OBJ say-3fs 1pexc-OBJ
>
> And we arriving, eating, as soon as we finished, Nancy arriving, said to us, "Let's study at 8:00."

There is a third construction, used with both same and different subjects, which indicates that the action of the subordinate verb begins just prior to the action of the independent verb (and may continue during the time of the action of the independent verb). It is formed by adding an active nonfuture nominalizer to the verb root of the subordinate verb followed by the auxiliary verb *'bA-* 'be', also bearing an active nonfuture nominalizer. Both nominalizers agree in gender, number, and animacy with the subject of the subordinate clause. The construction is thus a nominalized form of the progressive aspect construction (cf. §2.3.1).

> (543) *[eta-jɨ   'bA-kɨ]   ɨ̃   'xã-Rɨ*
> leave-NFUT^MS^NMLZ be-NFUT^MS^NMLZ 3ms see-GER
>
> *bãxɨ-bE-te-Abẽ-jA*
> know-NEG-DYN-N/H3ms-REP
>
> When he left, he reportedly wasn't able to see.

(544) [õ 'xapi-A-jO   'bA-ko   bĩ
      3fs hear-CAUS-NFUT^FS^NMLZ be-NFUT^FS^NMLZ 2s^POS

      xakojɨ-Ij-E-RE]   xi   kɨrābĩ-RE   eta-Ako
      greet-STV-IN^PL^NMLZ-OBJ 1s^POS house-OBJ   leave-N/H^3fs
      When she heard your greeting, she came out of my house.

(545) ɨ-I   dākāxā-Ij-E-RE   dā   'bārē dākāxā-Ibā
      3ms-POS stand^up-STV-IN^PL^NMLZ-OBJ 3p   also   stand^up-N/H^3p
      When he stood up, they also stood up.

6.4.1.3 Earlier occurrence of the action of the subordinate verb.

The occurrence of the action of the subordinate verb before that of the independent verb is indicated by a gerund with the verbal suffix -buru 'after', optionally followed by the postposition 'jobo 'after'. The postposition 'jobo is sometimes marked by one of the temporal suffixes -I or -RE. This construction is used with both same and different subjects; different subject clauses normally contain an overt subject in the possessive case. Examples (546)–(548) include the postposition 'jobo.

(546) ke   te-Rĩ   dõ-I   'kari   [xura-te-Rĩ-buru   'jobo-I]
      thus do-GER   that-LOC   BT   cocoon-make-GER-AFTER   after-LOC

      põẽ-te-Ij-Abē
      person-become-STV-N/H^3ms
      So there after being metamorphosed, he is born.

(547) aru   kā-Rĩ   [bāxē   kā-Rĩ-buru   'jobo]
      and   sleep-GER 1pinc^POS sleep-GER-AFTER after

      kopai-dɨ-Ij-Abē-jA
      return-go-STV-N/H^3ms-REP
      And sleeping, after we sleep, he reportedly returns.

(548) aru   [jɨxē   dɨ-Rĩ-buru   'jobo-I]   kojɨ-jɨ   Julio
      and   1pexc^POS   go-GER-AFTER   after-LOC tell-NFUT^MS^NMLZ Julio

xawe   dɨ-jA-bã   xɨejo-wA
already go-STV-3p child-PL

And after our having gone, Julio was saying, "The children have already gone."

In (549) and (550) the postposition ʼjobo is absent.

(549) [õ-I   ke   a-Rɨ-burʉ]   jɨri-kakɨ   jɨ
      3fs-POS thus say-GER-AFTER laugh-N/H^1ms   1s
      After she said thus, I laughed.

(550) a-karã   jɨ̃xã   [bɨ̃   boa-ʼRɨ-burʉ]   da-wɨ   jɨ̃xã
      say-N/H^1pexc 1pexc 2s^POS kill-GER-AFTER come-NON3 1pexc

      a-karã   jɨ̃xã   ʼbãrẽ
      say-N/H^1pexc 1pexc also

      We said, "After you beat us, we came," we said also.

6.4.1.4 Later occurrence of the action of the subordinate verb.
The occurrence of the action of the subordinate verb after that of the independent verb is indicated by marking the subordinate verb (either dynamic or stative) with a future tense subordinating suffix, followed by the postposition xɨpoka 'before' which is sometimes marked by one of the -RE or -I temporal suffixes. (xɨpo-xã-ka (head-DIM-PART) 'a little before' is also sometimes found.) The subordinating suffix agrees in gender and number with the subject of the subordinate verb. The feminine and animate plural forms of this subordinating suffix can be analyzed as consisting of the corresponding near future tense verb suffixes (see (156) on page 47) followed by the inanimate plural nominalizer, i.e., the abstract general nominalizer, -E: -koxɨje 'feminine singular' and -Rãxɨje 'animate plural'. The masculine singular form is less transparently related, being -kɨje instead of the expected *-kɨxɨje. For simplicity, we gloss all these subordinating suffixes using (BEFORE). These suffixes used in this adverbial clause construction are similar to those used in the second of the two constructions which mark most subordinate clauses the action of which is subsequent to that of the independent clause (see §6.2).

The same forms are used with both same and different subjects. As with other adverbial clauses, the subordinate clause generally precedes the independent clause.

(551) bābā-Rɨ̃bɨ̃-RE   [xi   bue-I-jābī-I   xaro-kije
      first-CLS:time-OBJ 1s^POS study-STV-CLS:building-LOC send-BEFORE^MS

      xipoka-RE] bāxi-ka-jɨ-bU   'ɨ̃-RE
      before-OBJ know-BEN-NFUT^MS^NMLZ-be   3ms-OBJ
      First, before I send (him) to school, I advise/counsel (him).

The two examples (552) and (553) illustrate the less common pattern in which the adverbial clause follows the independent clause.

(552) kari-RE   xẽdī'ā-RE-wɨ   [bāxẽ   wiaxe-RE dɨ̃-Rāxije   xipoka]
      now-OBJ   petition-OBJ-PL 1pinc^POS   trip-OBJ go-BEFORE^PL before
      Now let's petition (God) before we go on our trip.

(553) ke   bA-RU   'koxixi-Iwɨ-bU   [jɨ̃xẽ
      thus   be-IF   gather-NFUT^PL^NMLZ-be   1pexc^POS

      xawa-te-Rāxije   xipoka-I]
      eat^a^meal-do-BEFORE^PL   before-LOC
      Therefore, we are gathering before we eat our big meal.

6.4.1.5 Subordinate verb marks beginning point. There are two constructions which indicate that the action of the subordinate clause marks the beginning point in time of the action of the independent clause. Either construction may be used with both same and different subjects. The more common of these constructions is marked by a stative verb stem bearing the inanimate plural nominalizer, i.e., the abstract general nominalizer, *-E* or a time classifier such as *-Rɨ̃bɨ̃* 'time'. The resulting nominalized verb is further marked by the suffix *-b(ɨ̃)ā* 'identity' (see §3.3.7) and the case marker *-ta* 'goal, limit' (see §3.3.9.5). For simplicity, we gloss the combination of the identity suffix and the limit suffix *-bɨ̃āta* or *-bāta* as 'since'. This construction is illustrated in (554) and (555).

(554) obe-RIwɨ   xɨejo-wA jai-xE-bU   ['patu
      be^many-NFUT^PL^NMLZ   child-PL die-COND-be   coca

      bẽbẽ-I-põẽ-wA   dẽ   da-Ij-E
      work-STV-AG^NMLZ-PL   3p^POS   come-STV-IN^PL^NMLZ

ʹbA-ke-bɨ̄āta]   xɨo-Ij-E-RE   bãxẽ
be-NFUT^PL^NMLZ-SINCE   cure-STV-IN^PL^NMLZ-OBJ   1pinc^POS

kɨ-wA-bE-RU
exist-CAUS-NEG-IF

Many children would have died since the coca workers came, if we hadn't had medicines.

(555) ʹdõ-pe   ʹpa-Ij-E   kɨ-bE-wɨ   kãrẽxā
      that-SIM   be^similar-STV-IN^PL^NMLZ   exist-NEG-NON3   yet

[bābā-Rɨbɨ̄-bāta]
first-CLS:time-SINCE

It hasn't been like that yet, since the beginning.

A second construction in which the subordinate clause marks the beginning point in time of the action of the main verb, consists of a stative verb stem suffixed by a time classifier such as -*Rɨbɨ̄* 'time', -*xārāwɨ* 'day', or -*ɨxɨ* 'year', followed by the postposition ʹ*jobo* 'after, later, behind'. The postposition is often case marked by the -*RE* object suffix.

(556) kaij-E   wai-ʹjA-wɨ   kūɨʹdātɨrɨ ij-E
      all-IN^PL^NMLZ   happen-STV-NON3   same   this-IN^PL^NMLZ

      wai-ʹIj-E   ʹbA-ke-pe-REka
      happen-STV-IN^PL^NMLZ   be-NFUT^IN^PL^NMLZ-SIM-CERT

      xɨ̄bẽ-RI-xɨ̄-kɨ-I   i-xārāwɨ-RE
      blue/green-NMLZ-DIM-MS-POS   this-CLS:day-OBJ

      kɨ-E-ja-I-Rɨbɨ̄   ʹjobo-RE
      exist-IN^PL^NMLZ-make-STV-CLS:time   after-OBJ

Everything is happening exactly as it has happened since the time when God created this world.

6.4.1.6 Subordinate verb marks end point. A subordinate clause which indicates the end point in time of the action of the independent clause is formed by adding to a stative verb stem the inanimate plural

Subordination

nominalizer, i.e., the abstract general nominalizer, *-E* or a temporal classifier such as *-Rɨbɨ̃* 'time' followed by the case marker *-ta* 'goal, limit' (see §3.3.9.5). The adverbial clause begins with the adverb *pɨ* 'as far as, until'.

This construction is used with both same and different subjects. Unlike the other subordinate clauses of temporal relations, which usually precede the independent clause, the subordinate clause of end point in time generally follows the independent clause.

(557) *ke   te-Rĩ   ˈjowa-bE-RExa-Abẽ-jA   ˈdã-RE [pɨ   dẽ*
      thus do-GER accompany-NEG-HPAST-N/H^3ms-REP 3p-OBJ until 3p^POS

    bẽbẽ-I-Rõ-RE   bɨoxa-Ij-E-ta]
    work-STV-IN^SG^NMLZ-OBJ finish-STV-IN^PL^NMLZ-GOAL

Thus doing, he reportedly didn't accompany them until they finished their work.

(558) *ˈke-Rõ-RA   ja-ijɨ-wɨ   bẽã-Rõ*
      thus-IN^SG^NMLZ-UNIQUE do-DES-NON3 be^good-IN^SG^NMLZ

    ij-E   bẽbẽ-Ij-E-RE   xi   xabo-kɨ-I
    this-IN^PL^NMLZ work-STV-IN^PL^NMLZ-OBJ 1s^POS chief-MS-POS

    ja-Ikõxẽ-Ij-E-RE   jɨ-RE [pɨ   xi
    make-AUTH-STV-IN^PL^NMLZ-OBJ 1s-OBJ until 1s^POS

    bɨoxa-Ij-E-ta   di-E-RE]
    finish-STV-IN^PL^NMLZ-GOAL this-IN^PL^NMLZ-OBJ

I only want to do well this work which my boss commands/ permits me to do until I finish it.

(559) *bẽã-ja-kɨjɨ-bẽ   bãxã-RE bãxẽ   bãũ-wA-RE*
      be^good-do-FUT^MS^NMLZ-FUT^3s 1pinc-OBJ 1pinc^POS enemy-PL-OBJ

    xarɨwa-Rĩ   [pɨ   bãxẽ   jai-Rɨbɨ̃-I-ta]
    get^rid^of-GER until 1pinc^POS die-CLS:time-LOC-GOAL

He will save us from (lit., getting rid of) our enemies until we die.

6.4.2 Locative adverbial clauses

Locative adverbial clauses are formed as relative clauses modifying a locative noun such as *dō-RE* (that-OBJ) 'there'. Since the noun that is relativized is a locative noun, the verb agrees with that noun by bearing the inanimate singular nominalizer, i.e., abstract specific nominalizer, *-Rō*; the underlying subject appears in its possessive form. As with other relative clauses, relative tense is expressed by the use of the auxiliary verb *'bA-* 'be'.

(560) *āībā-boa-kixi-wɨ   dō-RE   [pābū-Ri-RE   xi*
 animal-kill-NRFUT^MS-NON3 that-OBJ armadillo-CLS:3D-OBJ 1s^POS

 'xā-I-Rō   'bA-karō-RE]
 see-STV-IN^SG^NMLZ be-NFUT^IN^SG^NMLZ-OBJ
 I'll hunt there, where I saw the armadillo.

6.4.3 Logical adverbial clauses

There are five logical relations which may be expressed in Cubeo by adverbial clauses: purpose, cause (or grounds or reason), condition, concession, and comparison.

6.4.3.1 Purpose. Unlike most adverbial clauses, a subordinate clause giving the purpose for the action of the independent clause of the sentence generally follows that independent clause.

A subordinate purpose clause, the subject of which is different from the subject of the independent clause, is very similar to the temporal adverbial clause of later occurrence (see §6.4.1.4). That is, the subordinate verb (either dynamic or stative) takes a future subordinating suffix which agrees with its subject, followed by the noun suffix *-pe* 'similarity' (see §3.3.5). Again, we gloss the resulting composite forms as wholes for simplicity: *-kijepe* 'different subject purpose, masculine singular or inanimate'; *-koxjepe* 'different subject purpose, feminine singular'; and *-Rãxjepe* 'different subject purpose, animate plural'.

The construction is the same for both negative and affirmative purpose clauses.

Except in direct address, the subordinate verb is followed by the verb *a-* 'say' with a nominalizer agreeing in animacy, person, number, and gender with the subject of the independent verb. This verb serves as an auxiliary verb in this construction, and the complements of the subordinate purpose verb follow the auxiliary verb, as seen in (561) and (562).

(561) jɨ-RE xɨejo-kɨ-RE epe-Ibã   xi-bɨ'kɨ-wA   bue-I-Rõ-I
     1s-OBJ child-MS-OBJ put-N/H^3p   1s^POS-adult-PL teach-STV-IN^SG^NMLZ-LOC

  [xi   bãxi-kijepe   a-Iwɨ   ape-Rõ   xi
  1s^POS know-PUR^DS   say-NFUT^PL^NMLZ   other-IN^SG^NMLZ   1s^POS

  bãxi-bE-Rõ-RE]
  know-NEG-IN^SG^NMLZ-OBJ

  From (when I was) a child, my parents put me in a school in order that I learn something that I didn't know.

(562) jɨ-RE dã   'ɨ-te-Rã-bã   [xi   kaja-te-koxijepe
     1s-OBJ 3p   want-DYN-R/D^PL^ASM-3p   1s^POS   help-do-PUR^DS

  a-Iwɨ   Nancy-RE]
  say-NFUT^PL^NMLZ   Nancy-OBJ

  Evidently they wanted me to help Nancy (lit., wanted in order that I help).

Examples (563) and (564) are in the context of direct address, and, therefore, the verb *a-* 'say' does not appear.

(563) aru ke   te-Rĩ   jɨxẽ   ã-Ij-E-RE   'bãrẽ   bɨkɨ-RE
     and thus do-GER 1pexc^POS eat-STV-IN^PL^NMLZ-OBJ also   grow-OBJ

  ja-xA-kɨ   jɨxã-RE   ['bixa-bE-kijepe]   aru   ['xu-wA
  make-IMP-MS   1pexc-OBJ get^ruined-NEG-PUR^DS   and   worm-PL

  ã-bE-Rãxijepe]
  eat-NEG-PUR^DS

  And cause our food to grow for us also, in order that it not get ruined and in order that the worms not eat it.

(564) kaja-te-xA-kɨ   jɨxẽ-pa-kɨ   jɨxẽ   dɨ-Rãxi-Rõ
     help-do-IMP-MS   1pexc^POS-parent-MS   1pexc^POS go-NRFUT^PL-IN^SG^NMLZ

    [oko   oka-bE-kijepe]
    water rain-NEG-PUR^DS
Our Father, help our trip (lit., future going), in order that it not rain.

The marked order is shown in (565), in which the purpose clause precedes the independent clause.

(565) aru [ɨ-I   ārɨ-bE-te-bE-kijepe   a-jɨ]
      and 3ms-POS remember-NEG-do-NEG-PUR^DS say-NFUT^MS^NMLZ

      kai-Rɨbɨ   bāxi-ka-jɨ-bU   ɨ-RE
      all-CLS:time   know-BEN-NFUT^MS^NMLZ-be   3ms-OBJ
In order that he not forget, I am always advising him.

When the subject of the subordinate purpose clause is the same as the subject of the independent clause, the subordinate verb is marked by a future nominalizer (see (159) on page 49) which agrees with the subject in gender and number. As with the purpose clause of different subject, the purpose clause of same subject generally follows the independent clause.

(566) tu-I-pāwã-I   ēbē-Rɨ   xia-jo-kū-RE
      arrive-STV-CLS:port-LOC descend-GER river-CLS:cone-CLS:hump-OBJ

      xaxi'e-bI   [dɨ-kiji   xia-I]
      scoop^out-3ms   go-FUT^MS^NMLZ   river-LOC
Going down to the port, he recently scooped (the rain water) out of the canoe in order to travel on the river.

(567) aru 'ko-wɨ-A   po-I-Rɨbɨ-A-RE   bāxā põē-wA
      and flower-CLS:tube-PL   bloom-STV-CLS:time-PL-OBJ   1pinc person-PL

      'bārē wo-Ij-Awɨ   i-Rā-RE   būbɨ-wA-RE   [dē   'koro-RE
      also seek-STV-N/H^1pinc   this-PL-OBJ   bee-PL-OBJ   3p^POS liquid-OBJ

      ɨ-Rāxiwɨ]
      get-FUT^PL^NMLZ
And during the season when the flowers bloom, we people habitually look for these bees in order to get their honey.

(568) kari   jābī   korika   baxi   dɨ-Iwɨ-bU   jɨ̃xã
      today   night   middle   right^at go-NFUT^PL^NMLZ-be 1pexc

   xiwa-I   [ea-Rãxiwɨ   jɨ̃xẽ   kɨ-Rõ-RE]   aru
   upstream-LOC   arrive-FUT^PL^NMLZ   1pexc^POS   live-IN^SG^NMLZ-OBJ and

   [dɨ̃-Rãxiwɨ   'kari bue-I-põẽ-kɨ-RE   xarɨwa-Rɨ̃]
   go-FUT^PL^NMLZ   BT   teach-STV-AG^NMLZ-MS-OBJ   get^rid^of-GER

   Tonight, right in the middle of the night, we are going upstream in
   order to get to our town and to get away from the teacher.

(569) aru   õ   bɨ̃õ-ko   ['xã-xũã-kojo]
      and   3fs úquira-FS   egg-put^on^the^ground-FUT^FS^NMLZ

   xua-I-do   xua-I-do   ja-Ij-Ako
   nest-STV-CLS:broad   nest-STV-CLS:broad   make-STV-N/H^3fs

   And she, the *úquira* (bird), in order to lay eggs, she habitually makes
   a nest.

Example (570) shows the marked order in which the subordinate clause precedes the main verb (note also the use of the focus suffix *-ta*).

(570) 'xãkɨ   dõ-I   [jɨ-RE   ixɨ-Rõ-RE   'xã-kojo-ta]
      INTNT   that-LOC   1s-OBJ   hurt-IN^SG^NMLZ-OBJ   see-FUT^FS^NMLZ-FOC

   te-kebã-wɨ
   do-ASM-PERS

   There, in order to see (what) my illness (was), she (the nurse) did
   (that).

6.4.3.2 Cause, grounds, and reason. A subordinate clause which gives the cause, grounds, or reason for the action of the independent verb is formed by nominalizing a stative verb stem with the inanimate plural nominalizer, i.e., the abstract general nominalizer, *-E*, and following this nominalized verb with the noun *boxe* 'payment'. The construction is the same for both same and different subjects. Reason, grounds, and cause clauses generally follow the independent clause.

(571) doa-Rɨ   da-kebā-wɨ   [dē   dēō   kɨ-wA-bE   boxe]
paddle-GER come-ASM-PERS 3p^POS gasoline exist-CAUS-NEG payment
They came paddling because they didn't have gasoline.

The less common order, in which the reason clause precedes the independent clause, is illustrated in (572).

(572) [xi   'kɨ-ba   'bixa-I-Rō   'bA-karō-RE
1s^POS louse-CLS:broad be^lost-STV-IN^SG^NMLZ be-NFUT^IN^SG^NMLZ-OBJ

ō-I   ea-Ij-E   boxe]   toroxi-wɨ
3fs-POS find-STV-IN^PL^NMLZ payment be^happy-NON3
Because she found the comb I had lost, I am happy.

6.4.3.3 Condition. Conditional clauses are subordinate clauses which give the condition for the action of an independent verb. Like most subordinate clauses, a conditional clause usually precedes the independent clause. However, the way in which switch-subject and relative tense are marked in conditional clauses differs significantly from the way these are marked in other subordinate clauses.

If the subjects of the subordinate and independent clauses are different, the suffix *-RU* 'if' is added to the verb of the subordinate clause in place of gender/number suffixes. The *-RU* suffix follows derivational suffixes and other inflectional suffixes, such as the negative. The subject of the subordinate clause may optionally be expressed by a possessive noun phrase.

If the subjects of the subordinate and independent clauses are the same, the main verb of the subordinate clause is nominalized with a nonfuture nominalizer (see (150) on page 46). The main verb is then followed by the auxiliary verb *bA-RU* (be-IF) 'be'. If the subject of the subordinate clause is expressed, it is in the nominative case.

The condition may be a real one or a contrary-to-fact (irrealis) one. An irrealis condition is expressed by using the conditional aspect (described on page 50) in the independent clause; a real or possible condition is expressed by the use of other tenses in the independent clause.

(573)–(575) are examples of real or possible conditions.

(573) [tā-Rɨ   bātɨ-Ij-E   jaxu-RU] bēā-wɨ
kick-GER be^complete-STV-IN^PL^NMLZ play-IF be^good-NON3

> di-Rɨ-RE
> this-CLS:3D-OBJ
>
> If you play only kicking it (a soccer ball), that is good.

(574) *[bɨ̃xẽ kuja-bE-RU] kɨ-kɨjɨ-bẽ   bɨ̃xã-RE*
2p^POS bathe-NEG-IF exist-FUT^MS^NMLZ-FUT^3s 2p-OBJ
If you don't bathe, he (the sandman) will be on you.

(575) *[kore-ijɨ-ko   bA-RU] kore-xA-ko*
wait^for-DES-NFUT^FS^NMLZ be-IF wait^for-IMP-FS
If you want to wait, wait.

Examples of unreal or contrary-to-fact conditions are given in (576) and (577).

(576) *[bɨ̃xã bãũ-kɨ-wA-RIwɨ   bA-RU 'dã-RE]*
2p   enemy-exist-CAUS-NFUT^PL^NMLZ be-IF 3p-OBJ

   bãũ-kɨ-wA-xE-bU   jɨ̃xã-RE 'bãrẽ
   enemy-exist-CAUS-COND-be 1pexc-OBJ also
   If you (all) were to oppose them, you would also be opposing us.

(577) *[jɨ̃xẽ bẽbẽ-Rĩ daxoka-RU] bẽã-bE-xE-bU   dõ*
1pexc^POS work-GER stop-IF be^good-NEG-COND-be that
If we were to stop working, that would not be good.

Example (578) shows the marked order in which the conditional clause follows the independent clause.

(578) *bẽã-Awɨ̃   [ã-RU ãũrõ-RE]*
be^good-N/H^IN^3 eat-IF cassava-OBJ
It's good if you eat cassava.

For same subject conditionals, the auxiliary verb plus conditional suffix are occasionally omitted in informal speech, leaving the conditional clause expressed simply by a nominalized verb.

(579) ʼkɨ̄-xɨ̄-kɨ   ʼtaro-RE   kɨ-kɨ   ʼō-RE   xē-xE-bU
      small-DIM-MS swing-OBJ exist-NFUT^MS^NMLZ 3fs-OBJ grab-COND-be
      If the little boy were in the swing, he would grab her (a butterfly).

(580) [ō ɨ-ko]   da-kojo-bē̃
      3fs want-NFUT^FS^NMLZ come-FUT^FS^NMLZ-FUT^3s
      If she wants to, she'll come.

(581) [dã ɨ-RIwɨ]   da-Rãxārã-bã
      3p want-NFUT^PL^NMLZ come-INDEF^FUT^PL-3p
      If they want to, they'll come.

6.4.3.4 Concession. A concessive adverbial clause ('although...') is formed by nominalizing the subordinate verb with a nonfuture nominalizer (see (150) on page 46) which agrees with the subject in number and gender, then adding the suffix *-wareka* 'concession, different subject' or the suffix *-wakari* 'concession, same subject'. These suffixes may be composed of the individual morphemes *-wa-RE-ka* 'individually-OBJ-DUB' or *-wa-REka* 'individually-CERT', and *-wa-kari* 'individually-BT', respectively; *-ʼkari* is a discourse particle used to mark the major events in a narrative (see Salser and Salser 1979).

Like most adverbial clauses, a concessive subordinate clause generally precedes the independent clause.

(582) [dēō-RE   kɨ-wA-RIwɨ-wareka]   ʼxã-jOwA-bE-te-wɨ
      gasoline-OBJ exist-CAUS-NFUT^PL^NMLZ-CNCS^DS see-CAUS-NEG-DYN-NON3

      pōē-deko-xã-jOwA-Ij-E-RE   oka-Ij-E
      person-reflection-see-CAUS-STV-IN^PL^NMLZ-OBJ rain-STV-IN^PL^NMLZ

      boxe
      payment
      Although they had gas (for the generator), we didn't show films, because it rained.

(583) [ɨ̃ boxe-ja-jɨ-wareka]   ʼje-RE
      3ms payment-make-NFUT^MS^NMLZ-CNCS^DS what-OBJ

Subordination 181

> *boxe-ja-bE-te-kakɨ*   *jɨ*
> payment-make-NEG-DYN-N/H^1ms   1s
> Even though he paid (me), I didn't buy anything (lit., I didn't buy what).

(584) *[jɨ da-ijɨ-kɨ-wakari]*   *dāpī-RExa-kakɨ*
      1s come-DES-NFUT^MS^NMLZ-CNCS^SS put^up^with-HPAST-N/H^1ms
      Although I wanted to come, I put up with it (not being allowed to come).

(585) *aru ke te-Rī [ābē-te-ijɨ-RI-kū-wakari]*   *da-wA-RE*
      and thus do-GER bad-do-DES-NMLZ-CLS:hump-CNCS^SS come-CAUS-OBJ

      da-Awɨ̃   *jɨ̃xā-RE*
      come-N/H^IN^3   1pexc-OBJ
      And then, although the plane was wanting to go bad (have mechanical problems), it kept on coming, bringing us.

(586) *aru ke te-Rī [ābē-te-Iwɨ-wareka]*   *da-karā*
      and thus do-GER bad-do-NFUT^PL^NMLZ-CNCS^DS come-N/H^1pexc

      kārēxā
      still
      And then, although it (the airplane) was damaged, still we came.

6.4.3.5 Comparison. A subordinate clause can express a comparison of similarity or equality between its action and the action of the independent verb, i.e., a manner adverbial clause. It has a relative clause structure headed by the inanimate proximate pronoun *jo* 'this' (see (253) on page 83) with the suffix *-pe* 'similarity' (see §3.3.5), followed by a relative clause the verb of which is marked by the inanimate plural nominalizer, i.e., the abstract general nominalizer, *-E* plus the suffix *-pe* 'similarity'. If the auxiliary verb *'bA-* 'be' is used to mark relative time, it takes the *-pe* 'similarity' suffix.

A subordinate clause which expresses a comparison between its action and the action of the independent verb may either precede or follow that independent clause.

(587) *kaja-te-ijɨ-wɨ*   *bɨ̄xā-RE [ꞌjo-pe xi-pa-kɨ-I*
      help-do-DES-NON3 2p-OBJ   this-SIM 1s^POS-parent-MS-POS

kaja-te-Ij-E-pe   jɨ-RE]
help-do-STV-IN^PL^NMLZ-SIM 1s-OBJ
I want to help you as my father has helped me...

(588) ['jo-pe jɨxe-bɨkɨ-wA   dẽ   ja-Ij-E-pe]
this-SIM 1pexc^POS-adult-PL 3p^POS do-STV-IN^PL^NMLZ-SIM

ja-Rã-xA-RE   jĩxã
do-IMP^AN^PL-IMP-OBJ 1pexc
As our parents/ancestors do, let us do.

(589) ape-Rĩbĩ   ja-jA-bã   dã ['jo-pe xabo-kɨ-I
other-CLS:time do-STV-3PL 3p this-SIM chief-MS-POS

ja-Ikõxẽ-Ij-E   'bA-ke-pe]
do-AUTH-STV-IN^PL^NMLZ be-NFUT^IN^PL^NMLZ-SIM
...sometimes they have done/are doing as the chief had commanded to do...

(590) pɨ̃õ-jɨ̃-RE   xẽ-xA-kɨ   ['jo-pe xi
blow-CLS:funnel-OBJ grab-IMP-MS this-SIM 1s^POS

xẽ-Ij-E-pe]
grab-STV-IN^PL^NMLZ-SIM
Hold the blowgun like I'm holding it.

6.4.4 Event clauses

Subordinate clauses in isolation, i.e., without an independent clause, are often used as titles of stories. The construction resembles other subordinate clauses in that the verb is nominalized (with an inanimate singular nominalizer, i.e., an abstract specific nominalizer); the underlying subject appears in the possessive case, and tense marking (generally prior time) is marked using the auxiliary verb 'bA- 'be'.

(591) [jĩ̃xẽ   da-I-Rõ   'bA-karõ]
1pexc^POS come-STV-IN^SG^NMLZ be-NFUT^IN^SG^NMLZ
Our arrival (lit., 'our having come')

(592) [xi   bābã-te-I-Rõ   'bA-karõ
      1s͡POS new-become-STV-IN͡SG͡NMLZ be-NFUT͡IN͡SG͡NMLZ

   bāka-Rõ-I]
   jungle-CLS:place-LOC
   When I got lost in the jungle (lit., my having gotten lost in the jungle).

Appendix 1
Affixes and Glosses

This appendix lists the various affixes discussed in the text, together with their glosses, the abbreviations of those glosses, and the sections in which the affixes are discussed. A few particles which function as discourse markers are also listed but are not discussed in this grammar (see Salser and Salser 1979).

ʹkari	backbone tag	BT	
ʹxākɨ	narrator intent	INTENT	

Prefixes

ʹa-		which	4.1.4
ādī-	that, those (farther away)	that	3.3.1
ape-	other, another	other	3.3.1
bāxẽ-	our (inclusive) (used with kinship terms)	1pinc^POS	4.1.5
bī-	your (singular) (used with kinship terms)	2s^POS	4.1.5
bĩxẽ-	your (plural) (used with kinship terms)	2p^POS	4.1.5
dẽ-	their (used with kinship terms)	3p^POS	4.1.5
di-/dī	this, that, these, those (anaphoric)	this	3.3.1
i-́	this, these (nearby)	this	3.3.1
ĩ-I-	his (used with most kinship terms)	3ms^POS	4.1.5
jĩxẽ-	our (exclusive) (used with kinship terms)	1pexc^POS	4.1.5
ō-I-	her (used with most kinship terms)	3fs^POS	4.1.5
xi-	my (used with kinship terms)	1s^POS	4.1.5

'xi-   his, her (used with some kinship terms)   3s^POS   4.1.5

Classifiers

-ba	broad, flat	CLS:broad
-baxu	bodylike	CLS:body
-bERExa	genus	CLS:genus
-bẽ	threadlike	CLS:thread
-bɨ	oblong	CLS:oblong
-bo	small, round	CLS:round
-boka	ropelike	CLS:rope
-boxɨ	bundlelike	CLS:bundle
-bũ	vinelike	CLS:vine
-do	broad	CLS:broad
-ɨxɨ	year	CLS:year
-ja	riverlike	CLS:river
-jabe	seedlike	CLS:seed
-jãbĩ	buildinglike	CLS:building
-jãbĩ	night	CLS:night
-jĩ	funnel shaped	CLS:funnel
-jo	slender, pointed, cylindrical	CLS:cone
-joka	leaflike	CLS:leaf
-kajawa	racklike	CLS:rack
-kawabɨ	branchlike	CLS:branch
-kaxe	coverlike	CLS:cover
-kobe	holelike	CLS:hole
-koro	liquidlike	CLS:liquid
-kuru	baglike	CLS:bag
-kɨ	treelike	CLS:tree
-kɨporɨ	like the mouth of a river	CLS:mouth
-kũ	hump shaped	CLS:hump
-'pãwã	portlike	CLS:port
-pɨe	basketlike	CLS:basket
-pũrãwɨ	side	CLS:side
-Rɨ	small, 3D	CLS:3D
-Rɨ̃bĩ	time	CLS:time
-Rõ	place	CLS:place

Appendix 1

-tãkũ	rapids	CLS:rapids	
-tɨkarɨ	short, narrow, cylindrical	CLS:cylinder	
-tɨra	circular	CLS:circle	
-'tõkũ	boxlike	CLS:box	
-tuku	roomlike	CLS:room	
tʃrã-	base/supportlike	CLS:base/support	
-wa	large, broad, flat	CLS:table	
-we	flat, thin	CLS:flat	
-wɨ	tubular	CLS:tube	
-xarabo	forked	CLS:forked	
-xãrãwɨ	day	CLS:day	

Other suffixes

(reduplication of last syllable of the stem)	iterative	ITER	2.2.2.5
-A	plural (inanimate noun)	PL	3.1.1
-A	nonrecent past and present habitual (glossed separately only in interrogative)	N/H|	2.2.2.1
-A	causative	CAUS	2.2.3.2
-Abẽ	witnessed third masculine singular, nonrecent past and present habitual	N/H^3ms	2.2.2.5
-Ako	witnessed third feminine singular, nonrecent past and present habitual	N/H^3fs	2.2.2.5
-apa	emphatic	EMPH	2.3.2
-Awɨ	witnessed first plural inclusive, second, or inanimate subject, nonrecent past and present habitual	N/H^1pinc, N/H^2, and N/H^IN^3	2.2.2.5
-bã	identical	IDENT	3.3.7
-bã	witnessed third plural, recent past, present durative, and near future	3p	2.2.2.5
-bã	third plural animate, future	FUT^3p	2.2.2.5

-bA	be, interrogative	be^INTR	2.1.3
-bA	nonsecond, interrogative present	INTR	2.2.2.1
-bãrã	passive plural nominalizer	PSV^PL^NMLZ	2.2.3.2
-bãta	since (subordinate clause)	SINCE	6.4.1.5
-bE	be, third animate singular indicative	be^3s	2.1.3
-bE	negative	NEG	2.2.2.3
-bE	third singular future, of doubt	FUT^3s^DUB	2.2.2.5
-be	third animate singular, assumed, recent past and present durative	R/D^3s^ASM	2.2.2.5
-bẽ	third animate singular, probable, recent past and present durative	R/D^3s^PROB	2.2.2.5
-bẽ	third singular animate, future	FUT^3s	2.2.2.5
-bEbu	be, probable, second and third	be^PROB	2.1.3
-bI	third masculine singular, witnessed, recent past, present durative, and near future	3ms	2.2.2.5
-bĩ	identical	IDENT	3.3.7
-bĩã	identical	IDENT	3.3.7
-bĩãta	since (subordinate clause)	SINCE	6.4.1.5
-bIko	third feminine singular, witnessed, recent past present durative, and near future	3fs	2.2.2.5
-bɨ	masculine singular (noun)	MS	3.1.2
-bɨ	passive masculine singular nominalizer	PSV^MS^NMLZ	2.2.3.2
-bõ	feminine singular (noun)	FS	3.1.2
-bõ	passive feminine singular nominalizer	PSV^FS^NMLZ	2.2.3.2

Appendix 1

-bũ	first, second, or inanimate, probable, recent past and present durative	R/D^NON3^PROB	2.2.2.5
-bũ	first, second, and inanimate, probable, recent past and present durative	R/D^NON3^PROB	2.2.2.5
-bũ	first, second, and inanimate, future	FUT^NON3	2.2.2.5
-bU	be	be	2.1.3, 2.2.2.5
-bU	nonthird singular future, of doubt	FUT^NON3^DUB	2.2.2.5
-bu	first, second, and inanimate, assumed, recent past and present durative	R/D^NON3^ASM	2.2.2.5
-buru	after (subordinate clause)	AFTER	6.4.1.3
-du	frustrative	FRUS	2.2.2.2
-E	inanimate plural nonfuture nominalizer	IN^PL^NMLZ	2.2.2.5, 3.1.4.2
-ERE	when (subordinate clause, different subject, plural)	WHEN^DS	6.4.1.2
-EREka	while (subordinate clause, different subject)	WHILE^DS	6.4.1.1
-I	stativizer	STV	2.2.1
-I	possessive	POS	3.3.9.2
-I	locative, temporal	LOC	3.3.9.2
-I	intensifier (on adverbs)	INTNS	4.3.3
-Ibã	witnessed, third plural, habitual nonrecent past and present	N/H^3p	2.2.2.5
-Ij	stativizer	STV	2.2.1
-ijɨ	desiderative	DES	2.2.2.2
-ikɨ	narrator focus or perspective[7]	NARR^FOC	
-Ikõxẽ	authoritative	AUTH	2.2.3.2
-itʃɨ	irrealis, nonpresent	IRR	2.2.2.2

---

[7]This discourse morpheme is not treated in this grammar, see Salser and Salser (1979).

-Iwɨ	animate plural nonfuture nominalizer	NFUT^PL^NMLZ	2.2.2.5
-Ixɨro	irrealis, present	IRR	2.2.2.2
-jA	reportative	REP	2.2.2.4
-jA	stativizer	STV	2.2.2.5, 2.2.1
-jArã	plural, probable, recent past and present durative	R/D^PL^PROB	2.2.2.5
-je	inanimate plural imperative	IMP^IN^PL	2.2.2.1
-jE	inanimate, probable, recent past and present durative	R/D^IN^PROB	2.2.2.5
-jɨ	desiderative	DES	2.2.2.2
-jɨ	masculine singular nonfuture nominalizer	NFUT^MS^NMLZ	2.2.2.5
-jɨ	masculine singular, probable, recent past and present durative	R/D^MS^PROB	2.2.2.5
-jO	feminine singular nonfuture nominalizer	NFUT^FS^NMLZ	2.2.2.5
-jO	feminine singular, probable, recent past and present durative	R/D^FS^PROB	2.2.2.5
-ka	benefactive	BEN	2.2.3.2
-ka	past (subordinate verbs)	PST	6.2
-ka	narrator doubt[8]	DUB	
-ka	partitive	PART	3.3.8
-kako	while (subordinate clause, same subject, feminine singular)	WHILE^SS	6.4.1.1
-kako	witnessed, first feminine singular, nonrecent past and present habitual	N/H^1fs	2.2.2.5
-kakɨ	while (subordinate clause, same subject, masculine singular)	WHILE^SS	6.4.1.1

---

[8]This discourse morpheme is not treated in this grammar; see Salser and Salser (1979).

Appendix 1

-kakɨ	witnessed, first masculine singular, nonrecent past and present habitual	N/H^1ms	2.2.2.5
-karã	witnessed, first plural exclusive, nonrecent past and present habitual	N/H^1pexc	2.2.2.5
-karõ	nonfuture inanimate singular nominalizer (on verb 'bA- 'be')	NFUT^IN^SG^NMLZ	6.2
-kawɨ	while (subordinate clause, same subject, animate plural)	WHILE^SS	6.4.1.1
-kawɨ	nonfuture animate plural nominalizer (on verb 'bA- 'be')	NFUT^PL^NMLZ	6.2
-ke	instrument, accompaniment	INST	3.3.9.3
-ke	nonfuture inanimate plural nominalizer (on verb 'bA- 'be')	NFUT^IN^PL^NMLZ	6.2
-ke	partitive, inanimate plural	PART^IN^PL	3.3.8
-kebã	assumed, nonrecent past	ASM	2.2.2.4, 4.2.2.5
-kije	inanimate plural indefinite future nominalizer	FUT^IN^PL^NMLZ	2.2.2.5
-kije	before (subordinate clause, masculine singular)	BEFORE^MS	6.4.1.4
-kijepe	purpose (subordinate clause, different subject, masculine singular and inanimate)	PUR^DS	6.4.3.1
-kirõ	inanimate singular indefinite future nominalizer	FUT^IN^SG^NMLZ	2.2.2.5
-kixi	masculine singular near future	NRFUT^MS	2.2.2.5
-kɨ	masculine singular nonfuture nominalizer	NFUT^MS^NMLZ	2.2.2.5, 6.2
-kɨ	masculine singular, assumed, recent past and present durative	R/D^MS^ASM	2.2.2.5
-kɨ	masculine singular imperative	IMP^MS	2.2.2.1

-kɨ	masculine singular (noun), nonfeminine (adjective)	MS	3.1.2
-kɨjɨ	masculine singular indefinite future nominalizer	FUT^MS^NMLZ	2.2.2.5
-ko	feminine singular nonfuture nominalizer	NFUT^FS^NMLZ	2.2.2.5, 6.2
-ko	feminine singular, assumed, recent past and present durative	R/D^FS^ASM	2.2.2.5
-ko	feminine singular imperative	IMP^FS	2.2.2.1
-ko	feminine singular (noun and adjective)	FS	3.1.2
-kojo	feminine singular indefinite future nominalizer	FUT^FS^NMLZ	2.2.2.5
-kõxẽ	authoritative	AUTH	2.2.3.2
-koxi	feminine singular, near future	NRFUT^FS	2.2.2.5
-koxije	before (subordinate clause, feminine singular)	BEFORE^FS	6.4.1.4
-koxijepe	purpose (subordinate clause, different subject, feminine singular)	PUR^DS	6.4.3.1
-O	causative	CAUS	2.2.3.2
-OwA	causative	CAUS	2.2.3.2
-pe	similarity	SIM	3.3.5, 6.4.3.5
-põẽ	agentive nominalizer	AG^NMLZ	3.1.4.3
-RA	only this kind, only of the kind or nature of whatever is being focused on[9]	UNIQUE	
-Rã	specific locative, specific temporal	LOC	3.3.9.4
-Rã	plural nominalizer (in independent purpose clauses)	PL^NMLZ	2.3.3
-Rã	plural, assumed, recent past and present durative	R/D^PL^ASM	2.2.2.5
-Rã	plural animate (noun)	PL	3.1.2

---

[9]This discourse morpheme is not treated in this grammar; see Salser and Salser (1979).

-Rã	animate plural imperative	IMP^AN^PL	2.2.2.1
-Rãxãrã	animate plural indefinite future nominalizer	FUT^PL^NMLZ	2.2.2.5
-Rãxi	plural, near future	NRFUT^PL	2.2.2.5
-Rãxiwɨ	animate plural, indefinite future, of doubt, nominalizer	FUT^PL^DUB^NMLZ	2.2.2.5
-Rãxije	before (subordinate clause, animate plural)	BEFORE^PL	6.4.1.4
-Rãxijepe	purpose (subordinate clause, different subject, animate plural)	PUR^DS	6.4.3.1
-RE	first, second, and animate assumed, recent past and present durative	R/D^ASM	2.2.2.5
-RE	object	OBJ	3.3.9.1
-REka	certainty	CERT	3.3.4
-RExa	historical past	HPAST	2.2.2.5
-RI	nonsecond interrogative, past	PST^INTR	2.2.2.1
-RI	nominalizer	NMLZ	3.1.4.1
-RIwɨ	animate plural nonfuture nominalizer	NFUT^PL^NMLZ	2.2.2.5
-Rĩ	gerund	GER	6.4.1.2
-Rɨ̃	interrogative, second person	2^INTR	2.2.2.1
-Rõ	inanimate singular imperative	IMP^IN^SG	2.2.2.1
-Rõ	inanimate singular nonfuture nominalizer	NFUT^IN^SG^NMLZ	2.2.2.5, 3.1.4.2
-Rõbĩwã	feminine plural (noun)	FP	3.1.2.1
-RõRE	when (different subject, singular)	WHEN^DS	6.4.1.2
-RU	if (subordinate clause)	IF	6.4.3.3
-ta	focus[10]	FOC	
-ta	goal, limit	GOAL	3.3.9.5
-te	dynamicizer	DYN	2.2.1

---

[10]This discourse marker is not discussed in this grammar; see Salser and Salser (1979).

-tʃĩã	emphatic (used by male speakers)	EMPH	(discourse marker, not treated in this grammar)
-wA	causative	CAUS	2.2.3.2
-wA	plural animate (noun)	PL	3.1.2
-wa	accustomed	ACST	2.2.2.5
-wa	separation	SEP	3.3.6
-wakari	alone, by oneself	SELF	3.3.6
-wakari	concession (subordinate clause, same subject)	CNCS^SS	6.4.3.4
-wareka	concession (subordinate clause, different subject)	CNCS^DS	6.4.3.4
-wɨ	witnessed, first, second, and inanimate, recent past and present durative; first and second near future	NON3	2.2.2.5
-wɨ	any person, nonrecent past (in context of *-kebã* 'assumed')	PERS	2.2.2.5
-wɨ	plural (adjective and quantifier)	PL	4.2
-xã	associative	ASC	3.3.3
-xA	imperative	IMP	2.2.2.1
-xE	conditional	COND	2.2.2.5
-xi	future first interrogative	FUT^1^INTR	2.2.2.1
-xĩ	diminutive	DIM	3.3.2
-xIda	optative frustrative	OPT^FRUS	2.2.2.2
-xɨ	irrealis, present	IRR	2.2.2.2

Appendix 2
Practical Orthography

As discussed in §2.2, all of the consonants except the voiceless stops and the voiceless affricate /tʃ/ have oral and nasal allophones. In some cases, the allophones are written in the practical orthography, viz., /b/ is written as *b* or as *m*, /d/ is written as *d* or as *n*, and /j/ as *y* or as *ñ*, depending on whether the consonant precedes an oral or nasalized vowel. This is because, in the practical orthography, the first nasalized vowel in a word is indicated by a tilde, unless it is preceded by a nasal consonant, in which case the vowel is not marked as nasalized because all vowels in such an environment are nasalized in Cubeo, e.g., *ãvʉ* /ãwĩ/ 'I ate recently', but *nʉmemi* /dĩbẽbĩ/ 'he is not going'. The phoneme /r/ is always written as *r*, regardless of its nasalization. Inherently nasal suffixes are written with the tilde on the first vowel, even when suffixed to a nasal root, e.g., *cũracũ* /kĩrã-kũ/ (rock-CLS:hump) 'rock' and *nʉicõjemi* /dĩ-ɨkõxẽ-bĩ/ (go-AUTH-3MSG) 'he commands (someone) to go'.

In the practical orthography /ɨ/ is written as *ʉ*, /k/ as *c* or *qu*, /tʃ/ as *ch*, /x/ as *j*, /j/ as *y*, and /w/ as *v*. The letter *d* also occurs in the practical orthography because of the high frequency of use of the verb root *ja-* (often pronounced [ða]) 'do, make, cause', even though [ð] can generally be analyzed as an allophone of /j/ (also discussed in §2.2).

Words borrowed into Cubeo from Spanish are for the most part spelled as they are in Spanish, including the accent mark, e.g., *colegio* 'school' has *g*, *finca* 'farm' has *f*, *kilo* 'kilogram' has *k*, *lino* 'linen' has *l*, *camello* 'camel' has *ll*, *sacerdote* 'priest' has *s*, and *José* is written with an accent mark, even though according to the stress rules of Cubeo, the vowel in this word would be automatically stressed. Final consonants on borrowed names, however, are neither pronounced nor written before a suffix:

Víctoi 'Victor's' (morphophonemically, *Víctor-i* (Víctor-POS). The Cubeos now consider some borrowed words to be Cubeo words, such as *úru* from *oro* 'gold'.

The primary stress of a Cubeo word usually falls on the second syllable. If not, the primary stressed syllable is marked in the practical orthography by an acute accent mark, as in Spanish. For example:

náme   /ˈdãbẽ/   rainbow

jatɨódobe   /xatɨˈojobe/ She's cooking.

Compound nouns and compound verbs are often written without spaces, particularly if one of the members of the compound is a root. Our marking of word breaks in the examples of this grammar occasionally deviates from the word breaks used in the practical orthography.

References

Ardila, Olga. 1988. La sub-familia lingüística Tucano-Oriental: Estado actual y perspectivas de investigación. Tercer Seminario-Taller para el Estudio Preliminar del Atlas Etnolingüístico Colombiano. Bogotá. Instituto Caro y Cuervo.

López, Manuel and Pedro López. 1986. Pãmié coyɨiye. 2a edición. Lomalinda, Meta, Colombia: Editorial Townsend.

Mithun, Marianne. 1991. Active/agentive case marking and its motivations. Language 67:510–46.

Salser, J. K., Jr. 1971. Cubeo phonemics. Linguistics 75:74–79.

—— and Neva Salser. 1979. Some features of Cubeo discourse and sentence structure. In Robert E. Longacre (ed.), Discourse grammar: Studies in indigenous languages of Colombia, Panama, and Ecuador 2:253–72. Summer Institute of Linguistics and the University of Texas at Arlington Publications in Linguistics 52. Dallas.

Waltz, Nathan E. and Alva Wheeler. 1972. Proto Tucanoan. In Esther Matteson (ed.). Comparative studies in Amerindian languages. Janua Linguarum, Series Practica 127, 119–49. The Hague: Mouton.

Summer Institute of Linguistics and
The University of Texas at Arlington
Publications in Linguistics

Recent Publications

130. **Cubeo grammar: Studies in the languages of Colombia 5,** by Nancy L. Morse and Michael B. Maxwell. 1999.
129. **Aspects of Zaiwa prosody: An autosegmental account,** by Mark W. Wannemacher. 1998.
128. **Tense and aspect in Obolo grammar and discourse,** by Uche Aaron. 1998.
127. **Case grammar applied,** by Walter A. Cook, S.J. 1998.
126. **The Dong language in Guizhou Province, China,** by Long Yaohong and Zheng Guoqiao, translated from Chinese by D. Norman Geary. 1998.
125. **Vietnamese classifiers in narrative texts,** by Karen Ann Daley. 1998.
124. **Comparative Kadai: The Tai branch,** ed. by Jerold A. Edmondson and David B. Solnit. 1997.
123. **Why there are no clitics: An alternative perspective on pronominal allomorphy,** by Daniel L. Everett. 1996.
122. **Mamaindé stress: The need for strata,** by David Eberhard. 1995.
121. **The Doyayo language: Selected studies,** by Elisabeth Wiering and Marinus Wiering. 1994.
120. **A discourse analysis of First Corinthians,** by Ralph Bruce Terry. 1995.
119. **Discourse features of ten languages of West-Central Africa,** ed. by Stephen H. Levensohn. 1994.
118. **Epena Pedee syntax: Studies in the languages of Colombia 4,** by Phillip Lee Harms. 1994.
117. **Beyond the bilingual classroom: Literacy acquisition among Peruvian Amazon communities,** by Barbara Trudell. 1993.
116. **The French imparfait and passé simple in discourse,** by Sharon Rebecca Rand. 1993.
115. **The function of verb prefixes in Southwestern Otomí,** by Henrietta Andrews. 1993.
114. **Proto Witotoan,** by Richard P. Aschmann. 1993.
113. **A pragmatic analysis of Norwegian modal particles,** by Erik E. Andvik. 1992.
112. **Retuarã syntax: Studies in the languages of Colombia 3,** by Clay Strom. 1992.
111. **Studies in the syntax of Mixtecan Languages 4,** ed. by C. Henry Bradley and Barbara E. Hollenbach. 1992.
110. **Windows on bilingualism,** by Eugene Casad. 1992.
109. **Switch reference in Koasati discourse,** by David Rising. 1992.
108. **Phonological studies in four languages of Maluku,** ed. by Donald A. Burquest and Wyn D. Laidig. 1992.
107. **Language in context: Essays for Robert E. Longacre,** ed. by Shin Ja J. Hwang and William R. Merrifield. 1992.
106. **Tepetotutla Chinantec syntax: Studies in Chinantec languages 5,** by David Westley. 1991.
105. **Studies in the syntax of Mixtecan languages 3,** ed. by C. Henry Bradley and Barbara E. Hollenbach. 1991.
104. **Sentence repetition testing for studies of community bilingualism,** by Carla F. Radloff. 1991.
103. **An autosegmental approach to Shilluk phonology,** by Leoma G. Gilley. 1992.
102. **Tone in five languages of Cameroon,** ed. by Stephen C. Anderson. 1991.
101. **Barasano syntax: Studies in the languages of Colombia 2,** by Wendell Jones and Paula Jones. 1991.

100. **A reference grammar of Southeastern Tepehuan,** by Thomas L. Willett. 1991.
99. **Tense and aspect in eight languages of Cameroon,** ed. by Stephen C. Anderson and Bernard Comrie. 1991.
98. **The structure of Thai narrative,** by Somsonge Burusphat. 1991.
97. **Can literacy lead to development? A case study in literacy, adult education, and economic development in India,** by Uwe Gustafsson. 1991.
96. **Survey on a shoestring: A manual for small-scale language surveys,** by Frank Blair. 1990.
95. **Syllables, tone, and verb paradigms: Studies in Chinantec languages 4,** ed. by William R. Merrifield and Calvin R. Rensch. 1990.
94. **Ika syntax: Studies in the languages of Colombia 1,** by Paul S. Frank. 1990.
93. **Development and diversity: Language variation across time and space (A Festschrift for Charles-James N. Bailey),** ed. by Jerold A. Edmondson, Crawford Feagin, and Peter Mühlhäusler. 1990.
92. **Comanche dictionary and grammar,** ed. by Lila W. Robinson and James Armagost. 1990.
91. **Language maintenance in Melanesia: Sociolinguistics and social networks in New Caledonia,** by Stephen J. Schooling. 1990.
90. **Studies in the syntax of Mixtecan languages 2,** ed. by C. Henry Bradley and Barbara E. Hollenbach. 1990.
89. **Comaltepec Chinantec syntax: Studies in Chinantec languages 3,** by Judi Lynn Anderson. 1989.
88. **Lealao Chinantec syntax: Studies in Chinantec languages 2,** by James E. Rupp. 1989.
87. **An etymological dictionary of the Chinantec languages: Studies in Chinantec languages 1,** by Calvin R. Rensch. 1989.
86. **Comparative Kadai: Linguistic studies beyond Tai,** ed. by Jerold A. Edmondson and David B. Solnit. 1988.
85. **The verbal piece in Ebira,** by John R. Adive. 1989.
84. **Insights into Tagalog: Reduplication, infixation, and stress from nonlinear phonology,** by Koleen M. French. 1988.
83. **Studies in the syntax of Mixtecan languages 1,** ed. by C. Henry Bradley and Barbara E. Hollenbach. 1988.
82. **Dinka vowel system,** by Job Malou. 1988.
81. **Aspects of Western Subanon formal speech,** by William C. Hall. 1987.
80. **Current trends and issues in Hispanic linguistics,** ed. by Lenard Studerus. 1987.
79. **Modes in Dényá discourse,** by Samson Negbo Abangma. 1987.
78. **Tense/aspect and the development of auxiliaries in Kru languages,** by Lynelle Marchese. 1986.
77. **Discourse features of Korean narration,** by Shin Ja Joo Hwang. 1987.
76. **Hixkaryana and linguistic typology,** by Desmond C. Derbyshire. 1985.
75. **Sentence initial devices,** ed. by Joseph E. Grimes. 1986.
74. **English phonetic transcription,** by Charles-James N. Bailey. 1985.
73. **Pragmatics in non-Western perspective,** ed. by George Huttar and Kenneth J. Gregerson. 1986.
72. **Senoufo phonology, discourse to syllable (a prosodic approach),** by Elizabeth Mills. 1984.
71. **Workbook for historical linguistics,** by Winfred P. Lehmann. 1984.
70. **Babine & Carrier phonology: A historically oriented study,** by Gillian L. Story. 1984.
69. **Affix positions and cooccurrences: The PARADIGM program,** by Joseph E. Grimes. 1983.

68. **Syntactic change and syntactic reconstruction: A tagmemic approach,** by John R. Costello. 1983.
67. **Pragmatic aspects of English text structure,** by Larry B. Jones. 1983.
66. **Phonology and morphology of Axininca Campa,** by David L. Payne. 1981.
65. **A generative grammar of Afar,** by Loren F. Bliese. 1981.
64. **A framework for discourse analysis,** by Wilbur N. Pickering. 1980.
63. **Discourse grammar in Ga'dang,** by Michael R. Walrod. 1979.
62. **Nung grammar,** by Janice E. Saul and Nancy F. Wilson. 1980.
61. **Predicate and argument in Rengao grammar,** by Kenneth J. Gregerson. 1979.
60. **A grammatical description of the Engenni language,** by Elaine Thomas. 1978.
59. **The functions of reported speech in discourse,** by Mildred L. Larson. 1978.
58.2. **Discourse studies in Mesoamerican languages 2: Texts,** ed. by Linda K. Jones. 1979.
58.1. **Discourse studies in Mesoamerican languages 1: Discussion,** ed. by Linda K. Jones. 1979.
57. **The deep structure of the sentence in Sara-Ngambay dialogues, including a description of phrase, clause, and paragraph,** by James Edward Thayer. 1978.
56.4. **Southern Uto-Aztecan grammatical sketches: Studies in Uto-Aztecan grammar 4,** ed. by Ronald W. Langacker. 1984.
56.3. **Uto-Aztecan grammatical sketches: Studies in Uto-Aztecan grammar 3,** ed. by Ronald W. Langacker. 1982.
56.2. **Modern Aztec grammatical sketches: Studies in Uto-Aztecan grammar 2,** ed. by Ronald W. Langacker. 1979.
56.1. **An overview of Uto-Aztecan grammar: Studies in Uto-Aztecan grammar 1,** by Ronald W. Langacker. 1977.
55. **Two studies in Middle American comparative linguistics,** by David Oltrogge and Calvin R. Rensch. 1977.
54. **Studies in Otomanguean phonology,** ed. by William R. Merrifield. 1977.
53. **Grammatical analysis,** by Kenneth L. Pike and Evelyn G. Pike. 1977.
52.3. **Discourse grammar: Studies in indigenous languages of Colombia, Panama, and Ecuador 3,** ed. by Robert E. Longacre and Frances Woods. 1977.
52.2. **Discourse grammar: Studies in indigenous languages of Colombia, Panama, and Ecuador 2,** ed. by Robert E. Longacre and Frances Woods. 1977.
52.1. **Discourse grammar: Studies in indigenous languages of Colombia, Panama, and Ecuador 1,** ed. by Robert E. Longacre and Frances Woods. 1976.
51. **Papers on discourse,** ed. by Joseph E. Grimes. 1978.

For further information or a full listing of SIL publications contact:

International Academic Bookstore
Summer Institute of Linguistics
7500 W. Camp Wisdom Road
Dallas, TX 75236-5699

Voice: 972-708-7404
Fax: 972-708-7433
Email: academic.books@sil.org
Internet: http://www.sil.org

www.ingramcontent.com/pod-product-compliance
Lightning Source LLC
Chambersburg PA
CBHW051523230426
43668CB00012B/1717